Good News, Great Joy

AN ADVENT STUDY ON THE POWER AND PERFECTION OF JESUS

This study belongs to:

_____

_____

THE DAILY GRACE CO.®

Unlock Your Digital Study

Did you know you can access your new study right from your phone?
Follow these simple steps, and you will be on your way to diving deeper into God's Word.

Download The Daily Grace Co.® App

AVAILABLE FOR FREE IN THE APP STORE AND GOOGLE PLAY

Search for Your New Study

LOCATE YOUR STUDY IN THE DAILY GRACE CO.® APP

- Select the "Studies" tab found at the bottom of the home page in the app.
- Select the pink "+" button to bring up all available studies.
- Click on your new study.

Apply Your Access Code

EMAILED TO YOU AFTER PURCHASE

- Copy the access code from your email, and enter it into the "Unlock Study with Access Code" box found on our app.
- You are all set! Now that you have downloaded the app, found your study, and applied your access code, you can begin your study virtually!
- If you did not receive an email with an access code after the purchase of your new study, check your spam folder. If you still cannot find your access code, contact our Customer Delight team at info@thedailygraceco.com.

OTHER APP FEATURES

VIDEOS   COMMUNITY   BIBLE   BLOG   PODCAST   AND MORE!

In This Study

Study Suggestions

We believe that the Bible is true, trustworthy, and timeless and that it is vitally important for all believers. These study suggestions are intended to help you more effectively study Scripture as you seek to know and love God through His Word.

SUGGESTED STUDY TOOLS

☐ Bible

☐ Double-spaced, printed copy of the Scripture passages that this study covers (You can use a website like www.biblegateway.com to copy the text of a passage and print out a double-spaced copy to be able to mark on easily.)

☐ Journal to write notes or prayers

☐ Pens, colored pencils, and highlighters

☐ Dictionary to look up unfamiliar words

Pray

Begin your study time in prayer. Ask God to reveal Himself to you, help you understand what you are reading, and transform you with His Word (Psalm 119:18).

 Read Scripture

Before you read what is written in each day of the study itself, read the assigned passages of Scripture for that day. Use your double-spaced copy to circle, underline, highlight, draw arrows, and mark in any way you would like to help you dig deeper as you work through a passage.

 Memorize Scripture

Each week of the study begins with a memory verse. You may want to write the verse down and place it somewhere you will see it often. We also recommend spending a few minutes memorizing the verse before you complete each day's study material.

 Read Study Content

Read the daily written content provided for the current study day.

 Respond

Answer the questions that appear at the end of each study day.

How to Study the Bible

The inductive method provides tools for deeper and more intentional Bible study.
To study the Bible inductively, work through the steps below after
reading background information on the book.

Observation & Comprehension
KEY QUESTION: WHAT DOES THE TEXT SAY?

After reading the daily Scripture in its entirety at least once, begin working with smaller portions of the Scripture. Read a passage of Scripture repetitively, and then mark the following items in the text:

- Key or repeated words and ideas
- Key themes
- Transition words (e.g., therefore, but, because, if/then, likewise, etc.)
- Lists
- Comparisons and contrasts
- Commands
- Unfamiliar words (look these up in a dictionary)
- Questions you have about the text

Interpretation
KEY QUESTION: WHAT DOES THE TEXT MEAN?

Once you have annotated the text, work through the following steps to help you interpret its meaning:

- Read the passage in other versions for a better understanding of the text.
- Read cross-references to help interpret Scripture with Scripture.
- Paraphrase or summarize the passage to check for understanding.
- Identify how the text reflects the metanarrative of Scripture, which is the story of creation, fall, redemption, and restoration.
- Read trustworthy commentaries if you need further insight into the meaning of the passage.

Application

Bible study is not merely an intellectual pursuit. The truths about God, ourselves, and the gospel that we discover in Scripture should produce transformation in our hearts and lives. Answer the following questions and prompts as you consider what you have learned in your study:

- What attributes of God's character are revealed in the passage?

- Consider places where the text directly states the character of God, as well as how His character is revealed through His words and actions.

- What do I learn about myself in light of who God is?

- Consider how you fall short of God's character, how the text reveals your sin nature, and what it says about your new identity in Christ.

- How should this truth change me?

- A passage of Scripture may contain direct commands telling us what to do or warnings about sins to avoid in order to help us grow in holiness. Other times, our application flows out of seeing ourselves in light of God's character. As we pray and reflect on how God is calling us to change in light of His Word, we should be asking questions like, "How should I pray for God to change my heart?" and "What practical steps can I take toward cultivating habits of holiness?"

Introduction

We are so glad you have decided to study *Good News, Great Joy* this Advent season. Our prayer is that this study draws you closer to Jesus and that you will enter Christmas Day with a renewed sense of awe for all our Savior has done.

We know that the Advent season brings with it so many things: joy, decorations, parties, and a general feeling of excitement for what lies ahead. We also know that the best-laid plans can fall by the wayside when the busyness and stress of the holidays set in. That is why we want to use this introduction section to set you up for success as much as we can. Below, we have included some information and tips to help you make the most of this Advent study as you prepare your heart for the celebration of Christ's birth and, ultimately, His second coming.

ABOUT THIS STUDY

Good News, Great Joy examines the different offices of Christ and how He perfectly fulfills the roles of Prophet, Priest, King, and Messiah. This resource begins on the fourth Sunday before Christmas and ends on Christmas Day. The calendar provided on pages 12–13 provides a quick look at which readings you should complete each day to stay on track. We suggest allowing fifteen to thirty minutes to complete each day's devotional content.

Each week begins with an Advent candle lighting and memory verse. If you are new to the Advent candle lighting tradition, it is helpful to know what the candles represent and how often they are lit. There are five Advent candles: hope, peace, joy, love, and the Christ candle. Traditionally, each Sunday, you will light one new Advent candle. This means that on the first Sunday of Advent, you will light the hope candle. On the second Sunday, you will light the hope and peace candles, and on the third Sunday, you will light the hope, peace, and joy candles, and so on and so forth.

In addition to leading you through Advent candle lighting, each week of this study will also examine a different office of Christ. If you are new to studying the offices of Christ, you can learn more on pages 14–15. We hope that by studying and understanding how

Christ is the fulfillment of each of these roles, you will grow closer to Him and find a new love and appreciation for all that Christ has done for you.

BEFORE YOU BEGIN

As we mentioned previously, we know that the best-laid plans can often go awry during the busy Christmas season. However, we truly believe that the best way to celebrate Christmas is by setting your focus on the One this holiday is all about. Therefore, we recommend taking a look at your calendar and planning out when you will complete each study day. It also may help to find a friend or family member to work through this study with to keep you accountable.

Finally, we pray this resource keeps Christ at the center of it all this holiday season. May this study bring you great delight in seeing God's goodness and grace displayed toward us through sending His Son, and may your eyes and heart be opened anew to the good news of the gospel.

The best way to celebrate Christmas is by setting your focus on the One this holiday is all about.

2023 Advent Study Calendar

Week 1: *Jesus is the perfect Prophet who fulfills every prophecy and brings us hope.*	
Sunday, December 3rd	*Candle Lighting: Hope* *Memory Verse: John 1:5*
Monday, December 4th	*What is the Role of a Prophet?*
Tuesday, December 5th	*Different Times and in Different Ways*
Wednesday, December 6th	*The Anticipated Prophet*
Thursday, December 7th	*Jesus: The Perfect Revelation*
Friday, December 8th	*Jesus: The Fulfillment of Prophecy*
Saturday, December 9th	*Week 1 Application*
Week 2: *Jesus is our Great High Priest who gives us peace.*	
Sunday, December 10th	*Candle Lighting: Peace* *Memory Verse: Isaiah 1:18b*
Monday, December 11th	*What is the Role of a Priest?*
Tuesday, December 12th	*Our Need for a Priest*

Wednesday, December 13th	*The Anticipated Priest*
Thursday, December 14th	*Jesus: The Great High Priest*
Friday, December 15th	*Jesus: Our Priest*
Saturday, December 16th	*Week 2 Application*

Week 3: *Jesus is the King of kings who fills us with joy.*

Sunday, December 17th	*Candle Lighting: Joy* *Memory Verse: Psalm 100:4*
Monday, December 18th	*What is the Role of a King?*
Tuesday, December 19th	*The Rejection of the King*
Wednesday, December 20th	*The Anticipated King*
Thursday, December 21st	*Jesus: The King of Kings*
Friday, December 22nd	*Jesus: The Kingdom of Christ*
Saturday, December 23rd	*Week 3 Application*

Christmas: *Jesus Christ is the Messiah who loves us so much He came to save us.*

Sunday, December 24th	*Candle Lighting: Love* *Memory Verse: Isaiah 9:6* *Who is the Messiah?*
Monday, December 25th	*Candle Lighting: Christ Candle* *Jesus: The Messiah Is Here!*

Introduction to the Offices of Christy

What do you think of when you consider a person of authority? Maybe you think of the president of a country, the CEO of a company, or the chairman of a board. A position of authority can be referred to as an office. For example, the Executive Office of the President is not a large working space with a desk and computer. Instead, it refers to a group of people who receive authority to work alongside the President of the United States in matters that affect the country. But did you know that Jesus is considered to have different offices? While Scripture does not use the language of "office" specifically, based on what we see and learn about Jesus from the Bible, there are three offices that Jesus bears: Prophet, Priest, and King. While this study will dive more deeply into each of these offices, it is helpful to first have a general understanding of what each of these offices means.

PROPHET

Jesus is the true and better Prophet. Though God used prophets in the Old Testament to speak God's words to His people, Jesus is the very Word of God (John 1). Jesus came to earth and took on flesh to share God's truth and wisdom with people and provide eternal life through the words He taught and by His death and resurrection.

PRIEST

Jesus is our Great High Priest (Hebrews 4:14) who reconciled mankind to God through His own sacrifice on the cross. While the priests in the Old Testament made offerings on behalf of God's people, Jesus offered Himself as a sacrifice on our behalf, providing permanent forgiveness for our sin.

KING

The Old Testament is full of earthly kings who ruled over Israel and other nations. But all of these kings fall short in light of Jesus, who is the one true King. Jesus is King because He rules and reigns over all things. Christ inaugurated God's kingdom through His life, death, resurrection, and ascension. And through Jesus, we are able to be part of the kingdom of God.

MESSIAH

Connected to all three of these offices is the title of Messiah. While Messiah is not considered an official office, the truth that Jesus is the Messiah enhances our understanding of who Jesus is. Messiah means "Anointed One," and throughout Scripture, the name Messiah refers to the promised Savior who would rescue and deliver God's people from their sins. Advent is the season in which we remember and rejoice over the Messiah, Jesus, who came to save us and set us free.

Advent is a time of anticipation, a season of waiting as we count down the days until Christmas. In this season, we place ourselves in the shoes of the Israelites, who anticipated the promised Messiah who would redeem people from their sins, reconcile people to God, and restore God's kingdom. We ready ourselves for Christmas, not only by setting up our trees and wrapping presents but by preparing our hearts through God's Word. This study will help you do just that. Through this study, you will grow deeper in your understanding of the baby born in Bethlehem: Jesus, who is our Prophet, Priest, King, and Messiah. You will learn how Jesus perfectly fulfills each of these offices and how He is faithful to redeem, reconcile, and restore.

As you grow in your understanding of who Jesus is, so will your excitement during the season of Advent grow, for the celebrated baby at Christmas has done more than we could ever imagine. He is our Prophet, Priest, King, and Messiah, who cleanses our hearts, unites us to the Father, and grants us a permanent place in God's kingdom. Though presents sit ready to be unwrapped under our Christmas trees, Jesus is the greatest gift we could ever receive.

Advent is the season in which we remember and rejoice over the Messiah, Jesus.

WEEK ONE

Prophet

Jesus is the perfect Prophet who fulfills every prophecy and brings us hope.

Candle Lighting

Hope

Today, we will light the hope candle and remember
that Jesus is our hope — yesterday, today, and forever.

Father,

*As we light this first candle of Advent, we thank You for the hope You brought
to the world over two thousand years ago. Thank You for sending Your Son
as the fulfillment of a promise You made to Your people thousands of years
ago. We praise You that, through Jesus, our sins have been washed away
and that we can live with hope for a day when tears will flow no more.*

We pray this in Your Son's precious name,

Amen

Memory
Verse

That light shines in the darkness, and yet the darkness did not overcome it.

JOHN 1:5

DAY ONE

God protected
the prophets He
sent out and used
them to declare
His promises and
admonishments.

What Is the Role of a Prophet?

Read Deuteronomy 13:1–5, Deuteronomy 18:9–22

We know that wise men, shepherds, and angels are part of the Christmas story, but did you know that prophets are also part of the Christmas story? While we do not see prophets show up in the actual story of Christ's birth, the prophets in the Bible are intricately tied to the baby born in Bethlehem. Their messages and ministries were intentionally used by God to point to the child to come, the child who would be the fulfillment of God's promises. So before we get to that starry night in Bethlehem before we get to the angel's chorus and the shepherd's wonder, and before we get to the cries of a newborn in a manger, let us go backward in history and meet these prophets who impact the Advent narrative.

In the Bible, a prophet's main role was to be a mouthpiece for God. They would speak on behalf of God by relaying God's Word to the people. Prophets always spoke the words of the Lord and derived their authority from God alone. Every genuine prophet in Scripture had a moment in which God came directly to him and gave that prophet the authority to speak for Him. For instance, in Jeremiah 1:9–10, the prophet Jeremiah recounts how God gave him the authority to speak for Him when he wrote: "Then the Lord reached out his hand, touched my mouth, and told me: I have now filled your mouth with my words. See, I have appointed you today over nations and kingdoms to uproot and tear down, to destroy and demolish, to build and plant."

These verses reveal how God put His words inside Jeremiah to speak and how God appointed him specifically to be a prophet for the people of Israel.

While prophets did speak to future events and foretold God's plans of judgment or restoration, prophets were primarily used by God to lead the Israelites in their faithfulness to Him. Second Chronicles 24:19 tells us how God "sent them prophets to bring them back to the Lord; they admonished them, but the people would not listen." Prophets would use the messages God gave them to encourage the people to remember the holiness of the Lord, call them to repent from their sins, and challenge them to remain obedient to God's covenant. Often, prophets placed themselves in difficult situations and faced persecution for the messages they delivered to God's people. Nevertheless, God protected the prophets He sent out and used them to declare His promises and admonishments.

You may be wondering, *Why were there prophets in Scripture if God could speak directly to man?* In Exodus 20:18–21, the Israelites witnessed the effects of God's glory from afar as He met with Moses atop Mount Sinai. When they saw the thunder, lightning, and smoke on the mountain that accompanied God's presence, the people were afraid. So, in Exodus 20:18–21, the Israelites asked Moses to meet with God on their behalf and to tell them God's words instead of having God speak to them directly. Deuteronomy 18:16 references this past situation as one reason why God gave and sent prophets to His people.

Scripture also tells us of false prophets who were not genuine prophets of God. These prophets were self-appointed rather than appointed by God and therefore spoke with their own authority rather than the authority of the Lord. These false prophets often used certain practices to determine and declare the truth. They would sometimes use forms of divination like fortune telling, spells, or searching the entrails of animals to discover messages from God (Deuteronomy 18:9–10). A defining factor of a false prophet would be someone who leads people away in their worship of God rather than one who spurs them on in their worship. God warns against these kinds of people in Deuteronomy 13:1–3 and commands His people not to listen to prophets who encourage them to follow and worship other gods.

> The establishment of prophets in Scripture reveals how God desires to speak to His people.

Another characteristic of a false prophet would be the failure to consistently provide predictions that came true. God tells His people in Deuteronomy 18:20–22 how they can recognize a message that is not from Him: if the messenger speaks in God's name, but their message does not come true. If this happens, they have made presumptions rather than speaking something directly from the Lord.

The establishment of prophets in Scripture reveals how God desires to speak to His people. While the Israelites resisted having God speak to them directly, God still made it possible for His people to hear His words through the prophets. God's words to the prophets also reveal intimacy as God chose them to hear and relay His words. Prophecy in the Bible shows us how God does not remain at a distance but comes near to His people in intimate ways. God's use of prophets in Scripture also attests to His desire to give wisdom and direction to His people. It was kind of the Lord to raise up prophets to help guide and lead His people in their faithfulness to Him. God is also gracious to give warnings to His people and promises of hope and restoration through the prophets.

And while prophets in the Old Testament relayed God's words, there was a time coming when God would speak to His people directly. One day, in the little town of Bethlehem, the Word of God would be born as a baby, and the people would receive God's revelation face to face.

Study Questions

01 / How did today's study deepen your understanding of prophets?

02 / Why do you think there were (and still are) people who claim to have a message from God when they really do not?

03 / Why is it important to listen to and obey the Word of God? How can you practically listen to and obey God's Word?

Notes

God is a gracious God, and He pursues His people no matter the condition of their hearts.

Different Times and in Different Ways

Read Isaiah 1:18–20, Ezekiel 14:6–7

On the night Jesus was born, something spectacular happened. While humble shepherds attended to their flocks, an angel suddenly appeared to them, proclaiming "good news of great joy that will be for all the people" (Luke 2:10). This news would change everything, and the shepherds accepted the angel's message with wonder and delight. The response of these shepherds contrasts greatly with the response of God's people to His messengers in the Old Testament. God's prophets often proclaimed messages that seemed like anything but "good news of great joy." But the words of the prophets in the Old Testament mattered just as much as the words of the heavenly herald in the Christmas story.

Hebrews 1:1 tells us that "long ago God spoke to the ancestors by the prophets at different times and in different ways." Each Old Testament prophet served a specific purpose in the history of God's people, the Israelites. The first time the word "prophet" appears in Scripture is in Genesis 20:7 when God refers to Abraham as a prophet. The next well-known prophet to come after Abraham was Moses. While God used Abraham to establish the nation of Israel, it was Moses whom God used to lead Israel to the Promised Land that God promised to Abraham. Although Abraham was faithful to the Lord, Deuteronomy 34:10 states how no prophet arose in Israel who was like Moses because God knew Moses face to face. Moses had an intimate relationship with the Lord, and even though he failed in many ways, he was God's instrument to guide the people in their faithfulness to the Lord.

Unfortunately, the further we journey through the Old Testament, the greater God's people grew in their wickedness. They rebelled against the Lord and desired to take matters into their own hands rather than submit themselves to God. One primary example of Israel's rebellion was when Israel demanded to have a king like their surrounding nations (1 Samuel 8). God used a prophet by the name of Samuel to speak to the people of Israel during this time. It was Samuel's task to find the king whom God chose to lead the Israelites and to speak to the king on God's behalf. Just like the prophets before him, Samuel sought to encourage Israel's faithfulness to God as their ultimate King, even though they had now chosen someone to rule over them. After the first king of Israel failed, Samuel found and anointed David, whom God specifically chose to lead the Israelites.

David was far from a perfect king, but by God's grace and faithfulness, the nation of Israel flourished under his reign. They were a united people who were encouraged by David to worship and obey the Lord. Sadly, this all changed when David died. When David's son, Solomon, took the throne, it seemed as if Solomon would follow in his father's footsteps. But Solomon eventually turned his heart away from the

God's grace shines even in the darkness of judgment, for God promised to restore and redeem His people.

Lord, influencing the hearts of God's people to turn away as well. Israel's situation only worsened as Solomon's son, Rehoboam, took the throne, and Rehoboam's actions caused the kingdom of Israel to split. Now, Israel was a divided kingdom. The broken nation reflected the brokenness of the hearts of God's people, who no longer desired to worship and obey the Lord.

But God is a gracious God, and He pursues His people no matter the condition of their hearts. Out of His grace, God continued to provide prophets to encourage repentance and renewed worship of the Lord. In the initial stages of the divided kingdom, God appointed the prophets Elijah and Elisha. Elijah, in particular, is considered one of the most important prophets in Israel's history, and he is known to have greatly impacted Israel's returned worship of God. Both Elijah and Elisha were also given power by God to do miraculous works. The words and works of these prophets revealed the glory of God, encouraging the Israelites to turn from idols who paled in comparison to the one true God.

And while there were moments of returned worship and repentance under Elijah and Elisha's influence, the Israelites would always resume their rebellious ways and worship of other gods. The majority of kings who took the throne over the two kingdoms were wicked, and God's people continued to do what was evil in God's sight. Yet God did not give up on His people, even though they had been unfaithful to Him. God continued to send prophet after prophet to both kingdoms to encourage the kings to obey the Lord and the people to repent of their sin. We receive detailed accounts of these prophecies in the prophetic books of Scripture, categorized as the Major and Minor Prophets.

The Major and Minor Prophets are often perceived as being all about "doom and gloom." These books contain prophecies of judgment upon Israel and surrounding nations. And because of Israel's constant unrepentance, even with the prophets' warnings, these prophecies came true as God's people were overcome by other nations and taken into exile. God's words of judgment were just because of the seriousness of Israel's sin and the wickedness of their hearts. Thankfully, God did not only speak judgment upon His people. God's grace shines even in the darkness of judgment, for God promised to restore and redeem His people. God used both the Major and Minor Prophets to declare His promised purposes to save His people and bring them to Himself.

The Old Testament prophets teach us about God's jealousy for His people, the seriousness of our sin, and God's faithfulness to redeem and restore, even though His people rebel against Him. Yet the failure of God's people to listen to the prophets and maintain faithfulness to the Lord sets the stage for Jesus, the one true Prophet who will succeed in guiding people to obey and worship the Lord (Hebrews 1:1–4). He will proclaim good news of great joy that will establish genuine repentance and true heart change.

> God used both the Major and Minor Prophets to declare His promised purposes to save His people.

Study Questions

01 / What does Israel's rebellion reveal about the human heart?

02 / How is God's grace evident through the words of the prophets?

03 / How does the gospel encourage our repentance and worship of God?

Notes

Timeline of Major and Minor Prophets

C. 848 BC
The Vision of Obadiah

C. 793 BC
Jonah Sent to Nineveh

C. 760 BC
The Words of Amos

C. 740 BC
*Isaiah's Vision
and Commission*

C. 735 BC
*The Word of the
Lord to Micah*

C. 725 BC
Hosea's Prophecies

C. 640 BC
The Vision of Nahum

C. 638 BC
*The Word of the
Lord to Zephaniah*

C. 627 BC
The Call of Jeremiah

C. 625 BC
*The Oracle
to Habakkuk*

C. 600 BC
*The Word of
the Lord to Joel*

C. 592 BC
*Ezekiel's First
Temple Vision*

C. 586 BC
*Lamentations
is Written*

C. 582 BC
*Daniel Interprets
Nebuchadnezzar's
Dream*

C. 573 BC
*Ezekiel's Second
Temple Vision*

C. 520 BC
*The Word of the
Lord to Zechariah*

C. 520 BC
*The Word of the
Lord to Haggai*

C. 430 BC
*The Word of the Lord
to Malachi*

Throughout Israel's history, many prophets spoke the word of the Lord to His people. The information below briefly highlights each prophet's ministry. It is important to note that the kingdom of Israel split into two in c. 931 BC (1 Kings 12). The northern kingdom was called Israel, and the southern kingdom was called Judah. Because of this, we have identified which kingdom each prophet spoke to, noting that some prophesied to both kingdoms and some prophesied to the surrounding nations. As you read about both the Major and Minor Prophets, remember that all of these prophets ultimately point to our need for a true and better Prophet, Jesus Christ, whom we celebrate at Christmas.

Major Prophets

ISAIAH

Prophesied to: Judah

Main Message: God's judgment of Judah because of the Israelites' unfaithfulness; God's promises of restoration, especially through a promised Messiah

Key Themes:

- ✧ God's just judgment
- ✧ The promised Messiah
- ✧ God's grace
- ✧ God's gift of restoration

JEREMIAH

Prophesied to: Judah

Main Message: Judah's sinfulness and their need for repentance, as well as God's promises of restoration

Key Themes:

- ✧ God's just judgment
- ✧ God's gift of restoration
- ✧ The new covenant

LAMENTATIONS

Prophesied to: Judah

Main Message: Grief over Judah's sins and judgment

Key Themes:

- ✡ Trust in God's sovereignty
- ✡ Lament
- ✡ Hope in God's restoration

EZEKIEL

Prophesied to: Judah

Main Message: Warning of God's judgment against Judah and God's promises to restore Judah and Jerusalem

Key Themes:

- ✡ God's just judgment
- ✡ God's gift of restoration
- ✡ Worship restored

DANIEL

Prophesied to: Judah and surrounding kingdoms

Main Message: God's plan to save and restore His people from all oppressors

Key Themes:

- ✡ God's sovereignty and faithfulness
- ✡ God's just retribution
- ✡ God's eternal and supreme kingdom

Minor Prophets

HOSEA

Prophesied to: Israel

Main Message: The coming Assyrian exile and the need for repentance

Key Themes:

- ✡ God's covenantal love
- ✡ God's just judgment
- ✡ God's gift of restoration

JOEL

Prophesied to: Israel

Main Message: God's judgment through the Day of the Lord, the need for repentance, and God's promises of restoration

Key Themes:

- ✡ God's just judgment
- ✡ God's gift of restoration
- ✡ The gift of the Spirit

AMOS

Prophesied to: Israel

Main Message: God's judgment by Assyrian exile, the need for repentance, and God's promises of restoration

Key Themes:

- ✡ God's heart for justice
- ✡ God's gift of restoration

OBADIAH

Prophesied to: Israel and Judah

Main Message: God's judgment against Edom and Israel's promised restoration

Key Themes:

- ✡ God's sovereignty
- ✡ God's heart for justice and just retribution
- ✡ God's gift of restoration

JONAH

Prophesied to: Nineveh

Main Message: God's warning of judgment if Nineveh does not repent, reflecting Israel's need for repentance

Key Themes:

- ✡ God's grace and compassion
- ✡ Repentance

MICAH

Prophesied to: Israel and Judah

Main Message: God's judgment upon Israel but also God's restoration

Key Themes:

- ✡ The promised Deliverer
- ✡ God's promised deliverance
- ✡ Retribution for injustice

NAHUM

Prophesied to: Nineveh

Main Message: God's judgment upon Nineveh for not repenting

Key Themes:

- ✡ God's just judgment
- ✡ God's gift of restoration

HABAKKUK

Prophesied to: Judah

Main Message: God's judgment upon Babylon

Key Themes:

- ✡ God's justice
- ✡ God's sovereignty to use bad for good

ZEPHANIAH

Prophesied to: Judah

Main Message: Judgment for both Judah and surrounding nations but also God's promise of restoration

Key Themes:

- ✡ God's just judgment
- ✡ God's gift of restoration

HAGGAI

Prophesied to: Judah

Main Message: The initiation of the reconstruction of the temple

Key Themes:

- ✡ God's faithfulness
- ✡ Restored worship

ZECHARIAH

Prophesied to: Judah

Main Message: Judah's sin and the need for repentance, as well as God's promises of restoration

Key Themes:

- ✡ The promised Messiah
- ✡ God's sovereignty
- ✡ Repentance

MALACHI

Prophesied to: Israel

Main Message: Israel's need to repent and the Day of the Lord

Key Themes:

- ✡ A promised Deliverer
- ✡ God's just judgment
- ✡ God's desire for worship and faithfulness

Only Jesus
can truly turn
our hearts to the
Lord and keep
them there by
His grace.

The Anticipated Prophet

Read Deuteronomy 18:15–18, Luke 1:11–17

We help our kids count down the days until Christmas with Advent calendars full of chocolate. We look forward to gathering with friends and family we do not often see throughout the year on Christmas Day. We grow excited to open that one special present we have asked to receive. Anticipation breeds delight, especially when we are waiting for something that brings us joy. The Israelites knew what it was like to wait with anticipation. Nestled between words about true prophets in the Old Testament, we find a promise of a Prophet to come. And while the Israelites might not have anticipated Him when they were rebellious and wayward, they were likely anticipating a prophet as they went hundreds of years without hearing from God.

In Deuteronomy 18:15–18, Moses shares God's promise to raise up a prophet. Most Bible interpreters believe that with this promise, God was speaking about the line of prophets who would arise after Moses died. God promised that these prophets would speak His words and come from among His people. Just like Moses, God promised that these future prophets would receive God's words in their mouths and tell all that God commanded them to say. And as we saw in our study yesterday, God did indeed raise up prophets for the people of Israel after Moses's death. Yet the people did not heed God's command in Deuteronomy 18:15 that they must listen to these prophets. While some did listen to the prophets God sent and some repentance did occur, the nation of Israel, on the whole, continued to do what was wrong in God's eyes.

But the Israelites were then impacted greatly by something they probably never expected: God stopped sending prophets, and the people stopped receiving the word of the Lord. After the Israelites were brought out of exile and restored to their land, God did not speak for approximately four hundred years. The last prophet recorded in Scripture is the prophet Malachi, and the book of Malachi finishes with these words: "Look, I am going to send you the prophet Elijah before the great and terrible day of the Lord comes. And he will turn the hearts of fathers to their children and the hearts of children to their fathers. Otherwise, I will come and strike the land with a curse" (Malachi 4:5–6). With these final words, prophecy ceased for a time. Because of the sudden cessation of prophecy, Bible interpreters believe that the Israelites began to view Deuteronomy 18:15–18 as a prophecy about one particular person who would come. And Malachi 4:5–6 seems to confirm this.

During the four hundred years of silence, the Israelites were likely in a time of anticipation. As the years went by and God still had not provided His promised Prophet, the Israelites probably thought, *When will this promised Prophet come? Will God speak to us again?* It is possible that because of Malachi 4:5–6, people expected the Prophet Elijah to come again. But God's mention of Elijah is best understood as a description of the person coming rather than Elijah returning himself. This Prophet would be like Elijah and would carry on Elijah's work by turning the hearts of God's people to the Lord.

Though the Israelites could not have predicted it then, we now know that this Prophet did come, and He was preceded by another who was sent to prepare the way for Him (Luke 3:4). In Luke 1:11–17, we read how the angel Gabriel appeared to a man named Zechariah. Gabriel told Zechariah how his wife would bear a son who would have an incredible destiny. This boy would be given God's Spirit and would turn many hearts to the Lord. Gabriel's words are very similar to those in Malachi 4:5–6, especially with the mention of Elijah (Malachi 4:5, Luke 1:17). Just as Zechariah might have thought, we can find ourselves wondering, *Is this the promised Prophet?* Later on in Luke 1, Zechariah prophesies this about his son, "And you, child, will be called a prophet of the Most High, for you will go before the Lord to prepare his ways" (Luke 1:76).

While Zechariah's son, John the Baptist, would be *a* prophet of the Most High, he would not be *the* Prophet God promised. Instead, John the Baptist would be a herald

As we count down the days until Christmas, may our hearts be soft and open to Jesus.

for the promised Prophet to come — the One who would be not only a prophet but also the Lord, the Messiah, God in the flesh. This promised Prophet is Jesus, who would go on to turn hearts to the Lord through an agonizing death on the cross. But would the people heed God's words to listen to Jesus, the true promised Prophet of God?

We see the answer to that question in John 7:40, when some people saw the miraculous works Jesus performed and said, "This truly is the Prophet" (John 7:40). However, while some people recognized Jesus as God's prophet and listened to His words, others rejected Him (John 7:41). After so many years of anticipation, God's people did not welcome Jesus as God's true promised Prophet. This rejection would be like us slamming the door in the face of the person we had been excited to see on Christmas Day or opening a gift we had desired, only to then toss it aside in disgust.

However, even with this rejection, Jesus remained faithful to teaching God's words. But unlike the prophets before Him, Jesus did what those prophets could not do by saving God's people from their sin. While the prophets helped encourage obedience and worship, only Jesus can truly turn our hearts to the Lord and keep them there by His grace. This Advent season, we have a choice to make. Will we reject the baby in the manger who died for us, or will we receive Him? As we count down the days until Christmas, may our hearts be soft and open to Jesus because unlike the Israelites, this season of anticipation is not a time of silence but celebration. Jesus has come, and He now draws all His children to Himself, teaching us to listen to Him and grow in obedience as He transforms our hearts.

Study Questions

01 / How would you feel as an Israelite during the four hundred years of silence?

02 / Why does it matter that God remained faithful to provide the promised Prophet?

03 / Why did the people reject Jesus, even though He was the anticipated Prophet?

Notes

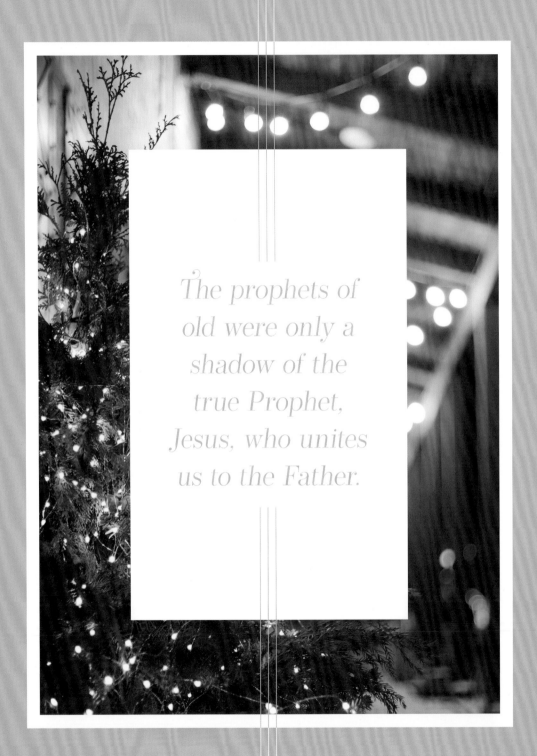

The prophets of old were only a shadow of the true Prophet, Jesus, who unites us to the Father.

Jesus: The Perfect Revelation

Read Hebrews 1:1–2, John 1:1, John 14:9

*T*he Israelites lived without a prophet's words for four hundred years. During these years, the Israelites eventually came under Roman rule. They had returned to their land from exile, but they faced heavy taxation and oppression from the Roman government. As such, the Israelites once again found themselves in a place of hardship. Throughout this time, there was no word from God, no prophet giving the people encouragement and instruction from the Lord. But this all changed one night in Bethlehem. That night, the Word of God broke through the silence, and heaven met earth like never before. The anticipated Prophet came, yet He was completely different from what people expected. The Word of God was a baby boy born in a manger.

Yet this child was unlike those who came before Him. While He grew up and began sharing God's words with the people, He claimed an authority that the prophets of old did not possess. Yes, this man's authority to proclaim God's words came from God, but He also claimed to share equality with the One who provided Him authority. This was because Jesus—the true Prophet, God's promised Prophet—is God in the flesh.

John 1:14 tells us, "The Word became flesh and dwelt among us. We observed his glory, the glory as the one and only Son from the Father, full of grace and truth." The Word is Jesus Christ, who was with God in the beginning and shares God's nature. It was God's plan from the start to send a Prophet who would be set apart from the rest who came before Him. Jesus is distinct from the prophets because Jesus did not only speak

God's words—He is the Word of God, the revelation of God in human form. While those before Him revealed God's wisdom and instruction, Jesus is the perfect revelation. Only Jesus can communicate God's truth and wisdom perfectly because He is God.

Jesus revealed the Father in a way the prophets could not because He enabled mankind to be face-to-face with God Himself. Those who saw Jesus speak heard God's words from the very lips of God. This is why Jesus tells His disciples in John 14:9 that those who see Him have seen the Father. To see, hear, and know Jesus is to see, hear, and know God. However, Jesus is also distinct from the prophets because He did not only speak on behalf of God. He called people to follow Him and experience new life through Him.

Jesus declares in John 14:6 that He is the only way to God. Jesus reveals the Father to humanity, but He also reveals the way to know the Father—through Him. Those who believe in Jesus and follow Him receive a relationship with God and eternal life. Through Christ, we receive new hearts and a new way of life that is dedicated to the Lord. Therefore, Jesus is the answer for our wayward hearts and misaligned worship.

God's revelation remained consistent throughout time and culminated in Jesus Christ.

While the past prophets encouraged God's people to follow God and His law, they were still sinful humans themselves. Yet Jesus did not waver in His obedience to God. He remained faithful to the Lord and did what God's people could not by meeting all the requirements of God's law. Jesus lived the perfect life that we could never live and died the death that we deserve. But through His death and resurrection, those who trust and believe in Jesus receive the ability to be faithful to the Lord. With our hearts cleansed from sin and with the help of the Holy Spirit, we are enabled to walk in the newness of life that Christ gives us.

Each one of us is separated from God because of our sin. Desperately though we may try, we cannot do anything on our own to bridge the chasm between us and God that sin has created. But this is why God gave us Jesus. The prophets of old were only a shadow of the true Prophet, Jesus, who unites us to the Father. The cross of Christ bridges the gap between us and God. Through the grace of Christ, we are able to run to the open arms of the Father and live as the people God created us to be. Sin kept us from obeying and worshiping the Lord as we should, but the new hearts we receive from Christ turn us away from our sinful pursuits to follow the Lord. Even when we stray in our faithfulness to the Lord, the grace of Christ brings us back, and the Spirit enables us to keep pursuing the Lord.

This Advent, consider God's incredible grace to send His people His Word. Consider God's faithfulness to provide salvation even when it seemed like He was silent. God's revelation remained consistent throughout time and culminated in Jesus Christ. Even in those years of silence, God remained faithful to bring His people to Himself. Yet He did not send a mere man to do this, but He sent His own Son.

Whatever you may be experiencing this Advent season, do not allow those situations and emotions to keep you from marveling at Jesus Christ. Do not lose sight of the new life that Jesus Christ has given you or offers you. In the past, God spoke through the prophets, but now, He has spoken to us through His Son. And when we listen to Jesus and follow Him, our lives are transformed. The baby born in Bethlehem changed everything, so let us respond to Him with adoration and praise.

Study Questions

01 / How was Jesus distinct from the prophets before Him?
Why is Jesus more than a prophet?

02 / Read Mark 8:34–38. How are our lives changed by following Christ? Why is the cost to follow Christ worth it?

03 / How does the life that Jesus gives you motivate your obedience to God?

Notes

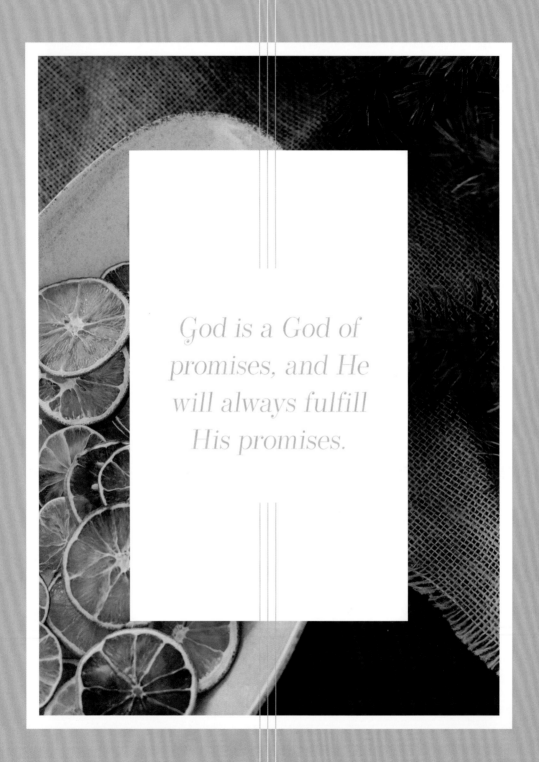

God is a God of promises, and He will always fulfill His promises.

Jesus: The Fulfillment of Prophecy

Read Luke 24:25–27, 1 Peter 1:10–12

The day after Christmas can feel pretty disheartening. The excitement of Christmas fades once the day has passed. The presents have all been unwrapped, the Christmas tree is ready to be taken down, and a regular routine begins again. We might combat these feelings of disappointment by looking ahead to the next Christmas. Children may get started on their Christmas lists for next year early, and parents may feel content when taking down the tree, knowing that the day will come for it to be decorated again. Hope is fueled by looking ahead. Whether it be Christmas Day or another anticipated event, our hope grows by looking ahead to what we know will happen.

Many prophecies in the Old Testament involved looking ahead. God, in His faithfulness, partially fulfilled His promises for Israel—such as releasing them from exile and returning them to their land—but there was still something to hope for. Israel was still under foreign rule, the temple was not what it used to be, and the promised Messiah had not come. Yet the Israelites could find hope as they read the prophecies God gave them and looked ahead to their fulfillment.

Though they were unrepentant and wayward, God provided glimpses of grace through prophecies. God gave the prophets prophecies of restoration, such as in Ezekiel 34:27b, which says, "They will know that I am the Lord when I break the bars of their yoke and rescue them from the power of those who enslave them." God declared prophecies of forgiveness, such as in Isaiah 1:18, which says, "'Come, let's settle this,' says the Lord.

'Though your sins are scarlet, they will be as white as snow; though they are crimson red, they will be like wool.'" God also provided prophecies of a new covenant that He would establish with His people (Jeremiah 31), and God gave prophecy after prophecy of the chosen Messiah, who would be God's agent of salvation and restoration (Isaiah 9:6, Jeremiah 33:14–15).

While many of the prophecies God gave the Israelites contained warnings and punishment, God remained faithful to always provide prophecies that fostered hope. Even before God used prophets, He spoke promises to His people, forming covenants with them that promised a future of abundance, freedom, and peace. God's words of promise even trace back to the garden of Eden, where God Himself first declared how the Messiah would defeat Satan (Genesis 3:15). God is a God of promises, and He will always fulfill His promises.

First Peter 1:10–12 tells us how the prophets in the Old Testament searched through past and current prophecies to determine when and how the Messiah would come. These verses show how the Holy Spirit foretold what the Messiah would accomplish and also how He would suffer. Therefore, the prophets were given a general understanding of the Messiah, and they looked ahead to His coming. Through prophets like Isaiah, we are able to read prophecies of the birth, life, and death of Jesus that the Holy Spirit gave to the prophets. But unlike the prophets, we have witnessed these prophecies fulfilled.

While many prophecies were partially fulfilled in Israel's history, all of the prophecies in the Old Testament ultimately point us toward Jesus and are fulfilled in Him. We can see this for ourselves in the Christmas stories we often read during Advent. The Gospel of Matthew repeatedly shows how certain events fulfilled prophecies in Scripture. The virgin birth and Jesus being born in Bethlehem, for example, are but two of these many fulfillments (Matthew 1:22–23, Matthew 2:5–6).

God's promises of redemption, salvation, forgiveness, and restoration all find their fulfillment in Jesus Christ.

But it would be Jesus's death on the cross and His resurrection from the dead that would ultimately fulfill God's promises. God's promises of redemption, salvation, forgiveness, and restoration all find their fulfillment in Jesus Christ. Through Jesus's death and resurrection, those who repent and believe in Him are released from their bondage to sin, saved from the punishment of their sin, forgiven of all of their sins, and restored in their relationship with God. Therefore, Jesus is not only the true and better Prophet but the fulfillment of every prophecy in Scripture.

Second Corinthians 1:20 tells us how "every one of God's promises is 'Yes' in him." God has declared His great faithfulness by fulfilling His promises through Christ, even the covenantal promises spoken to Abraham, Issac, and David. However, though many of God's promises have been fulfilled through Christ, we still await the day when God's promises of complete redemption and restoration will be fulfilled when Jesus returns to make all things new. Like the prophets and the Israelites, we look ahead to when all of God's promises will be complete in Christ. And because so many prophecies have already been fulfilled in Christ, we have hope that God will fulfill His every promise through Christ.

As we wait in the tension between the cross and glory, we do not wait without hope. This Advent season points us to Christ's first coming, but it also points us to the Second Advent, when Christ will come again. Because we know that Christ has already come, we can know with confidence that Christ will return. But just like the disappointment we may feel after Christmas Day, we might wrestle with feelings of discouragement and discontentment while waiting for Christ's return. Yet we can rekindle our hope by looking back at what God has done through Christ and what He will do when Jesus returns. We can rejoice in what has been fulfilled while anticipating and hoping in what has not yet been fulfilled.

Our hearts find hope and joy by coming to God's Word, God's special revelation to us. Because of Christ's grace and the gift of the Holy Spirit, God speaks to us through His Word, and we respond with obedience, delight, and praise. So, in this Advent season, rest in God's promises through His Word and look ahead to when Jesus will completely fulfill each and every one.

> *Jesus is not only the true and better Prophet but the fulfillment of every prophecy in Scripture.*

Study Questions

01 / Read Luke 24:44. How is God's Word all about Jesus?

02 / How does the truth that God has fulfilled many prophecies in Christ foster your hope?

03 / How can you look ahead this Advent season? How does God's Word benefit you as you look ahead?

Notes

Week One Application

Before we begin a new week of study, take some time to apply and share the truths of Scripture you learned this week. Here are a few ideas of how you could do this:

01. Schedule a meet-up with a friend to share what you are learning from God's Word.

02. Use these prompts to journal or pray through what God is revealing to you through your study of His Word.

a. *Lord, I feel…*

....

....

....

b. *Lord, You are…*

....

....

....

c. *Lord, forgive me for…*

....

....

....

d. Lord, help me with…

....

....

....

03. Spend time worshiping God in a way that is meaningful to you, whether that is taking a walk in nature, painting, drawing, singing, etc.

04. Paraphrase the Scripture you read this week.

....

....

....

....

....

....

....

....

05. Use a study Bible or commentary to help you answer questions that came up as you read this week's Scripture.

06. Use highlighters to mark the places you see the metanarrative of Scripture in one or more of the passages of Scripture that you read this week. (See *The Metanarrative of Scripture* on page 174.)

Prophecies Fulfilled by Jesus or Involving Jesus

IN THE BOOK OF MATTHEW

PASSAGE	EVENT	FULFILLMENT OF
Matthew 1:20–23	*Jesus is born of a virgin and named Immanuel.*	Isaiah 7:14
Matthew 2:5–6	*Jesus is born in Bethlehem, in the land of Judea.*	Micah 5:2
Matthew 2:14–15	*Jesus's parents take Him to Egypt to hide from Herod.*	Hosea 11:1
Matthew 2:16–18	*Herod kills all the boys two years old and younger to keep the promised Messiah from living.*	Jeremiah 31:15
Matthew 3:1–3	*John the Baptist prepares the way for Jesus.*	Isaiah 40:3

PASSAGE	EVENT	FULFILLMENT OF
Matthew 4:12–17	*Jesus goes to Zebulun and Naphtali before starting His ministry.*	Isaiah 9:1–2
Matthew 8:16–17	*Jesus heals the sick and demon-possessed.*	Isaiah 53:4
Matthew 10:34–36	*Jesus's message and the new way of life He calls people to bring conflict.*	Micah 7:6
Matthew 12:14–21	*Jesus's ministry is marked by humility.*	Isaiah 42:1–4
Matthew 13:13–15	*The people do not listen or understand Jesus's parables.*	Isaiah 6:9–10
Matthew 21:1–5	*Jesus rides on a donkey into Jerusalem.*	Zechariah 9:9
Matthew 26–27	*Jesus is beaten, mocked, and killed without retaliating.*	Isaiah 52:13–53:12
Matthew 26:31	*Jesus predicts His disciples will fall away from Him.*	Zechariah 13:7
Matthew 27:3–10	*The thirty pieces of silver that Judas received for betraying Jesus are used to purchase a field.*	Zechariah 11:12–13

WEEK TWO

Priest

Jesus is our
Great High Priest
who gives us peace.

Candle Lighting

Peace

Today, we light the peace candle, remembering
that Jesus, our Great High Priest, secured peace for
us — not just in our daily lives but for forever.

Father,

*As we light the peace candle today, we thank You that You gave us Jesus to be our
peace. We praise You for sending Your Son to take on our sin and shame and pay
the price we never could so that we could be with You forever. Because of Jesus,
nothing in this world can ultimately harm us, for we have salvation in You.*

We pray this in Your precious Son's name,

Amen

Memory Verse

Though your sins are scarlet,
they will be as white as snow;
though they are crimson red,
they will be like wool.

ISAIAH 1:18B

The beauty
of the tabernacle
and the priestly
garments were
meant to reflect
the glory
of the Lord.

What Is the Role of a Priest?

Read Leviticus 8–10, Numbers 3:1–10

*E*very year, as the holiday season approaches, our to-do lists grow, and the preparations for Christmas seem to multiply. From meals to gifts to travel, we spend precious time and effort preparing for Christmas Day. But in this season of Advent, do we spend as much time preparing our hearts for the celebration of our Savior's birth? This theme of preparation will mark our time in the Word this week as we look at the role of the priests in the Old Testament and how this role points to our perfect and better Priest, Jesus.

In order to fully appreciate Christ's role as Priest in our lives, we must understand the origins and purpose of this role. This might not seem particularly festive, but this is one of the roles Jesus embodies, and it should be celebrated just like we celebrate His roles as King and Messiah. Understanding the Old Testament role of the priest enables us to see the beautiful preparations God initiated to pave the way for Jesus to fulfill the role completely and perfectly.

The role of the priest was initiated after the Israelites left their bondage in Egypt and the Lord led them to Mount Sinai in the wilderness. It was there that they made their camp while Moses climbed the mountain to receive the Law. On the mountain, he also received the specifications for the building of the tabernacle, the anointing of the priests, and the sacrificial system (Exodus 25–31). In Exodus 25:8–9a, the Lord says to Moses, "They are to make a sanctuary for me so that I may dwell among them. You must make it according to all that I show you." The beauty of the tabernacle and the priestly garments were meant to reflect the glory of the Lord and evoke worship from the people. The consecration and cleansing of the priests to their sacred position displayed God's holiness and mankind's inability for perfection in their sinful state.

The office of the priesthood in the Old Testament held great honor, but more importantly, it held great responsibility. Priests filled a God-ordained position that enabled the people to seek forgiveness of sin and thus withhold the wrath of God from year to year. Leviticus 8–10 details the consecration of the priests. Moses himself would not be a priest, but he was God's chosen leader to anoint the tabernacle and the priests who served there. Numbers 3 also details how the tribe of Levi was chosen to assist Aaron in caring for the tabernacle and its furnishings. This was important because God's presence dwelt in the tabernacle, and it was the center of the Israelite camp and nation.

Leviticus 8 recounts the consecration of Aaron and his sons. These men were chosen by God. They were not chosen due to merit but because God had a plan to use them and their future generations for His glory. As these men came forward, they were first washed and then anointed with oil by Moses, which is a similar picture of the anointing of the Holy Spirit. This anointing marked them as set apart for God's purpose. A sin offering was required to atone for the sin of the priests, and a burnt offering was given as a pleasing aroma to the Lord. Then they were instructed to remain within the tent for seven days until their ordination was complete.

On the eighth day, the priests began the ministry of the tabernacle. The high priest was given the charge of atoning for the sin of the entire nation. Before he could fulfill that role, he had to first cleanse himself and offer a sacrifice for his own sin. Once complete, he offered the sin, burnt, grain, and fellowship offerings on behalf of the people (Leviticus 1–7). Aaron blessed the nation, and God accepted the offering of the people as His glory consumed the sacrifice in fire. This led the people to great worship. This same process would be followed for hundreds of years until the arrival of Christ, the final Priest, made it obsolete (Hebrews 8:13).

The contrast of the beautiful priestly garments with the spattered blood of the sacrificed animals should cause us to pause and consider what the Lord wanted the Israelites, and us, to learn from this process.

Christ, our Priest, brings us before the Father as holy vessels through the sacrifice of His life.

70

Hebrews 9:22 says, "without the shedding of blood there is no forgiveness." God ordained the sacrifice of innocent animals to atone for sin and delay His wrath. He ordained sinful men to enter the Holy of Holies, the place where His presence dwelt in the tabernacle, to remind mankind of their dependence on yearly atonement. Sin requires payment, and God provided a temporary process until His permanent solution, Jesus, arrived.

In Leviticus 10, we read how God gave a charge to the high priests to be holy and teach His statutes to the nation. Holiness and obedience were imperative. Aaron's sons Nadab and Abihu learned this lesson the hard way when they took the commands of the Lord and the sacred tabernacle lightly. Aaron and his remaining sons were charged to live lives of holiness, set apart for the ministry of the Lord. They were to model this for the nation and lead them to desire holiness and lives that reflected their love for and devotion to the God who saved them.

As believers, we are also called to holiness. We should look different from the world. Sin is deadly and causes separation from our holy God. But Christ, our Priest, brings us before the Father as holy vessels through the sacrifice of His life. During this Christmas season, may we seek holiness amidst the commercial focus of the holiday. First Peter 2:9 tells us, "But you are a chosen race, a royal priesthood, a holy nation, a people for his possession, so that you may proclaim the praises of the one who called you out of darkness into his marvelous light." Our Great High Priest, Jesus, has made us members of this royal priesthood. We now proclaim Him with our lives.

> Our Great High Priest, Jesus, has made us members of this royal priesthood. We now proclaim Him with our lives.

Study Questions

01 / Why was the priesthood important to the nation of Israel, and how did it display mankind's need for a Savior?

02 / Why did the priests have to atone for their sin before atoning for the sin of the nation? How did God show His acceptance of the sacrifice? Why is this important?

03 / What are some practical ways you can proclaim Christ during this Advent season? As a "royal priest" in God's kingdom (1 Peter 2:9), how should your life be marked by holiness?

Notes

Thankfully,
God did make
a way for our sin
debt to be wiped
away through
His Son, Jesus.

Our Need for a Priest

Read Leviticus 16, Hebrews 7:23–28

As you plan for Christmas, what usually takes the most preparation? It may be getting a tree, unboxing your cherished nativity set, or preparing that ever-important Christmas meal. Whatever it might be, we all take great pains in our preparations because Christmas is important, special, and worthy of our time and effort. This sentiment was the same for the Israelites as they observed the Day of Atonement. No day was more important or holy in their calendar year. And no role was more important than that of the high priest. Without him, atonement could not be made. Israel needed a priest, and as we study today, we will see how desperately we need one, as well.

Yesterday, we began the second week of Advent by studying the role of the priest. The role of the high priest was given to Aaron and his two younger sons, Eleazar and Ithamar, after the death of his two older sons, Nadab and Abihu (Leviticus 10). The role was generational. A high priest held the office for his lifetime, and when he died, the role passed to his son. Leviticus 16:32 says, "The priest who is anointed and ordained to serve as high priest in place of his father will make atonement." We also read in Hebrews 7:23, "Now many have become Levitical priests, since they are prevented by death from remaining in office." These verses remind us that these men were finite. Though they held an immensely important role, they, too, would die. But God used these men for the good of His people and His plan of redemption. Sin had to be paid for then, and it must be paid for now.

Preparations for the Day of Atonement were crucial and extensive. As we read the Leviticus 16 account, there are likely many unfamiliar terms. Defining these terms helps us unwrap this day and understand its significance in the life of Israel and how Jesus came to fulfill each and every aspect. Each year, the Day of Atonement occurred on the tenth day of the seventh month. Just as we know that Christmas falls on December 25 each year, this most holy day never came as a shock to the Israelites. It was on this day that the nation sought forgiveness for their sin. With each passing year, the wrath of God required atonement to stay His wrath until the next year.

On the Day of Atonement, the high priest had to first cleanse himself, then clothe himself in the priestly garments. Once enrobed, he would offer a sin offering and a burnt offering. The priestly garments represented the function of the high priest as the mediator between God and man. They were a reflection of the glory and beauty due to God. Once the high priest was cleansed and his sin atoned, he could then offer on behalf of the people. The sacrifice for the nation included both live and sacrificed animals with very specific instructions.

To atone for the nation's sin, two goats were brought before the high priest, and a lot was cast to see which would be the sacrifice and which would be the scapegoat. The term "scapegoat" likely sounds familiar as it is used even today to describe someone who bears the blame for others. This goat literally bore the sin of the nation as Aaron confessed over it "all the Israelites' iniquities and rebellious acts—all their sins" (Leviticus 16:21). The goat was then led into the wilderness and released there as a picture of removing the sin and guilt of the nation from the presence of the Lord and the camp.

The second goat was sacrificed, and its blood was placed on the mercy seat. This was the golden lid that covered the ark of the covenant where the Ten Commandments were kept. God said in Exodus 25:22, "I will meet with you there above the mercy seat." Behind the curtain in the inner tent, above the mercy seat, the God of the universe dwelt with His people. It was there that He accepted their sacrifice and forgave them for another year. This day was to be a permanent statute for the nation as their sin must be atoned for annually. God ordained this sacrificial system in His great mercy, yet all these preparations and rituals were not enough to completely wipe away the debt of Israel's sin, nor ours.

Thankfully, God did make a way for our sin debt to be wiped away through His Son, Jesus. When Jesus was born on that blessed Christmas night, the stars shone brightly,

That precious baby, born on Christmas Day so long ago, now gives us life.

the shepherds worshiped joyfully, and Mary treasured each moment in her heart (Luke 2:19–20). But that beautiful baby had the greatest purpose and mission in history. He grew into a man who would fulfill the role of High Priest perfectly. He had no need to cleanse Himself because He was sinless. God had come to the earth to physically walk among His people. Jesus became the mercy seat when He took on flesh and dwelt among us (John 1:14). Jesus was the scapegoat who bore our sin and shame on the cross. And Jesus was the final, once-for-all-time sacrifice as His blood flowed from calvary and covered us in forgiveness (Hebrews 10:10).

As our High Priest, Jesus took Himself behind the curtain in the most holy place. There, He offered His own blood as permanent atonement for our sin. God established the Day of Atonement as a permanent statute for the nation of Israel. Jesus replaced that statute with Himself and delivered the crushing blow to sin once and for all. That precious baby, born on Christmas Day so long ago, now gives us life—abundant life here on earth and a glorious eternity in His presence (John 10:10, Revelation 21:3). This Christmas, may our hearts celebrate the triumphant work of our Priest, Jesus, who gave His life to return us to the presence of the Father.

Study Questions

01 / What does the Day of Atonement teach you about God's character and the seriousness of sin? Why do we need atonement for our sin?

02 / Read the verses below, and explain how Jesus fulfilled each aspect of the Day of Atonement. Why is this important?

• Priest (Hebrews 7:24, 26–27)

• Scapegoat (2 Corinthians 5:21)

• Sacrifice (Hebrews 10:12–15)

• Mercy Seat (Romans 3:23–26)

03 / Is Jesus the "permanent statute" of your life (Leviticus 16:29–34)? If so, take some time to reflect on the moment of your salvation and your walk with the Lord since then, and record a prayer of thanksgiving and worship to our sacrificial Priest. If not, take some time to reflect on what you learned today, and write down any questions you still have.

Notes

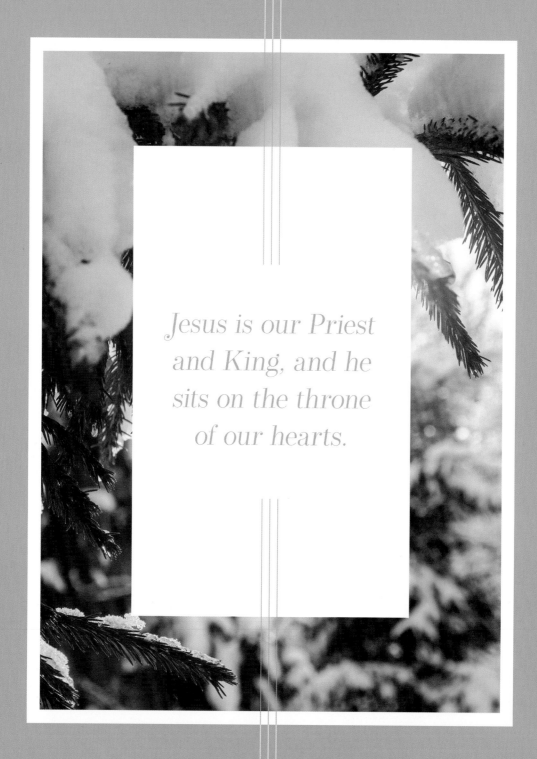

Jesus is our Priest and King, and he sits on the throne of our hearts.

The Anticipated Priest

Read Psalm 110, 1 Samuel 2:22–35

Christmas is a time of great anticipation. Children look forward to the magical season with the presents they hope to receive and the treats they hope to eat. Adults look forward to time spent with family members they might only see once a year. And the world, though gripped by sin, exhales in the hope of a season of rest and goodwill toward others. Anticipation marked that very first Christmas, as well, but for a very different reason. For thousands of years, the children of Israel awaited their Messiah. They awaited a Priest who could atone for their sin permanently and perfectly. On that starry night in Bethlehem, the world exhaled because the Priest had arrived.

As we have studied previously, the sacrificial system, the tabernacle, and the priests were all created to reflect the glory of God, atone for sin, evoke worship from the people, and display their obedience. But most importantly, it provided a way for God to dwell with man, though veiled by a curtain. This sacred process was always meant to be a temporary means to an end. It was always meant to make hearts anticipate the perfection to come. Though temporary, the priests were called to be holy men who led Israel to be holy. But they failed miserably.

Various places across the Old Testament detail the inability of priests to fulfill their roles. We have already read about the death of Aaron's sons, Nadab and Abihu, who disrespected the tabernacle (Leviticus 10:2). Today, we read about the two sons of Eli, who was the high priest in 1 Samuel 2. His sons, Hophni and Phinehas, openly sinned against the Lord and misused the offerings provided for the priests. The Lord required their life. But even in this hard story, God provided a glimpse of the anticipated, obedient, and perfect Priest in 1 Samuel 2:35: "Then I will raise up a faithful priest for myself. He will do whatever is in my heart and mind. I will establish a lasting dynasty for him, and he will walk before my anointed one for all time."

Other places in Scripture call out the priests for their failure to impart knowledge and holiness to the people. Because the priests forgot the Law, God promised to forget them and reject them as servants (Hosea 4:6). When they chose not to listen or honor the Lord's name, He cursed and rebuked them, rejected their descendants, and had them removed just like the waste from the animal sacrifices (Malachi 2:1–3). Priest after priest, failure upon failure. None were good enough; none were holy enough. The world longed for and anticipated a priest who was "holy, innocent, undefiled, separated from sinners, and exalted above the heavens" (Hebrews 7:26).

One of the greatest anticipatory passages of our coming Priest is Psalm 110. This is known as a royal psalm. Written by Israel's King David, this psalm does not simply describe David's accomplishments as king; it describes the eternal King who would sit on the Davidic throne forever (2 Samuel 7:16). The nation of Israel sang this psalm to celebrate God's covenant with David. But there are several striking distinctions in this psalm that set Jesus apart as a superior Priest, one who would complete the mission of His Father perfectly.

The first distinction is found in Psalm 110:1, which says, "This is the declaration of the Lord to my Lord: 'Sit at my right hand until I make your enemies your footstool.'" God is declaring Jesus's deity when He calls Jesus "Lord." Because of His deity, Jesus fulfills the Davidic covenant as the One who would sit on the throne forever and defeat His enemies, thus making them a footstool.

Secondly, Psalm 110:4 tells us, "The Lord has sworn an oath and will not take it back: 'You are a priest forever according to the pattern of Melchizedek.'" Not only is Jesus the eternal King, but He is also the eternal Priest. These dual roles have significant implications we will discuss further tomorrow, along with the significance of the name Melchizedek, but here in this royal psalm, we see that our anticipated Priest will also wear a crown and declare a new covenant to include Jews and Gentiles.

Christmas is a time when we can celebrate that Christ took on flesh and came to conquer sin and death.

The prophet and priest Zechariah, who prophesied to the group of Israelites that returned from exile, also spoke about this idea of a priest on the throne. Zechariah 6:13 says, "Yes, he will build the Lord's temple; he will bear royal splendor and will sit on his throne and rule. There will be a priest on his throne, and there will be peaceful counsel between the two of them." Jesus would come and perfect the priesthood, making the final sacrifice required for sin. He would then sit on the throne and rule over the temple built on the foundation of His sacrifice. That temple is not one made of brick and mortar but one made of believers who declare Christ as their Savior (1 Peter 2:5). We are now the temple where the Lord dwells. Jesus is our Priest and King, and He sits on the throne of our hearts.

Anticipation looks a little different for believers today. Christ has already come, but now we await His promised return. Christmas is a time when we can celebrate that Christ took on flesh and came to conquer sin and death. It is also a celebration and anticipation for His return when He will make all things new (Revelation 21:5). As we wait for that day, the Lord has given us all we need to love and serve Him well. We are His temple, and He has given us a mission to share the good news of the gospel. Philippians 3:20 reminds us why our anticipation is great; it is because "our citizenship is in heaven, and we eagerly wait for a Savior from there, the Lord Jesus Christ." May Christmas be a time when we joyfully prepare for Christ's return and anticipate the day we dwell with Him forever.

Study Questions

01 / How did the sacrificial system prompt anticipation for a better Priest? Why did the human priests fail so badly, and why was Jesus victorious?

02 / Why is Jesus's role as Priest unique in comparison to the earthly priests? How do the prophecies of His priesthood display God's sovereignty?

03 / Read the verses below. As we wait and anticipate Christ's second coming, how are believers called to live?

• Romans 12:1–2

• Titus 2:11–13

Notes

God has given both Jews and Gentiles all we need to understand this important role of Christ.

Jesus: The Great High Priest

Read Genesis 14:17–20, Hebrews 1:3, Hebrews 6:19–7:7, Hebrews 9:24–28

Every Christmas, there is that one family member who enjoys having fun with their gift-giving. Maybe they create an elaborate scavenger hunt to locate your gift, maybe they hand you the present exasperatingly wrapped inside another present, or possibly they give you a key to unlock a gift. Whichever method is used, the anticipation of the gift is heightened due to the events and obstacles surrounding it. As that first Christmas approached in Bethlehem, God had given clue after clue to His people that the Messiah was coming. With each passing year, the hope of the Savior grew. When He finally arrived, He was not what the world expected, but He was exactly what we needed. He was, and is, our Great High Priest.

The role of the high priest had great implications for the Jews. But for those of us who are not Jewish by birth, the necessity of a high priest can be difficult to understand. However, just like that family member who likes to give clues or a key to your gift, God has given both Jews and Gentiles all we need to understand this important role of Christ. One of those keys is the book of Hebrews. It is like no other in the New Testament as it specifically unlocks the mysteries of the priesthood and declares Jesus as the Great High Priest for all mankind. Specifically, it will help us understand our need for a High Priest and Jesus's superiority.

Yesterday, we read Psalm 110 and were introduced to a man named Melchizedek, as well as Jesus's dual roles of King and Priest. This ancient man and these dual roles tell us much about our Messiah and His fulfillment of the priesthood. Melchizedek is mentioned in only three places in Scripture—Genesis 14, Psalm 110, and the book of Hebrews. Genesis 14:18 tells us that Melchizedek was "king of Salem . . . he was a priest to God Most High." Salem was the ancient name for Jerusalem, and Melchizedek held the role of king and priest of God Most High in this important town. He was held in great honor and esteem, as evidenced by the offering Abram gave him. He was no ordinary man but instead singled out as a forerunner of Christ.

Hebrews further explains who Melchizedek was by explaining that he was a king of peace and a king of righteousness with no beginning or end (Hebrews 7:2–3). He resembled the Son of God. Psalm 110:4 affirms this by stating Christ is a priest forever in the order of Melchizedek. Some believe Melchizedek was a preincarnate appearance of Christ, while others believe he was a "type" of Christ, which can be defined as a person, object, or institution that serves as a shadow and points forward to the true substance of Christ. While that aspect of Melchizedek's identity will remain a mystery, we do know that Melchizedek pointed to Jesus and gave the Jews a glimpse of what to expect in the Messiah. The Savior of the world would be both a king and a priest.

Jesus is both the High Priest and the sacrifice.

The idea that one man held both the kingship and the priesthood would puzzle a devout Jew. The roles of priest and king were separate and distinct in the Jewish nation. The priests came from the tribe of Levi, while the kings came from the tribe of Judah. No king entered the temple to make atonement for the nation, and no priest sat on the throne to rule. Scripture clearly tells us that Jesus descended from the line of Judah and fulfilled the covenant made to David that his "throne will be established forever" (2 Samuel 7:16, Revelation 5:5). As a physical member of the tribe of Judah, Jesus could not be from the tribe of Levi. Instead, He was a priest of God Most High in the order of Melchizedek. God alone ordained Jesus's priesthood. And through these roles, He accomplished what no king or priest before or after Him could finish.

On that first Christmas night, this small child resting in a manger came to fulfill the role of Great High Priest. While the Jews hoped for a conquering king to destroy the Romans, Jesus came to conquer sin and death. Year after year, the Levitical priests sacrificed animals to seek atonement for sin, but Jesus, our Great High Priest, destroyed sin completely. He did this by taking Himself behind the curtain and offering His own spotless blood as a one-time sacrifice for all

(Hebrews 9:26). Jesus is both the High Priest and the sacrifice. Jesus made atonement for our sins, and we now enjoy God's presence as we await His return.

Jesus's roles as High Priest and King are intricately connected. One does not exist without the other. We will discuss Jesus as King in more detail next week, but for now, it is important to understand that only the Son of God could hold these two roles perfectly and complete them absolutely. The author of Hebrews encapsulates these roles in Hebrews 1:3b, which says, "After making purification for sins, he sat down at the right hand of the Majesty on high." As our Priest, Jesus made purification for sin. As our King, He sat down at the right hand of God. To sit down in first-century culture signaled that the work was complete. Jesus completed His work when He fulfilled His role as High Priest, atoned for all sin on the cross, and rose victoriously.

When Jesus came to dwell among mankind, He gave us the gift of eternal life through His completed work. But He also gave us the gift of knowing Him and unwrapping His character throughout our lives. With each new day, we can know our Savior more intimately and proclaim Him to others. The process of becoming more like Jesus is called sanctification. This journey is a gift that Jesus gives us to make us look less like the world and more like Him. This Christmas, the gift we can give our Savior is to be holy as He is holy. We turn our eyes toward Him and hope for the day when He takes us to the new heaven and new earth. There, sin will be no more, and the temple will be the "Lord God the Almighty and the Lamb" (Revelation 21:22).

With each new day, we can know our Savior more intimately and proclaim Him to others.

Study Questions

01 / Who was Melchizedek? Why is understanding his role important in understanding Jesus's role as High Priest?

02 / Why are Christ's roles as both Priest and King significant? How did Jesus accomplish what the Levitical priests could not?

03 / How can you grow in sanctification? What action steps can you take this Advent season to look more like Jesus to a watching world?

Notes

*The good news
of the gospel is
that Jesus came to
save the world.*

Jesus: Our Priest

Read Hebrews 10:11–14, Hebrews 10:19–23, Ephesians 2:11–22

Christmas is a time filled with love, anticipation, hope, and joy. But even in this happiest of seasons, feelings of envy creep in. Longing and coveting can overtake our hearts as we desire the gift someone else received. We may find ourselves wanting the same joy the gift brought to them. For those of us not born of Jewish heritage, the same could be said of the Jewish Messiah who was born that first Christmas night. To outsiders, it could easily seem like perhaps this Savior came to fulfill something for God's chosen people, and everyone else was simply excluded. Though they may not have realized it, the hearts of mankind envied this nation that now had the perfect Priest to atone for sin, as they longed for a Priest of their own.

The good news of the gospel is that Jesus came to save the world. Greeks, or Gentiles, do not have to be jealous of the Jews' Messiah because He came to be their Savior, as well. Romans 10:12 tells us, "there is no distinction between Jew and Greek, because the same Lord of all richly blesses all who call on him." Before Christ came, Greeks were excluded from the promises of God and without hope (Ephesians 2:12). However, Ephesians 2:13–14b tells us, "But now in Christ Jesus, you who were far away have been brought near by the blood of Christ. For he is our peace, who made both groups one and tore down the dividing wall of hostility." There is no need for envy because He is our Savior, too. He brought peace by becoming both High Priest and sacrifice, making atonement for all.

Over the past four days, we have briefly studied the Levitical priesthood and seen how Jesus came to fulfill the role of High Priest uniquely and perfectly. This role has great implications for both Jews and Greeks as Jesus offered Himself as the spotless sacrifice once and for all. While the Levitical priests entered the temple day after day, Jesus entered one time, offered Himself once, and sanctified those who believe forever (Hebrews 10:11–14). Clothed in the robes of righteousness, Jesus, our Priest, willingly went behind the curtain into the Holy of Holies and gave His life. On the cross, His body bore the pain, agony, and wrath of God that mankind deserved for their sin. It is through His torn and bleeding body that we draw near to the Father. The curtain in the temple has been torn in two by our Great High Priest, and we now have access to the presence of God Almighty.

For believers, access to the Father comes through the salvation Christ provides and the indwelling of the Holy Spirit. Jesus destroyed our need for the priesthood and the sacrificial system with His death and resurrection. The Apostle Paul tells us in Galatians 3:13a, "Christ redeemed us from the curse of the law by becoming a curse for us." Jesus tore down the barrier between God and man, and "in him we have boldness and confident access through faith in him" (Ephesians 3:12). We boldly walk into God's presence, robed in the righteousness of Christ, to worship and petition our heavenly Father.

Believers draw near to the presence of the Father in a way the ancient Hebrews could not. Their hope for forgiveness rested in equally sinful men and their ability to follow the sacrificial instructions. But Jesus, our Great High Priest, has sprinkled our hearts clean with His blood of atonement. His completed work heals us inwardly and makes us right before the Father eternally. Envy has no place in our hearts because the God of Abraham, Isaac, and Jacob is our God, too. The promises and covenants He made thousands of years ago find their completion in Christ. Through His sacrifice, we are heirs of the promise. Galatians 3:29 proclaims, "And if you belong to Christ, then you are Abraham's seed, heirs according to the promise." The nation God promised to Abraham so long ago includes all who call on the name of Jesus for salvation. Christian Jews and Greeks alike will worship Jesus around the throne one day.

We boldly walk into God's presence, robed in the righteousness of Christ, to worship and petition our heavenly Father.

Our Great High Priest enables us to hold fast and stand firm in our confession of hope until He comes again for His children. Our confession is that Jesus Christ is Lord. We hope in His salvation, forgiveness, and return. He is the Priest of our hearts, interceding on our behalf before the Father in heaven (Hebrews 7:25). One day, He will return for us and take us home to the new heaven and new earth. The Apostle John saw this glorious day in Revelation 7:9–10 when he said:

> After this I looked, and there was a vast multitude from every nation, tribe, people, and language, which no one could number, standing before the throne and before the Lamb. They were clothed in white robes with palm branches in their hands. And they cried out in a loud voice: Salvation belongs to our God, who is seated on the throne, and to the Lamb!

Salvation is for all who call on the name of Jesus Christ. Believers are now members of God's holy nation and chosen people (1 Peter 2:9). The gift of the Savior that first Christmas night was not just for the Jews but for the world. This Advent season, we celebrate that Jesus is our Priest, and we worship the sacrificial Lamb who sits on the throne.

Study Questions

01 / How does Jesus provide access to the Father? How did He destroy the Levitical priesthood and sacrificial system?

02 / What is your confession of faith? In what ways do you hold fast and stand firm in your salvation?

03 / Write out each of the verses listed below. How do they remind you that Jesus is your Priest and that you belong to the family of God?

• Galatians 3:26

• Ephesians 2:19–20

• Philippians 3:20

Notes

Week Two Application

Before we begin a new week of study, take some time to apply and share the truths of Scripture you learned this week. Here are a few ideas of how you could do this:

01. Schedule a meet-up with a friend to share what you are learning from God's Word.

02. Use these prompts to journal or pray through what God is revealing to you through your study of His Word.

a. *Lord, I feel…*

....

....

....

b. *Lord, You are…*

....

....

....

c. *Lord, forgive me for…*

....

....

....

d. Lord, help me with…

....

....

....

03. Spend time worshiping God in a way that is meaningful to you, whether that is taking a walk in nature, painting, drawing, singing, etc.

04. Paraphrase the Scripture you read this week.

....

....

....

....

....

....

....

....

....

05. Use a study Bible or commentary to help you answer questions that came up as you read this week's Scripture.

06. Use highlighters to mark the places you see the metanarrative of Scripture in one or more of the passages of Scripture that you read this week.
(See *The Metanarrative of Scripture* on page 174.)

Jesus's Fulfillment of the Priesthood

TURBAN: The white turban covering the head of the priest signified submission to the Lord. It also held the diadem with a band of blue lace to bear the iniquity of the people before God (*Exodus 28:36–38*).

PLATE (DIADEM): Made of gold and placed on the front of the turban, the plate was engraved with the words "Holy to the Lord." It removed from God's presence any wrongdoing and made Israel's worship acceptable to the Lord (*Exodus 39:30–31*).

TUNIC: The tunic was white to represent the cleansing of the priest. It was made of fine woven linen and worn under the robe as an undergarment (*Exodus 28:39–43*).

BREASTPIECE: The breastpiece sat on top of the ephod. It displayed twelve precious stones, which represented each tribe of Israel. As the high priest sacrificed, the stones symbolized the presence of the nation before God to atone for their sin (*Exodus 28:15–30*).

EPHOD: Similar to a vest, the ephod was worn over the robe. It was ornate and inscribed with the names of the twelve tribes of Israel, with six names on one shoulder piece and six names on the other. Both shoulder pieces were made of onyx and used to fasten the ephod (*Exodus 28:6–14*).

ROBE: The robe was worn over the tunic and had small bells sewn on the bottom. The bells served a couple of purposes: 1) The sound reminded the people of the sacred work the priest did on their behalf. 2) The sound "alerted" God that the priest was coming to sacrifice before Him so that he would not die in the presence of the Holy God (*Exodus 28:31–35*).

Therefore, brothers and sisters, since we have boldness to enter the sanctuary through the blood of Jesus — he has inaugurated for us a new and living way through the curtain (that is, through his flesh) — and since we have a great high priest over the house of God, let us draw near with a true heart in full assurance of faith, with our hearts sprinkled clean from an evil conscience and our bodies washed in pure water. Let us hold on to the confession of our hope without wavering, since he who promised is faithful.

HEBREWS 10:19–23

CROWN OF THORNS: This crown was meant to mock Jesus. Though it was not gold and did not read "Holy to the Lord" like the diadem of the high priest, it was a symbol of humility as Jesus became obedient to death. His crown did not need to declare His holiness, for His life had already done it (*Matthew 27:29, Mark 15:17, John 19:2, Philippians 2:7–8*).

SIGN ON THE CROSS: The sign that hung on the cross above Jesus's head read "King of the Jews." Like the crown of thorns, though it was meant to mock Jesus, it became a symbol of Jesus's submission to the Father as He willingly went to His death on our behalf. Jesus was and is our Priest and King, not just for the Jews but for all who call on His name (*Matthew 27:37, Luke 23:38, John 19:19*).

PIERCED SIDE & NAIL WOUNDS: Each year, the priest entered the presence of the Lord with the names of the twelve tribes on the breastpiece and the ephod to represent the repentance of the nation before the Lord. Jesus entered the presence of the Father with a pierced side and the wounds from nails in His hands and feet to declare complete payment of sin for mankind. Jesus stands before the Father on our behalf with wounds that bring us eternal atonement (*John 19:34–37, Isaiah 53:5, 1 Peter 2:24*).

ROBE: As the guards stripped Jesus and cloaked Him in a robe of purple to humiliate and taunt Him, they could not see the robe of righteousness He already wore in His perfect nature. Jesus conquered sin and death, and the angels in heaven rejoiced as the King returned and took His rightful, royal place next to the Father (*Matthew 27:28, Mark 15:17–20, John 19:2, Philippians 2:9–11, Isaiah 53:12*).

CRUSHED BODY: When Jesus was crucified on the cross, He wore no white linen tunic to signify purification. He was the pure and spotless lamb of God. As He bore our sin, naked on the tree, He took Himself behind the curtain of the Holy of Holies and gave His life to save sinners (*Isaiah 53:11b, Hebrews 7:24–25*).

KING OF THE JEWS

WEEK THREE

King

Jesus is the King of kings who fills us with joy.

Candle Lighting

Joy

Today, we light the joy candle, remembering that Jesus, our King, invites us into His kingdom, which is filled with joy.

Father,

This world is filled with so much sorrow and sadness. However, we praise You that You are a God of joy! When we are sad, we can remember the joy of our salvation. We can remember that You care for and love us so much that You sent Your one and only Son to pay the price for our sins so that we could live with You forever. Thank You for giving us the joy of the world and the hope that brings us on our saddest days.

We pray this in Your Son's precious name,

Amen

Memory Verse

Enter his gates with thanksgiving and his courts with praise. Give thanks to him and bless his name.

PSALM 100:4

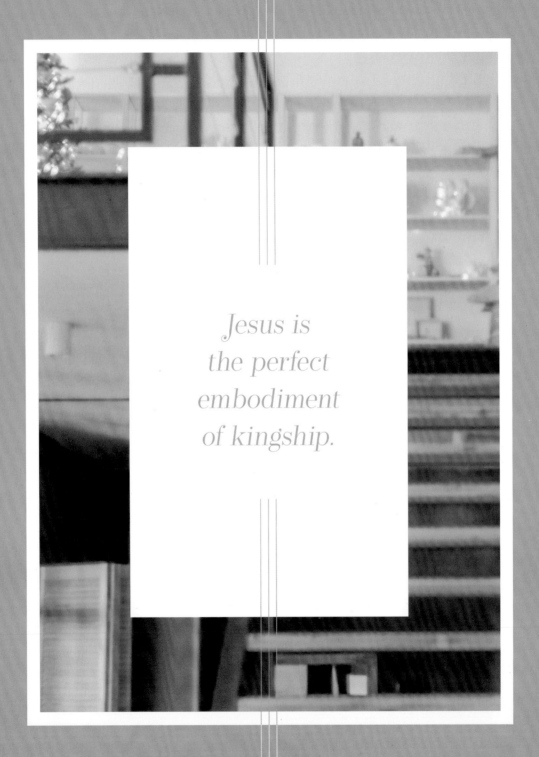

Jesus is
the perfect
embodiment
of kingship.

What Is the Role of a King?

Read Deuteronomy 17:14–20

There is something fascinating about royalty. We are drawn to the glamorous clothes, complex drama, and power-hungry decisions that plague dynasties throughout history. Many people enjoy watching shows and reading books with kings and queens as the main characters. We might feel so enraptured by nobility because it feels so distant from our lives today. Few monarchies still exist, and of those that do, most are little more than figureheads rather than the kings of the past who often possessed absolute power. Yet, since before the world began, there has been a King who rules over all of creation, and His power continues to shape our lives today and into eternity.

This all-powerful King, God, made Himself known to a man named Abram and established a covenant and a relationship with him. In Genesis 17:5–6, God said to Abram, "Your name will no longer be Abram; your name will be Abraham, for I will make you the father of many nations. I will make you extremely fruitful and will make nations and kings come from you." And God remained faithful to His promises, making Abraham the father of a great nation that later came to be known as Israel.

Several centuries later, however, the Israelites found themselves under the rule of an oppressive Pharaoh in a foreign country rather than under the kingship of a descendant of Abraham. But still, God remembered His people, sending Moses to save them from the evil kingship of Pharaoh. Once they were delivered, the Israelites began making their way to the Promised Land, where God would establish them as a nation, just as He promised

Abraham. And though God was sufficient to be their King, He knew His people would reject His kingship, desiring instead an earthly king like the nations surrounding them (1 Samuel 8:6–8). So, in His infinite wisdom, God provided the Israelites with specific instructions for the characteristics of a future king in Deuteronomy 17:14–20.

Why did Israel need a king at all? They already had the true King of heaven and earth on their side—the One who led them out of Egypt, parted the Red Sea, and sent manna from heaven as they wandered in the wilderness. But even though God provided for them as a good King, the people were quick to forget. Soon after God parted the Red Sea, the people complained about His lack of provision and wished to go back to the slavery of Egypt. When God sent manna, the people greedily stockpiled extra instead of trusting God to bring them what they needed each day. Even before the Israelites requested an earthly king, their hearts were far from God, their true King. God had promised nations and kings to come through Abraham's descendants, but Israel wanted more. They wanted a king who could fight their battles. They

wanted to be like "all the other nations" (1 Samuel 8:20). In their sin, they rejected God's good kingship for their own desires long before they ever asked for an earthly king.

So, in Deuteronomy 17:14–20, God lists three specific requirements for the future king of Israel. First, he must be chosen by God (Deuteronomy 17:15a). After all, it was God who truly knew what Israel needed, and out of His great love, God desired to provide for His people. Allowing God to choose Israel's leader would be an act of obedience and trust. Second, the king must come from the family line of Israel (Deuteronomy 17:15b). Though Israel was surrounded by foreign nations, it was always meant to be a nation that was set apart to worship God alone. Thus, any future king of Israel must be from the tribes of Israel and not a foreigner. Third, the king must obey and trust in God alone (Deuteronomy 17:16–20). He was not to acquire many horses, many wives, or much wealth for Himself. Instead, He was to trust and remain devoted to God alone.

These are not the requirements we would expect from a king. Most would imagine a king would need to be a great military

We live under the kingship of Jesus, who offers us freedom by His sacrificial death on the cross.

110

leader, wise, strong, handsome, and brave. God, however, does not require any of those characteristics in a king—only faithfulness to Him.

Sadly, no king of Israel was ever able to meet God's requirements fully. Even King David, who is widely regarded as Israel's best king, committed terrible acts of sin. As the years wore on and Israel's earthly kings failed to live up to God's instructions time and time again, the people desired a true and better King to come—a descendent of Abraham who would perfectly reign.

Thankfully, this perfect King came in the Son of God, Jesus Christ. Fully God and fully man, Jesus left His throne in heaven to live on earth and fulfill all the requirements for kingship. He was sent by God the Father and obedient to God's every command. He is from the line of Judah (Genesis 49:10)—one of God's chosen people. Rather than a palace, baby Jesus was placed into a lowly manger. In His time on earth, He amassed no great wealth, no vast army, or no noble family but instead lived by modest means. The Israelites desired a political leader with military prowess (1 Samuel 8:20) so that they could be like other nations. But Jesus came not to deliver His people from earthly enemies but to deliver them from sin. He came to earth not to be served but to serve us all by giving up His life on the cross so that we may be forgiven (Mark 10:45).

Jesus is the perfect embodiment of kingship. He uses His power to serve and save, and He invites us into His eternal kingdom. In this life, we must choose which king we will serve. Either we live under the kingship of the enemy, an oppressive ruler who enslaves us to sin, or we live under the kingship of Jesus, who offers us freedom by His sacrificial death on the cross. Which will we choose?

For even the Son of Man did not come to be served, but to serve, and to give his life as a ransom for many.

MARK 10:45

Study Questions

01 / How are the requirements for kingship in Deuteronomy different from the requirements for leadership in our modern-day governments and jobs?

02 / Why is leadership important in our lives? How do you most often respond to God's leadership?

03 / What do you put your trust in rather than trusting in God's provision?

Notes

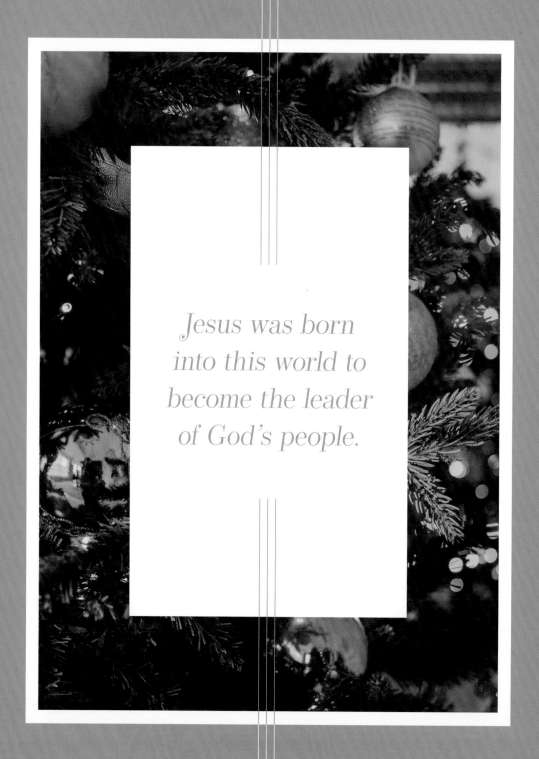

Jesus was born
into this world to
become the leader
of God's people.

The Rejection of the King

Read Judges 2, 1 Samuel 8:6–21

Rejection is a sharp blade capable of cutting to the deepest parts of us. You may have faced rejection in the form of a college you did not get into, a friend group that would not accept you, or a significant other who ended a relationship. The pain that comes after rejection is quick, yet the wound from it can last for years. And some of the most biting rejection comes when we offer to help someone who refuses our aid. We watch helplessly as they fall deeper into their pain but will not allow anyone to pull them out of it. In a similar way, time and time again, God sees His people fall into sin yet refuse to repent and return to Him for help.

After leading His people out of Egypt and through the wilderness, God gave Israel the Promised Land and commanded them to rely only on Him to protect and provide for them in it. God would be the King over this nation, and He would rule with justice, mercy, kindness, and power. This trust in God alone meant the Israelites could not make covenants with other nations for protection or worship other gods, or there would be consequences. Just as in today's world, where there are laws to ensure justice and punishments when those laws are broken, God created laws to ensure Israel's faithfulness and curses if Israel broke their promises to Him (Deuteronomy 28).

All of God's laws are good because He is good, and He will hold His people accountable because He is just. This is the kind of king we want. We want a king who creates laws for the good of us and our nation, and we want a king who upholds those laws to ensure justice.

However, Israel failed to keep their promises to God. Rather than trusting God to provide, they served the supposed gods of the storms, rain, love, and fertility to make sure they had agricultural success. We often do the same thing. We put our eggs in all the baskets we can. We pray to God but also work on our own to achieve what we want; we trust in God to provide but also stress over building up enough savings in case He does not; we know God made us and loves us but try to change everything we can about ourselves so that others will accept us. We cannot serve two kings. We are either citizens of one kingdom or enemies of it. While Israel still obeyed some of God's law, they ultimately rejected God as King by failing to serve Him alone. While Israel appeared to serve God and idols at the same time, in reality, they were actually rejecting God as King as they served false gods.

When most of us are rejected, we put as much distance between that person and us as possible. God, however, refuses to run from His people. He is not a ruler who locks the guilty in jail and throws away the key—He is One who offers mercy instead. He sent judges to lead the people back to His laws and the peace and joy that come from following them. When these good leaders ruled, the people thrived. Once they died, however, Israel returned to their treacherous ways. Over the years of the rule of the judges, Israel fell deeper into sin and betrayal of their King. By the time of the last judge, Samuel, Israel completely rejected God as King and demanded a human king to rule over them instead.

The more Israel trusted in the things of this world, the less they trusted in God's power. They abandoned the King who freed them from slavery in Egypt to once again enslave themselves to a human king who would take their children, crops, and animals to build up his own palace. Like Israel, we would rather bow to idols than God. We serve the things of this world that we think will provide us with success, comfort, and protection because we do not trust God to give us the things we need. We choose the rulers of this world over the King of heaven and earth. Because God is just, there are consequences when we betray His kingship. We all deserve death as a punishment for our treachery against Him (Romans 6:23).

Like Israel, we need a good ruler who can guide us back to God. Jesus was born into this world to become the leader of God's people. He lived in perfect obedience to God, showing us the path back into a relationship

We have a King who will never leave us and who sacrifices Himself to set His people free.

with our true King. He, too, was rejected by us and died under a mocking sign that read, "King of the Jews" (Matthew 27:37, Luke 23:38, John 19:19). Unlike the other leaders, though, Jesus did not stay in the grave, leaving us without a leader. He came back to life—eternal life—to reign over the kingdom of God. In doing so, Jesus freed us from the punishment of our betrayal by dying in our place on the cross. God forgives our sin because it has been paid for on the cross. Jesus's death shows us God's justice, mercy, and love all at once. We have a King who will never leave us and who sacrifices Himself to set His people free. Let all the citizens of God's kingdom celebrate His perfect, eternal, and just rule this Christmas season.

Study Questions

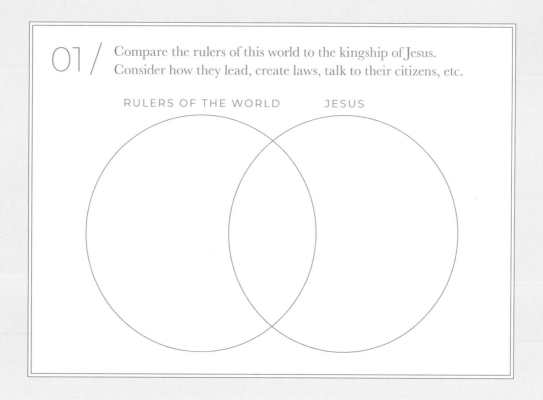

01 / Compare the rulers of this world to the kingship of Jesus. Consider how they lead, create laws, talk to their citizens, etc.

RULERS OF THE WORLD   JESUS

02 / Why would Israel reject God as King?

03 / How can you embrace God's authority rather than rejecting it?

Notes

Jesus's birth fulfilled the prophecies God gave His people.

The Anticipated King

Read Isaiah 9:1–7, Micah 5:1–6

Y ou awaken on Christmas morning to a pile of presents under the tree, and an enormous box covered in shiny wrapping paper catches your eye. You rush toward it and squeal in excitement because your name is written plainly on the top. You start to imagine what could be inside, hoping it is the toy you have begged for all year long. The anticipation mounts as you await your turn to open a gift, but when you rip off the paper, you find that it is not a toy like what you expected it to be but a book. You are disappointed because it is not what you anticipated.

This is what the Israelites experienced when waiting for the Messiah. For thousands of years, God's people looked to the heavens, wondering when He would arrive. Day after day, year after year, century after century, they waited. Where was this promised king to free them from oppression and corruption? When would the reign of peace and joy begin? They believed that this king would come and free them from the foreign rule that plagued them for centuries and restore Israel to the kingdom it had been so long before. Indeed, the King was coming, but He would not be what anyone expected.

After rejecting God's rule, God gave His people what they wanted—a human king named Saul. Although Saul led Israel well at first, he became ensnared in his own pursuit of glory over obedience to God and service of the people. The very thing that God warned Israel about came true. Because of Saul's disobedience, God replaced Saul with a new king named David.

David ruled Israel well and led them into a golden age of spiritual, economic, and military success. However, like all leaders before him, David died. The throne was passed to his son Solomon, who was wise, rich, and powerful. He was the very picture of what we likely imagine a king should be. However, Solomon also fell into the pit of selfish desires—he enslaved his own people in order to build up his kingdom and married foreign wives who led him away from God. Solomon's disobedience led to the disobedience of all of Israel (1 Kings 11:29–37), resulting in the nation of Israel splitting into two nations: the nation of Israel to the north and the nation of Judah to the south.

Israel and Judah both rode roller coasters of dynasties for decades, with some kings faithfully following God, resulting in the nation following Him as well, but other evil kings who led themselves and Israel away from their Creator. God continually sent prophets to beg the kings and people to return to Him, but each time, the people failed to do so long-term. After generations of disobedience, God allowed His people to be conquered by foreign armies, ending the reign of Israel and Judah's kings.

Even though the kings and people constantly turned away from God, He still offered them hope. The prophet Isaiah warned Israel of the imminent conquest of Assyria because of their rejection of God. As Isaiah painted a bleak picture of Israel's future, he also promised them that one day a new King would arise. This King will shine light into the darkest of nights, and He will break the rod of oppression that has held the people in bondage.

Unlike Saul and Solomon, this King is born for us (Luke 2:11). He will serve the people under His rule rather than command their service. This King will be a Prince of Peace, bringing rest and satisfaction to His kingdom. He will be a Wonderful Counselor full of wisdom to offer His people (Isaiah 9:6). And strangely, the prophet Micah tells us that He will come from a small, often-forgotten town called Bethlehem. This King will not be tucked away in a castle but exposed to us all. He will not be isolated from us but given for us. He will serve the lowly and forgotten rather than bow down to the rich and proud.

Isaiah prophesied this King would come from the line of David and reign forever. God's people heard this and imagined this new King would come just like David, a handsome and strong warrior who led a powerful army. They expected Him to overthrow their oppressor and reestablish

The Prince of Peace has arrived and will reign on earth in the hearts of all who receive Him.

a kingdom of Israel that would be as powerful as the nation under David. For hundreds of years, the Israelites waited for this King to appear. However, when He arrived, the people were confused.

This King was not handsome, powerful, or a military leader. Instead, He was a humble carpenter from Nazareth, a town that people did not expect anything good to come from (John 1:46). Jesus is not the King the people expected because He is so much more. The rulers of the world ultimately serve themselves. They use their appearances, power, and wealth to control others. Yet Jesus establishes a new kingdom where the King lays down His life for His people. Jesus did not come to rule over a piece of land but over the hearts of those who choose Him. He brings freedom from oppression, not by overthrowing governments but by freeing us from the burden of sin. Jesus is the greatest gift the world will ever receive, even if He came in a package no one would have expected.

Jesus's birth fulfilled the prophecies God gave His people. Just like David, Jesus ushers in a golden age for all who follow Him. It is not a golden age of wealth and power, but for those in His kingdom, it is one of joy and peace that starts now and lasts into eternity. The Prince of Peace has arrived and will reign on earth in the hearts of all who receive Him. The wait for the King is over. Jesus is here.

Study Questions

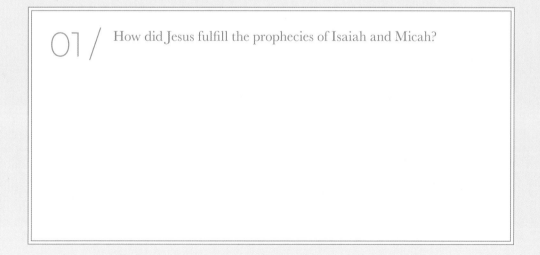

01 / How did Jesus fulfill the prophecies of Isaiah and Micah?

02 / What is the danger of putting our trust in human leaders?

03 / Do you feel like you are living in a golden age under the rule of Jesus? Why or why not?

Notes

How to Verse Map

There are many ways to digest God's Word. You can read it silently, aloud, or with others, or you can even have the Bible read to you. You can read entire chapters or books of the Bible at a time or go verse by verse. One way to study Scripture deeply is to create a verse map. This process allows you to dig into the meaning of one or two verses at a time so that you can better understand the meaning and, thus, have greater intimacy with God.

The following analogy can best describe the process of verse mapping: Imagine looking at a great forest. From far away, you see thousands of trees that all look nearly identical. As you walk closer, you start to notice the subtle differences between each tree. Then, you stare closely at just one tree and notice each knot and leaf. Verse mapping allows you to look at just one passage in a forest of Scripture so that you can notice it for its unique beauty. Look at the verse map below for Philippians 2:9.

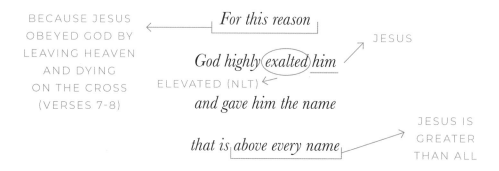

The goal of a verse map is to understand what the passage means and how it applies to our lives. To do this, you must research the passage by reading multiple translations, looking up cross-references (comparing this verse to other verses on the same subject), turning to trusted commentaries, and understanding grammar and sentence structure. This process may seem daunting at first, but take it one step at a time, and you might soon find the joy of studying God's Word through a verse map.

ON THE FOLLOWING PAGES YOU WILL CREATE A VERSE MAP FOR PHILIPPIANS 2:10–11.

1. Pray for understanding.

2. Read the passage carefully in multiple translations. You can find these on a Bible app or the internet. Write down any differences you see.

3. Notice the grammar and sentence structure. What verb tense is used? Are there any repeated words or phrases? What conjunctions (e.g., if, but, and) are there? Circle or underline anything that stands out to you.

4. Look at the context. What is happening before and after this passage that helps you understand the meaning?

5. Look at a commentary of this passage if you have one.

6. Apply. Ask yourself these three questions.

   a. What attribute of God do I notice in this passage?

   b. What do I learn about myself in light of God from this passage?

   c. How should this passage change the way I think, speak, or act?

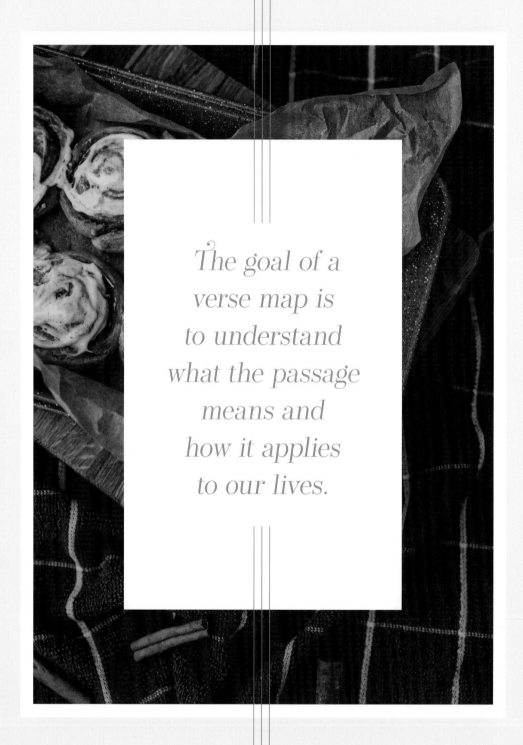

The goal of a
verse map is
to understand
what the passage
means and
how it applies
to our lives.

so that at the name of Jesus

every knee will bow —

in heaven and on earth

and under the earth —

and every tongue will confess

that Jesus Christ is Lord,

to the glory of God the Father.

PHILIPPIANS 2:10–11

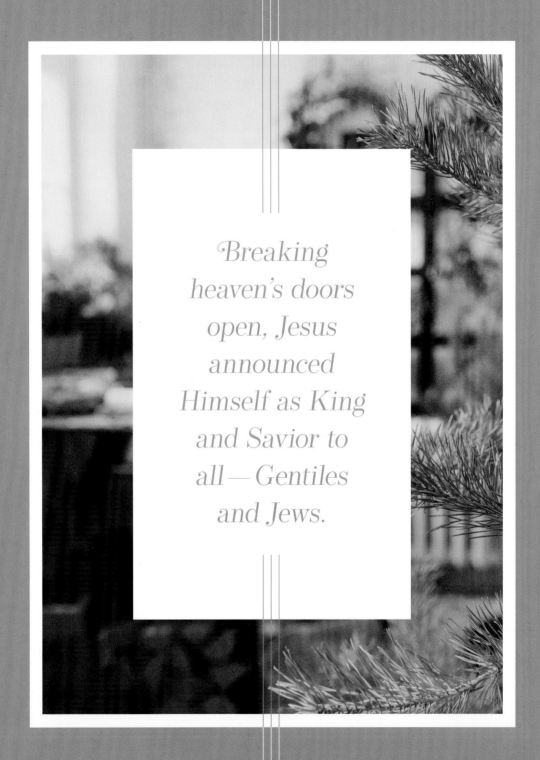

Breaking heaven's doors open, Jesus announced Himself as King and Savior to all—Gentiles and Jews.

Jesus: The King of Kings

Read Matthew 2:1–12, Philippians 2:9–11, Revelation 19:11–16

History remembers monarchs as beloved or evil. We assign them titles such as Catherine the Great, Ivan the Terrible, and Mad King George III. In reality, almost every past king possessed both admirable and abhorrent qualities. They were each loved by some and hated by others. In this Advent season, we await the coming of not just a king but the King of kings. This is the ruler who places all other rulers on their thrones, the only King who can truthfully be called "great" because there is no bad quality within Him.

Israel had been waiting for centuries for this promised King to appear. Yet when He came, He was rejected by His people just as His Father had been. Instead of God's people bowing before their long-awaited monarch, a group of foreign men from the east made their way to His side. Little is known about these men. Some call them the Magi, coming from the Greek word *magos*, which can denote someone from a priestly lineage, a sorcerer, or one who studies astronomy or dreams. In any case, these men follow a star in order to meet someone of great importance.

While Israel ignored the arrival of Jesus, the wise men traveled far for months or perhaps even years to celebrate Him. They went to Jerusalem to see this newborn King. At the time, Jerusalem was the seat of political and economic power in the area, making it the obvious location for a king to reside. The men entered the palace in Jerusalem but were surprised when they were told that the King they were searching for was not there but in a small town called Bethlehem. They then left the palace and headed toward a home far away from grandeur. The moment they set their eyes on this child monarch, they bowed down and worshiped, offering Him the finest gifts. It is important to note that the first people to bow to Jesus as King were not Jews but Gentiles. Jesus came to fulfill the promises of God to be the King of the Jews, but He did not stop there. Breaking heaven's doors open, Jesus announced Himself as King and Savior to all — Gentiles and Jews.

But not everyone was so excited about this new ruler. Herod was afraid of this young boy. Herod was the king of the Jews at this time in history, and he ruled under the authority of the Roman Empire. He fought his way to his seat of power and refused to allow it to be taken. Rather than bow down to another, Herod chose murder (Matthew 1:16–18). Even the rest of the scribes and scholars of Jerusalem who told the wise men where to find this boy stayed put in their homes rather than traveling the mere five miles between the two cities to see Him. By ignoring His presence, they rejected His kingship. We all react to the reign of Jesus. Either we rejoice that He rules over the world with justice and mercy, as the wise men did, or we rebel against His reign and try to keep all power for ourselves, as the rulers in Jerusalem did.

Although Jesus came to this earth quietly in humble circumstances and died a criminal's death on the cross, He now sits on an eternal throne in heaven. This suffering servant is now an exalted King. One day, Jesus will return to earth much differently than the way He first arrived. This second coming will not be mild and gentle but stunning and magnificent. The world will see Jesus as the true glorified King He is when He descends from heaven with an angelic army following behind. All nations will crumble before Him as the world sees His power is greater than any other. At this second coming, all of the enemies of God's kingdom will finally fall. Death, disease, hatred, corruption, shame, lust, and greed will evaporate like the morning dew as the sun shines upon it.

The reign of Jesus is not waiting on His second coming, however. It is already here. Jesus inaugurated His kingdom with His life, death, and resurrection. Dying for us, He opened a pathway into citizenship where we can find freedom. Unlike other kingdoms where one is born into citizen-

God's kingdom is unbound by ethnicity, race, or land boundary.

ship, entry into the kingdom of God is by choice. God's people are not from one region of the world or one people group. God's kingdom is unbound by ethnicity, race, or land boundary. None of us are initially born into it, but we can all be reborn as citizens of it when we accept the kingship of Jesus over our lives and the entire universe.

One day, Jesus will return to earth not as a baby but as a Warrior King. At that time, every knee will bow, just as the wise men did in His presence. All the world will know who the true King of kings is. In this season of celebration, let us praise God not only because Jesus came to the world two thousand years ago but also for the truth that He is coming again to rule over a new heaven and new earth as the King forevermore.

Study Questions

01 / Why is Jesus the King of kings?

02 / Compare the first coming of Jesus that we celebrate on Christmas to His second coming that is described in the book of Revelation.

FIRST COMING	SECOND COMING

03 / How does the description of Jesus in Revelation change the way you view Him?

Notes

Jesus reigns over all the earth, and the reality of His heavenly kingdom is revealed through the Church.

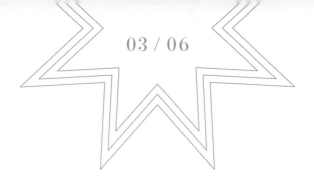

Jesus: The Kingdom of Christ

Read John 18:36, Ephesians 1:20–22, Ephesians 2:6

Whenever a major military battle was won, the ancient Romans held a triumph in the city. The victorious general, dressed in purple and gold and holding a scepter, rode through the streets in a laurel-laden chariot. This victor stood high above the crowd, looking down on them from his seat of power and prestige as a slave held a golden crown above his head. Great political leaders, musicians, sacrificial animals, and treasures from war all preceded this military leader in a parade that culminated in a great feast of celebration. But this triumph of glory only occurred after a great battle was waged and won.

Jesus fought the greatest battle in history against sin and death on the cross. Rather than conquering an emperor, He sacrificed for the people. This battle took all that Jesus physically had. He was beaten, lashed, humiliated, and tortured to death. But three days later, He rose again in victory. Jesus died a criminal's death but is now raised as royalty.

After Christ accomplished His redemptive work on the cross and rose from the grave, He went back to heaven as a victorious King. High above all the rulers of the earth, Jesus sits on a heavenly throne in power and glory at the right hand of God the Father. This is the position of greatest honor, showing the respect and love the Father has for His Son. All heavenly creatures bow down to Him as voices cry out His powerful name. Yet the kingdom of God is not isolated to heaven but has crashed into our world.

As previously discussed, shortly before Jesus began His three-year ministry, His cousin John the Baptist began preaching for the people to "repent, because the kingdom of heaven has come near" (Matthew 3:2). The King of heaven came down to earth, not to restore the long-gone kingdom of Israel but to create a new Messianic kingdom that had been promised to David so many years before.

This kingdom would prove far greater than the kingdom of Israel. It is not bound to one piece of land but covers the planet. It is not designated for one people group, but all believers, whether Jews or Gentiles, are welcomed as citizens. It is not bound by time but will last forever. This kingdom appears invisible to many but becomes more and more apparent to the world through God's people, the Church.

Jesus reigns over all the earth, and the reality of His heavenly kingdom is revealed through the Church. It is not great pastors, programs, or people that make the Church great—it is our powerful King. Jesus is the head of the Church, bringing more into its fold and guiding it with His Word. The kingdom begins in each of our hearts when we recognize the power of Jesus to save us from our sins and choose to enter into His kingdom. We then reveal His kingdom to the world as we live alongside other kingdom-minded people in the Church.

You are not the only subject of Jesus; you are one of many. We must live united with the whole kingdom of God here on earth to protect ourselves against the schemes of the enemy and show the lost where they might be found. We reveal God's kingdom as we live as its subjects. We obey and follow Jesus with our whole lives, showing that He is truly our King. His laws are the foundation of our community within the Church and our families. His promises are the hope we rest in. He is our ultimate authority.

Jesus is the One we bow before and the One to whom we owe our deepest allegiance.

Jesus is the One we bow before and the One to whom we owe our deepest allegiance. We recognize His ultimate authority above the lesser authorities of nations, political parties, or famous teachers. In this kingdom, we are not just ruled by a King, but we are one with Him. Just as two become one in marriage, we become one with Christ when we are saved. We are buried with Him in the ground and raised to new eternal life with Him as well. The Church, as the community of believers, has the power of Christ to help us live in obedience and proclaim the gospel to the nations. We are co-heirs to the kingdom of God alongside Jesus.

The kingdom of God is not like the kingdoms created in this world. The great and powerful Roman empire that paraded their victorious leaders and crucified Jesus is now nothing more than ruins. All empires fall, and all rulers meet the same fate—death. But the kingdom of God is in this world and yet stretches beyond it. It is eternal and will never fall. And its King, Jesus, defeated death and now sits on His throne forever. This is a King we can trust and a kingdom in which we can put our hope.

While Jesus inaugurated the kingdom of heaven in His earthly ministry, it will be fully consummated when He comes again. Heaven and earth will collide under the glorious rule of King Jesus, who will return to earth to fully eradicate death and sin. Until that glorious day, let all members of the Messianic kingdom live in loving obedience to our King and wait in hope for His triumphant return.

Study Questions

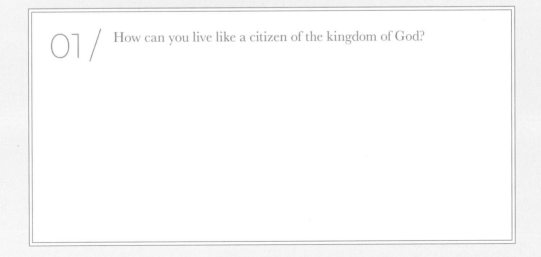

01 / How can you live like a citizen of the kingdom of God?

02 / Why do we need to be active participants in the Church?

03 / How do these passages change the way you view the role of the Church in God's kingdom?

Notes

Week Three Application

Before we begin a new week of study, take some time to apply and share the truths of Scripture you learned this week. Here are a few ideas of how you could do this:

01. Schedule a meet-up with a friend to share what you are learning from God's Word.

02. Use these prompts to journal or pray through what God is revealing to you through your study of His Word.

a. *Lord, I feel...*

....

....

....

b. *Lord, You are...*

....

....

....

c. *Lord, forgive me for...*

....

....

....

d. Lord, help me with...

....

....

....

03. Spend time worshiping God in a way that is meaningful to you, whether that is taking a walk in nature, painting, drawing, singing, etc.

04. Paraphrase the Scripture you read this week.

....

....

....

....

....

....

....

....

....

05. Use a study Bible or commentary to help you answer questions that came up as you read this week's Scripture.

06. Use highlighters to mark the places you see the metanarrative of Scripture in one or more of the passages of Scripture that you read this week.
(See *The Metanarrative of Scripture* on page 174.)

CHRISTMAS

Messiah

*Jesus Christ is
the Messiah
who loves us so
much He came
to save us.*

Candle Lighting

Love

Note: To be completed together with "Who is the Messiah?"

Today, we light the love candle. As we light the love candle, we can remember that Jesus is our Messiah and that He gave His life out of God's great love for us.

Father,

Thank You for loving us so much that You sent Your Son to take on our sins, die a sinner's death, and be raised to life three days later so that we can have eternal life with You. Father, we confess that we do not always love others in the way that You love us. We pray that we can better know Your love so that we can love You and others well. We pray that Your Spirit continues to make us Christlike so that people may see Your Son in us.

We ask this in Your precious Son's Name,

Amen

Memory Verse

For a child will be born for us,
a son will be given to us,
and the government will
be on his shoulders.
He will be named
Wonderful Counselor, Mighty God,
Eternal Father, Prince of Peace.

ISAIAH 9:6

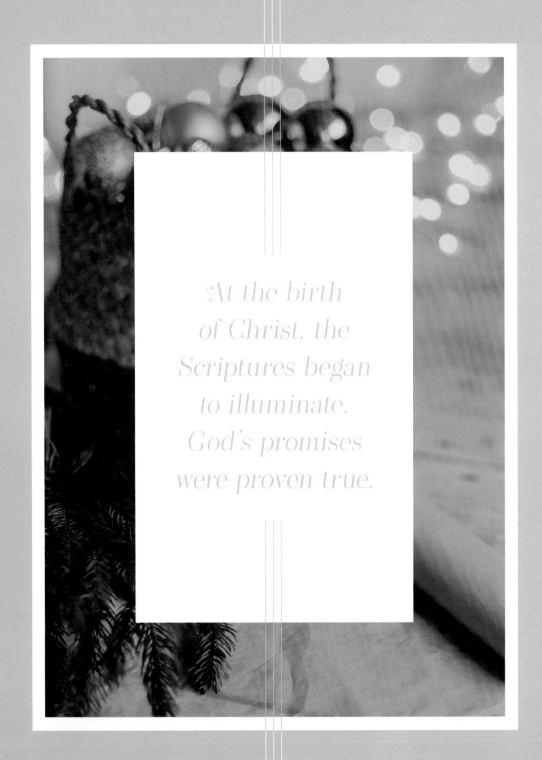

At the birth
of Christ, the
Scriptures began
to illuminate.
God's promises
were proven true.

04 / 01

Who Is the Messiah?

Read 1 Samuel 10:1, 1 Samuel 16:13, Luke 2:8–20

Winds rustle the grasses of the countryside in Israel. The night is quiet and still—much like every other night. Stars shine above while a group of shepherds faithfully tend to their flock. Little do they know, this night is not normal. This night will change the trajectory of not only their lives but of all human history. A bright light pierces the darkness, and the shepherds cower in fear. An angel of the Lord stands before them, sharing good news of great joy. The long-awaited Messiah has finally been born! Immediately, these shepherds leave their flocks on this hillside and venture toward Bethlehem, abandoning everything to lay eyes on this baby boy (Luke 2:8–20).

Why the haste? Why were these shepherds so desperate to meet this child?

Marked by oppression, poor leadership, and hearts prone to wandering, God's chosen people longed for a breath under wave after wave of hardship. This breath—this hope—is the Messiah. From moments after the Fall of Man in Genesis 3, God promised a Savior to finally end sin's grip on the world (Genesis 3:15). He promised a Messiah who would end oppression and break the chains of slavery for Israel. This Messiah would conquer enemies in God's name and eventually restore Israel to its promised glory. God's children would finally claim victory.

The hope of the Messiah passed down from generation to generation. Israel saw the kings of neighboring nations and begged God for one of their own. God granted their wish and chose Saul, handsome and a head taller than most, to be king of Israel. In 1 Samuel 10:1, Samuel, a faithful priest of the time, anointed and commissioned Saul, declaring him ruler of God's people.

In ancient Israel, priests and kings were anointed with olive oil to symbolize being chosen by God. These men were set apart for God's good works, responsible for guiding and leading Israel in obedience to the Lord. In fact, Messiah means "anointed one" or "chosen one." And so, with each anointing, Israel wondered, "Is this our Messiah?"

Sadly, Saul failed to obey God. The Lord removed His Spirit from Saul and instead chose David to reign over His people. We see David's anointing in 1 Samuel 16:13. Scripture tells us that God's Spirit came powerfully on David and even calls David a man after God's own heart (1 Samuel 13:14, Acts 13:22). In many ways, David fit the description of the Messiah. He defeated surrounding nations in God's name. Wealth and prosperity flowed into Israel. God's nation was feared by surrounding peoples. David sought the Lord's guidance in decisions. But, though David loved God, he was a sinner, just like us. David's leadership spiraled out of control when he slept with

Bathsheba and had her husband, Uriah, killed to cover up his mistake (2 Samuel 11). Though David is regarded as one of Israel's best kings, he was a mere shadow of the true and faithful King to come. Israel again was left waiting for their Messiah.

King after king was anointed to rule over Israel in the coming years. With each new king, Israel asked, "Is this our Messiah?" None of these kings proved worthy of the title. In the waiting, Israel often turned their heads away from God and toward gods of surrounding nations, hoping to somehow dig themselves out of oppression by their own strength. Even in the midst of Israel's unfaithfulness, God never removed His promise for future redemption. Our gracious Father still kept His plan intact, working in even the most despairing circumstances for Israel's good and His glory.

Though hope was thought to be lost, now, it is found. The Messiah has come.

The Messiah meant great hope and great joy for Israel, so much so that on the night of His birth, the shepherds ran through fields just to be in His presence. Scripture does not tell us that the shepherds took time to secure provision for their sheep or update their families on their whereabouts. Instead, they moved in haste to see hope fulfilled. Scripture tells us that these shepherds left the Messiah's presence glorifying and praising God, sharing the good news with anyone they met. The deep breath of redemption finally came to Israel.

As we look forward to Christmas Day, we can find a deeper reverence for this baby in a manger who we celebrate. We are reminded of the cries of God's children and the countless prayers lifted in longing—all dreaming of the day their Messiah would arrive. Second Corinthians 1:20 reads, "For every one of God's promises is 'Yes' in him. Therefore, through him we also say 'Amen' to the glory of God." At the birth of Christ, the Scriptures began to illuminate. God's promises were proven true. Years of waiting and wondering were now tenderly answered by the coos of a newborn boy. Though hope was thought to be lost, now, it is found. The Messiah has come.

Study Questions

01 / Even after the Fall of man and the continuous disobedience of Israel, God still kept His promise to provide a Messiah. What does this tell us about God's character?

02 / How did Israel's history impact their desire for a Messiah?

03 / Think about a time when you waited upon God.
What did you learn from that season?

Notes

Candle Lighting

The Christ Candle

Note: To be completed together with "Jesus: The Messiah is Here!"

Today, we light the Christ candle. As we light the Christ candle, we thank God for sending His perfect Son, who is the perfect Prophet, Priest, King, and Messiah, so that we can have eternal life with Him.

Father,

Today is the day we celebrate the birth that changed everything. We praise You that You are a faithful God who always fulfills His promises, even when we are unfaithful to You. Thank You for loving us so much that You sent Your one and only Son to walk this earth, to sympathize with us, and to die on the cross in our place so that we can approach Your throne with boldness. We love You. May You be praised forever and ever.

Amen

This newborn baby Mary comforted was the final Prophet, the Great High Priest, the everlasting King, and the long-anticipated Messiah.

Jesus: The Messiah Is Here!

Read Luke 2:19, Revelation 11:15

*D*o you have a favorite Christmas memory? Maybe your mind immediately goes to a gift from childhood that brings you joy. Maybe you can hear the laugh of a lost loved one. Or maybe you smell your mother's Christmas dinner. No doubt, Mary held onto Jesus's birth story in a similar way. Luke 2:19 reads, "But Mary was treasuring up all these things in her heart and meditating on them." Surely, years later, she could still smell the musty scent of the manger, hear Jesus's coos, and feel His little hand grip her fingers. Did Jesus radiate with hope as a newborn? Was there anything different about His cries? Were His eyes deep with compassion from the very beginning? This verse prompts us to pause and put ourselves in Mary's shoes. In her arms, she held the culmination of prayers answered and promises fulfilled. This boy was *God incarnate* and everything she—and her people—had been waiting for. This newborn baby Mary comforted was the final Prophet, the Great High Priest, the everlasting King, and the long-anticipated Messiah.

As we snuggle by the Christmas tree, sipping our coffee and relishing in this joyous season, let us reflect on what we have learned through these weeks of expanding our reverence of Jesus.

Jesus is the final Prophet—the only One who could perfectly communicate on behalf of God. He had no need to interpret visions or tell of a coming Savior. He is the dream that became a reality, the truth-teller with the very mind of God. Jesus is the Word of God. He invites us to know hope.

Jesus is the Great High Priest—the only One who sacrificed Himself on behalf of the people. He was the spotless Lamb whose sinless blood covered the sins of all humanity. Jesus tore down the dividing wall of hostility (Ephesians 2:14) and invited us into the Holy of Holies. Without fear or doubt, we can come near to the throne of God. He invites us to know peace.

Jesus is the everlasting King—the only One whose kingdom knows no end. He is the leader we long to follow, who executes perfect justice and rules in full wisdom. He is the compassionate ruler, the friend of the outcast, the One who elevates the poor and rewards the righteous. His kingdom is not threatened or shaken. Under His rule, our days are marked by endless praise. He invites us to know joy.

Jesus is the long-anticipated Messiah—the Chosen One in whom Israel placed their hope. He is the fulfillment of past promises and the confidence of our future. He is David's rightful heir. He is the heart of God in flesh. He is the hand of God—embracing His children, healing wounds, and dining in the presence of man. He invites us to know love.

Like Mary, take the time to treasure and meditate on these truths in your heart. Do you need hope? Do you long for peace? Do you thirst for joy again? Do you need to know you are deeply loved? In Christ, we discover the answers to our questions. We find our hunger appeased and our longings satiated. He is, in fact, everything we need.

And yet, like the Israelites waited for the Messiah, we, too, wait for His glorious return. Revelation 11:15 (NIV) proclaims, "The kingdom of the world has become the kingdom of our Lord and of his Messiah, and he will reign forever and ever." Our hearts long for this day—when Jesus will finally bring heaven to earth; when tears, pain, and suffering will be no more; when we can finally rest in the presence of our Savior. We know all too well the sting of sin, and we see brokenness on display in the world around us. Even Christmastime is marred by the Fall. We mourn unmet expectations, familial disagreements, plans that go awry, and loved ones who are no

We see the promises fulfilled. Jesus has come once, and He will come again.

longer with us. At Christmas, we celebrate but also grieve a world that desperately needs Jesus's return.

What is the difference between our waiting and the Israelites' waiting? We know Jesus came as a little baby in Bethlehem, sinless, humble, yet all-powerful. We know that He grew to perfectly serve God, healing and teaching along the way. We know He died a gruesome death on the cross, bearing the weight of our sins on His shoulders. We know He rose three days later, conquering the enemy and establishing full victory over death. We see the promises fulfilled. Jesus has come once, and He will come again. This time, we wait in confidence.

This waiting is not passive. We do not sit on our couches and continually watch our clocks for Jesus's return. No, this waiting is active. We have a job to do—a treasure to share. Throughout this study, we have seen Jesus prove Himself to be worthy over and over again. He is the Light of the World, the light that darkness will never overcome (John 1:5). Our broken bodies are the very vessels He chose to share this hope with the world (2 Corinthians 4:7–10). As we celebrate Christmas Day, may our hands and our lips praise Him. May we mourn with those whose Christmas may be painful. May we wash the dishes after Christmas dinner without grumbling. May we share the true gift of Jesus as we unwrap presents. May we let this renewed reverence of King Jesus, the Messiah, the final Prophet, and our Great High Priest deepen our joy.

The truth is, we will spend eternity growing in awe and wonder of our Savior—and it will never be enough. Let us again put ourselves in Mary's shoes, captivated by the glory of the newborn Messiah in her arms. Perhaps Mary knew these memories of Jesus's boyhood were worth more than gold. Perhaps, through her stories, the authors of the Gospels recounted Jesus's birth. Perhaps she knew coming generations needed these details of the humble beginnings of the King of kings. Jesus is worth more than any celebration we could throw, any words we could utter, any song we could sing. He is worthy of our hearts, our motivations, our time, and our resources. Jesus is worthy of our attention this Christmas and for all of our days forevermore.

Study Questions

01 / How are the requirements for kingship in Deuteronomy different from the requirements for leadership in our modern-day governments and jobs?

- Prophet

- Priest

- King

- Messiah

02 / Why can we have joy as we wait for Christ's return?

03 / Consider Luke 2:19. Is treasuring Jesus a regular habit of yours? How can you continue or begin to treasure Jesus in your life?

Notes

Word Study

Christos Χριστός	māšaḥ
• Greek for "anointed one," "Christ," or "Messiah" • Found in the New Testament 569 times	• Hebrew for "anoint" • Root of the word "Messiah" • Occurs in the Old Testament 69 times

Did you know that "Messiah" and "Christ" are synonyms—two words that mean the same thing? The Old Testament, written primarily in Hebrew, uses the word *māšaḥ* to describe anointing. This is where the word "Messiah" finds its origin. "Messiah" means "anointed one" or "chosen one," and this word was often used to describe a priest or king who was chosen by God to lead His people. An anointing was a special ritual performed at the beginning of one's service or reign, in which the anointed was covered with oil to symbolize being set apart by God. Often the Spirit of God then rested uniquely with the leader. In ancient Israel, "Messiah" held the weight of Israel's future on its shoulders. God promised to send a future Anointed One who would take away the sins of the world, conquer their enemies, and establish a kingdom that would never end.

The New Testament, written in Greek, translates "Anointed One" as "christos." In fact, Christ and Messiah are often used interchangeably between modern translations of the Bible, all with the root word "christos." "Christos" is referenced in the New Testament 569 times. The repetition of this word highlights a major theme of the Gospels and the entire New Testament—that Jesus is indeed the fulfillment of the prophecies of old. When we pray in reverence to Jesus Christ, we are, in fact, proclaiming that He is the beloved Chosen One of God, sent to redeem His people from slavery to sin and free them into His coming kingdom. The term "Christ" is rich with meaning, serving as a bridge that connects the promises and anticipation of the Old Testament with the hope fulfilled in the New Testament.

MĀŠAḤ IN THE OLD TESTAMENT

Clothe Aaron with the holy garments, anoint him, and consecrate him, so that he can serve me as a priest.

—Exodus 40:13

At this time tomorrow I will send you a man from the land of Benjamin. Anoint him ruler over my people Israel. He will save them from the Philistines because I have seen the affliction of my people, for their cry has come to me.

—1 Samuel 9:16

CHRISTOS IN THE NEW TESTAMENT

"But you," he asked them, "who do you say that I am?"
Peter answered, "God's Messiah."

—Luke 9:20

The woman said to him, "I know that the Messiah is coming" (who is called Christ). "When he comes, he will explain everything to us."

—John 4:25

This is eternal life: that they may know you, the only true God, and the one you have sent—Jesus Christ.

—John 17:3

Glossary

ATONEMENT: 1.) When the high priest would offer a sacrifice to God in order to cover Israel's sins and restore their relationship with God. 2.) The restoration of our relationship with God through Jesus's sacrifice on the cross, which, by grace, covered our sins and made a way for our forgiveness.

CONSECRATED: To be regarded as holy and set apart. Priests in the Old Testament were consecrated for their service to God in the temple. In Christ, all believers are consecrated by the blood of Christ, for it is Christ's blood that makes believers pure.

COVENANT: A binding agreement between two parties by which each party commits to fulfill certain conditions and receives certain benefits. When we speak about God's covenant generally, we refer to God's covenant that He made primarily with the people of Israel. These were promises to form the Israelites into one nation, bless them, give them a land to call their own, and deliver them through a promised Savior. But God also formed covenants associated with these blessings with Noah, Abraham, Moses, and David, and all of these covenants have been fulfilled through Christ.

ETERNAL: To last forever; something or someone that has no beginning or end.

GENTILE: A non-Jewish person.

GLORY: Splendor and high honor.

GOSPEL: 1.) The good news that God became flesh in Jesus, dwelt among us, fulfilled the Law given to us through Moses, paid the penalty for our sins with His death on the cross, and rose again on the third day so that we could be redeemed and restored to God. 2.) "Gospel" or "Gospels" describe one or more of the first-hand accounts of Jesus and His ministry (e.g., Matthew, Mark, Luke, and John).

GRACE: God's unmerited favor toward sinners.

HOLY/HOLINESS: To be set apart and pure. When referring to God, holiness is God's goodness, power, and majesty.

INCARNATION: The process by which Jesus took on human flesh and became completely human while maintaining His full deity.

INTERCESSION: To act on behalf of another. In the Old Testament, the priests interceded for God's people by making sacrifices on their behalf. On the cross, Jesus interceded for mankind by offering Himself as a sacrifice on behalf of mankind. Believers today intercede for other believers primarily by praying for them on their behalf.

MERCY: God's kindness and readiness to forgive, demonstrated through the salvation He gives believers through Christ.

PROMISED LAND: The land God promised to the Israelites where they would build their home and nation.

REDEMPTION: The process at the time of salvation by which Christ's grace delivers believers from the bondage of sin and gives them freedom in Christ.

REPENTANCE: The act of both confessing and turning away from sin in order to pursue obedience to God.

RESURRECTION: The process by which someone who is dead is brought back to life.

REVELATION: The act of revealing; to make something or someone known.

RIGHTEOUS/RIGHTEOUSNESS: To do and be what is morally just and right. The standard of righteousness is God, who is perfectly righteous. In Christ, we receive His righteousness in the place of our unrighteousness, causing us to be declared righteous in God's eyes.

SACRIFICE: An offering to God to give Him thanks or make atonement for sin.

SANCTIFICATION: The process of becoming holy—becoming more like Christ. We go through this lifelong process after accepting Jesus as our Lord and Savior.

SAVIOR: A title given to Jesus that describes Jesus as the One who ultimately provides salvation.

SCRIPTURE: In the New Testament, the Scriptures referred to the Law and Prophets of the Old Testament, but today, Scripture refers to God's Word as a whole — the Bible.

SIN: To miss the mark of obedience to God; to do, speak, or think anything that goes against God's law.

SOVEREIGNTY: God's complete control over all things and His ability to operate in and through creation as He so wills.

TABERNACLE: The portable place of worship in the Old Testament where God's presence would come to dwell with His people and where sacrifices were made out of thanks to God and for the forgiveness of sin.

TEMPLE: The building first built by King Solomon and rebuilt over the centuries where God's presence would come to dwell with His people, where sacrifices were made out of thanks to God and for the forgiveness of sin, and where people would gather to pray and learn from the Scriptures.

THE CHURCH: "The Church" (with a capital *C*) refers to all of God's people as a whole, whereas the terms "church" or "churches" (with a lowercase *c*) refer to local congregations made up of a portion of believers.

THE LAW: The Law refers to the collection of laws, or instructions for living, that God established for the people of Israel in the Old Testament. The Law was composed of moral, civil, and ceremonial laws that the people were to obey in order to please God and be formed into God's holy people.

TYPE/TYPOLOGY: A kind of analogy that the Old Testament uses to point to Christ. A "type" is a person, object, or institution that serves as a shadow, pointing forward to the true substance of Christ. An Old Testament "type of Christ" has similarities and differences to Christ, showing how the former is always an insufficient representation of the latter and thus points to Jesus as the true and better fulfillment.

Jesus is worth more than any celebration we could throw, any words we could utter, any song we could sing.

The Attributes of God

Eternal

God has no beginning and no end. He always was, always is, and always will be.

HAB. 1:12 / REV. 1:8 / IS. 41:4

Faithful

God is incapable of anything but fidelity. He is loyally devoted to His plan and purpose.

2 TIM. 2:13 / DEUT. 7:9 / HEB. 10:23

Good

God is pure; there is no defilement in Him. He is unable to sin, and all He does is good.

GEN. 1:31 / PS. 34:8 / PS. 107:1

Gracious

God is kind, giving us gifts and benefits we do not deserve.

2 KINGS 13:23 / PS. 145:8
IS. 30:18

Holy

God is undefiled and unable to be in the presence of defilement. He is sacred and set-apart.

REV. 4:8 / LEV. 19:2 / HAB. 1:13

Incomprehensible and Transcendent

God is high above and beyond human understanding. He is unable to be fully known.

PS. 145:3 / IS. 55:8-9
ROM. 11:33-36

Immutable

God does not change. He is the same yesterday, today, and tomorrow.

1 SAM. 15:29 / ROM. 11:29
JAMES 1:17

Infinite

God is limitless. He exhibits all of His attributes perfectly and boundlessly.

ROM. 11:33-36 / IS. 40:28
PS. 147:5

Jealous

God is desirous of receiving the praise and affection He rightly deserves.

EX. 20:5 / DEUT. 4:23-24
JOSH. 24:19

Just

God governs in perfect justice. He acts in accordance with justice. In Him, there is no wrongdoing or dishonesty.

IS. 61:8 / DEUT. 32:4 / PS. 146:7-9

Loving

God is eternally, enduringly, steadfastly loving and affectionate. He does not forsake or betray His covenant love.

JN. 3:16 / EPH. 2:4-5 / 1 JN. 4:16

Merciful

God is compassionate, withholding from us the wrath that we deserve.

TITUS 3:5 / PS. 25:10
LAM. 3:22-23

Omnipotent

God is all-powerful;
His strength is unlimited.

MAT. 19:26 / JOB 42:1-2
JER. 32:27

Omnipresent

God is everywhere;
His presence is near
and permeating.

PROV. 15:3 / PS. 139:7-10
JER. 23:23-24

Omniscient

God is all-knowing;
there is nothing
unknown to Him.

PS. 147:4 / I JN. 3:20
HEB. 4:13

Patient

God is long-suffering and
enduring. He gives ample
opportunity for people
to turn toward Him.

ROM. 2:4 / 2 PET. 3:9 / PS. 86:15

Self-Existent

God was not created
but exists by His
power alone.

PS. 90:1-2 / JN. 1:4 / JN. 5:26

Self-Sufficient

God has no needs
and depends on
nothing, but everything
depends on God.

IS. 40:28-31 / ACTS 17:24-25
PHIL. 4:19

Sovereign

God governs over
all things; He is in
complete control.

COL. 1:17 / PS. 24:1-2
1 CHRON. 29:11-12

Truthful

God is our measurement
of what is fact. By Him
we are able to discern
true and false.

JN. 3:33 / ROM. 1:25 / JN. 14:6

Wise

God is infinitely
knowledgeable and
is judicious with
His knowledge.

IS. 46:9-10 / IS. 55:9 / PROV. 3:19

Wrathful

God stands in opposition
to all that is evil. He enacts
judgment according to
His holiness, righteousness,
and justice.

PS. 69:24 / JN. 3:36 / ROM. 1:18

Timeline of Scripture

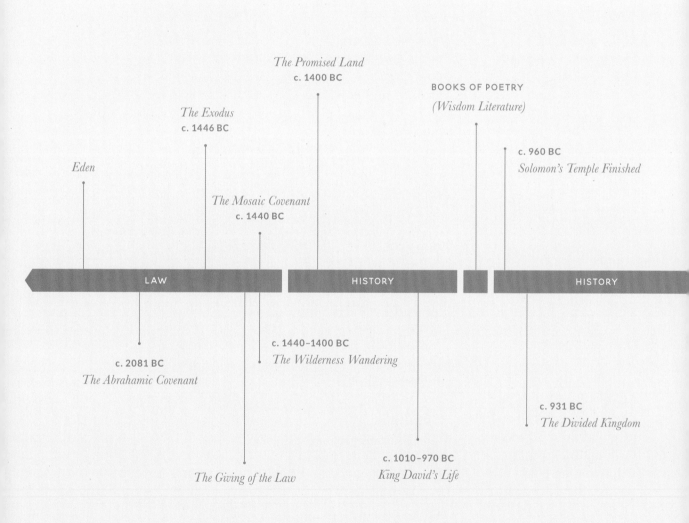

The Promised Land
c. 1400 BC

BOOKS OF POETRY
(Wisdom Literature)

The Exodus
c. 1446 BC

c. 960 BC
Solomon's Temple Finished

Eden

The Mosaic Covenant
c. 1440 BC

LAW

HISTORY

HISTORY

c. 1440–1400 BC
The Wilderness Wandering

c. 2081 BC
The Abrahamic Covenant

c. 931 BC
The Divided Kingdom

c. 1010–970 BC
King David's Life

The Giving of the Law

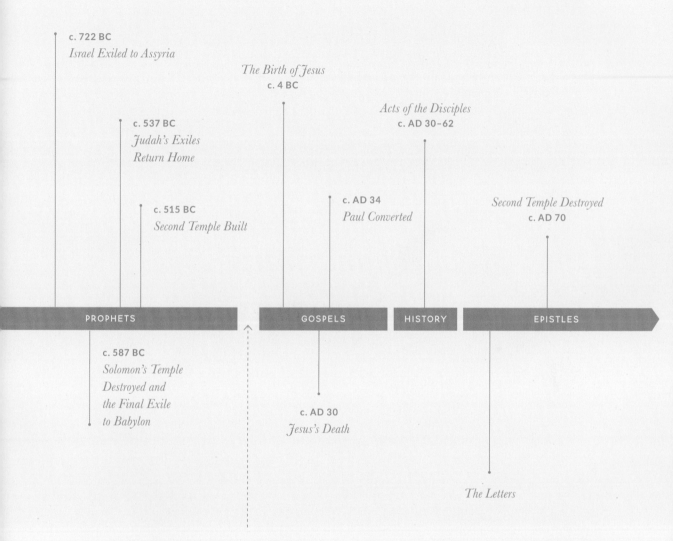

c. 722 BC
Israel Exiled to Assyria

The Birth of Jesus
c. 4 BC

Acts of the Disciples
c. AD 30–62

c. 537 BC
*Judah's Exiles
Return Home*

c. AD 34
Paul Converted

Second Temple Destroyed
c. AD 70

c. 515 BC
Second Temple Built

PROPHETS

GOSPELS

HISTORY

EPISTLES

c. 587 BC
*Solomon's Temple
Destroyed and
the Final Exile
to Babylon*

c. AD 30
Jesus's Death

The Letters

The Intertestamental Period

Metanarrative of Scripture

Creation

In the beginning, God created the universe. He made the world and everything in it. He created humans in His own image to be His representatives on the earth.

Fall

The first humans, Adam and Eve, disobeyed God by eating from the fruit of the Tree of Knowledge of Good and Evil. Their disobedience impacted the whole world. The punishment for sin is death, and because of Adam's original sin, all humans are sinful and condemned to death.

Redemption

God sent His Son to become a human and redeem His people. Jesus Christ lived a sinless life but died on the cross to pay the penalty for sin. He resurrected from the dead and ascended into heaven. All who put their faith in Jesus are saved from death and freely receive the gift of eternal life.

Restoration

One day, Jesus Christ will return again and restore all that sin destroyed. He will usher in a new heaven and new earth where all who trust in Him will live eternally with glorified bodies in the presence of God.

What Is *the Gospel?*

Thank you for reading and enjoying this study with us! We are abundantly grateful for the Word of God, the instruction we glean from it, and the ever-growing understanding it provides for us of God's character. We are also thankful that Scripture continually points to one thing in innumerable ways: the gospel.

We remember our brokenness when we read about the fall of Adam and Eve in the garden of Eden (Genesis 3), where sin entered into a perfect world and maimed it. We remember the necessity that something innocent must die to pay for our sin when we read about the atoning sacrifices in the Old Testament. We read that we have all sinned and fallen short of the glory of God (Romans 3:23) and that the penalty for our brokenness, the wages of our sin, is death (Romans 6:23). We all need grace and mercy, but most importantly, we all need a Savior.

We consider the goodness of God when we realize that He did not plan to leave us in this dire state. We see His promise to buy us back from the clutches of sin and death in Genesis 3:15. And we see that promise accomplished with Jesus Christ on the cross. Jesus Christ knew no sin yet became sin so that we might become righteous through His sacrifice (2 Corinthians 5:21). Jesus was tempted in every way that we are and lived sinlessly. He was reviled yet still yielded Himself for our sake, that we may have life abundant in Him. Jesus lived the perfect life that we could not live and died the death that we deserved.

The gospel is profound yet simple. There are many mysteries in it that we will never understand this side of heaven, but there is still overwhelming weight to its implications in this life. The gospel tells of our sinfulness and God's goodness and a gracious gift that compels a response. We are saved by grace through faith, which means that we rest with faith in the grace that Jesus Christ displayed on the cross (Ephesians 2:8–9). We cannot save ourselves from our brokenness or do any amount of good works to merit God's favor. Still, we can have faith that what Jesus accomplished in His death, burial, and resurrection was more than enough for our salvation and our eternal delight. When we accept God, we are commanded to die to ourselves and our sinful desires and live a life worthy of the calling we have received (Ephesians 4:1). The gospel compels us to be sanctified, and in so doing, we are conformed to the likeness of Christ Himself. This is hope. This is redemption. This is the gospel.

GENESIS 3:15

I will put hostility between you and the woman, and between your offspring and her offspring. He will strike your head, and you will strike his heel.

ROMANS 3:23

For all have sinned and fall short of the glory of God.

ROMANS 6:23

For the wages of sin is death, but the gift of God is eternal life in Christ Jesus our Lord.

2 CORINTHIANS 5:21

He made the one who did not know sin to be sin for us, so that in him we might become the righteousness of God.

EPHESIANS 2:8–9

For you are saved by grace through faith, and this is not from yourselves; it is God's gift—not from works, so that no one can boast.

EPHESIANS 4:1–3

Therefore I, the prisoner in the Lord, urge you to walk worthy of the calling you have received, with all humility and gentleness, with patience, bearing with one another in love, making every effort to keep the unity of the Spirit through the bond of peace.

BIBLIOGRAPHY

Week One

Baldwin, Joyce G. *Tyndale Old Testament Commentary: Haggai, Zechariah and Malachi*. Vol. 28. Downers Grove: InterVarsity Press, 1972.

Carson, D. A. *The Gospel according to John*. The Pillar New Testament Commentary. Grand Rapids: William B. Eerdmans Publishing Company, 1991.

Grudem, Wayne A. *Tyndale Old Testament Commentary: 1 Peter*. Vol. 17. Downers Grove: InterVarsity Press, 1988.

Guthrie, Donald. *Tyndale Old Testament Commentary: Hebrews*. Vol. 15. Downers Grove: InterVarsity Press, 1983.

Kranz, Jeffrey. "The Beginner's Guide to the Prophets in the Bible." Overview Bible. October 3, 2019. https://overviewbible.com/prophets/.

Kruse, Colin G. *Tyndale Old Testament Commentary: John*. Vol. 4. Downers Grove: InterVarsity Press, 2003.

Ligonier. "Christ our Prophet." *Ligonier Ministries*. May 15, 2017. https://www.ligonier.org/learn/devotionals/christ-our-prophet.

Morris, Leon. *Tyndale Old Testament Commentary: Luke. Vol. 3*. Downers Grove: InterVarsity Press, 1988.

O'Neal, Sam. "Who Were the Major Prophets in the Bible?" *Learn Religions*. February 23, 2019. https://www.learnreligions.com/introduction-to-the-major-prophets-in-the-bible-363402.

Storms, Sam. "What Does Scripture Teach About the Office of Prophet and Gift of Prophecy?" *The Gospel Coalition*. October 8, 2015. https://www.thegospelcoalition.org/article/sam-storms-what-does-scripture-teach-about-office-prophet-gift-prophecy/.

Thompson, J. A. *Tyndale Old Testament Commentary: Deuteronomy*. Vol. 5. Downers Grove: InterVarsity Press, 1974.

TOW Project. "Introduction to the Prophets." *Theology of Work Project*. Accessed May 11, 2022. https://www.theologyofwork.org/old-testament/introduction-to-the-prophets.

Walton, John and Andrew Hill. "Who Were the Minor Prophets?" Zondervan Academic. November 30, 2017. https://zondervanacademic.com/blog/minor-prophets.

Week Two

Dennis, Lane T. and Wayne Grudem, ed. *The ESV Study Bible*. Wheaton, IL: Crossway, 2008.

Kimbrell, Joanna. *Search the Word: Knowing & Loving God through Intentional Bible Study*. Edited by Jana White and Alli Turner. Hanover, MD: The Daily Grace Co., 2020.

Mohler Jr., Albert R. *Christ-Centered Exposition Commentary: Exalting Jesus in Hebrews*. Edited by David Platt, Daniel L. Akin, and Tony Merida. Nashville: B&H Publishing Group, 2017.

Week Three

Sproul, R. C. "The King Shall Come." Sermon. *Ligonier Ministries*. MP3 Audio. 20:29. https://www.ligonier.org/learn/series/coming-of-the-messiah/the-king-shall-come.

Sproul, R. C. "What Is the Kingdom of God?" *Ligonier Ministries*. September 13, 2021. https://www.ligonier.org/learn/articles/what-is-kingdom-god.

Strauss, Mark L. *Four Portraits, One Jesus: A Survey of Jesus and the Gospels*. Grand Rapids: Zondervan Academic, 2020.

Week Four

Alexander, T. D. "Jesus as Messiah." *The Gospel Coalition*. Accessed November 14, 2022. https://www.thegospelcoalition.org/essay/jesus-as-messiah/.

Blue Letter Bible. "Lexicon: Strong's H4886 - māšaḥ." *Blue Letter Bible*. Accessed November 15, 2022. https://www.blueletterbible.org/lexicon/h4886/csb/wlc/0-1/.

Blue Letter Bible. "Lexicon: Strong's G5547 - christos." *Blue Letter Bible*. Accessed November 15, 2022. https://www.blueletterbible.org/lexicon/g5547/csb/tr/0-1/.

Mathison, Keith. "The Davidic Covenant — The Unfolding of Biblical Eschatology." *Ligonier Ministries*. March 5, 2012. https://www.ligonier.org/learn/articles/davidic-covenant-unfolding-biblical-eschatology

Welchel, Huge. "Magi and the Eternal Effect of Our Work." *The Gospel Coalition*. December 30, 2013. https://www.thegospelcoalition.org/article/the-magi-and-the-eternal-effect-of-our-work/

Youngblood, Ronald F, ed. *Nelson's Illustrated Bible Dictionary*. Nashville: Thomas Nelson, 2014.

Thank you for studying
God's Word with us!

CONNECT WITH US
@thedailygraceco
@dailygracepodcast

CONTACT US
info@thedailygraceco.com

SHARE
#thedailygraceco

VISIT US ONLINE
www.thedailygraceco.com

MORE DAILY GRACE
The Daily Grace® App
Daily Grace® Podcast

Preface

This guide has been prepared for direct dissemination to the general public and is based on the most reliable hazard awareness and emergency education information available at the time of publication, including advances in scientific knowledge, more accurate technical language, and the latest physical research on what happens in disasters.

This publication is, however, too brief to cover every factor, situation, or difference in buildings, infrastructure, or other environmental features that might be of interest. To help you explore your interest further, additional sources of information have been included.

The guide has been designed to help the citizens of this nation learn how to protect themselves and their families against all types of hazards. It can be used as a reference source or as a step-by-step manual. The focus of the content is on how to develop, practice, and maintain emergency plans that reflect what must be done before, during, and after a disaster to protect people and their property. Also included is information on how to assemble a disaster supplies kit that contains the food, water, and other supplies in sufficient quantity for individuals and their families to survive following a disaster in the event they must rely on their own resources.

Are You Ready? is just one of many resources the Department of Homeland Security provides the citizens of this nation to help them be prepared against all types of hazards. The Department of Homeland Security's Ready Campaign seeks to help America be better prepared for even unlikely emergency scenarios. Information on how the public can be ready in case of a national emergency – including a possible terrorism attack involving biological, chemical, or radiological weapons – can be found by logging on to the Department of Homeland Security's web site, www.ready.gov, or by calling 1-800-BE-READY for printed information.

CERT

Following a disaster, community members may be on their own for a period of time because of the size of the area affected, lost communications, and impassable roads.

The Community Emergency Response Team (CERT) program supports local response capability by training volunteers to organize themselves and spontaneous volunteers at the disaster site, to provide immediate assistance to victims, and to collect disaster intelligence to support responders' efforts when they arrive.

In the classroom, participants learn about the hazards they face and ways to prepare for them. CERT members are taught basic organizational skills that they can use to help themselves, their loved ones, and their neighbors until help arrives.

Local government, or one of its representatives, sponsor CERT training in the community. Training consists of 20 hours of instruction on topics that include disaster preparedness, fire safety, disaster medical operations, light search and rescue, team organization, and disaster psychology. Upon completion of the training, participants are encouraged to continue their involvement by participating in training activities and volunteering for projects that support their community's disaster preparedness efforts.

For additional information on CERT, visit training.fema.gov/EMIWeb/CERT or contact your local Citizen Corps Council.

Citizen Corps

Citizen Corps provides opportunities for people across the country to participate in a range of measures to make their families, their homes, and their communities safer from the threats of crime, terrorism, public health issues, and disasters of all kinds. Through public education, training opportunities, and volunteer programs, every American can do their part to be better prepared and better protected and to help their communities do the same.

Citizen Corps is managed at the local level by Citizen Corps Councils, which bring together leaders from law enforcement, fire, emergency medical and other emergency management, volunteer organizations, local elected officials, the private sector, and other community stakeholders. These Citizen Corps Councils will organize public education on disaster mitigation and preparedness, citizen training, and volunteer programs to give people of all ages and backgrounds the opportunity to support their community's emergency services and to safeguard themselves and their property.

By participating in Citizen Corps programs, you can make your home, your neighborhood and your community a safer place to live. To find out more, please visit the Citizen Corps Web site, *www.citizencorps.gov* or visit *www.fema.gov*.

Activities under Citizen Corps include existing and new federally sponsored programs administered by the Department of Justice (Neighborhood Watch and Volunteers in Police Service), FEMA (Community Emergency Response Teams - CERT), and Department of Health and Human Services (Medical Reserve Corps), as well as other activities through Citizen Corps affiliate programs that share the common goal of community and family safety.

Certificate of Completion

As an option, credit can be provided to those who successfully complete the entire guide and score at least 75 percent on a final examination. To take the final examination, log on to training.fema.gov/emiweb/ishome.htm and follow the links for *Are You Ready? An In-depth Guide to Citizen Preparedness IS-22*. Those who pass the examination can expect to receive a certificate of completion within two weeks from the date the examination is received at FEMA. Questions about this option should be directed to the FEMA Independent Study Program by calling 1-800-238-2258 and asking for the Independent Study Office or writing to:

FEMA Independent Study Program
Emergency Management Institute
16825 South Seton Avenue
Emmitsburg, MD 21727

Facilitator Guide

Teaching others about disaster preparedness is a rewarding experience that results from knowing you have helped your fellow citizens be ready in the event a disaster should strike. As a tool to aid those who want to deliver such training, FEMA developed a Facilitator Guide with an accompanying CD-ROM for use with this *Are You Ready?* guide. The materials are appropriate for use in training groups such as school children, community organizations, scouts, social groups, and many others.

The Facilitator Guide includes guidelines on how to deliver training to various audiences, generic lesson plans for teaching disaster preparedness, and information on how to obtain other resources that can be used to augment the material in the *Are You Ready?* guide. The CD-ROM contains teaching aids such as electronic visuals that reflect key information and handouts that can be printed and distributed to reinforce what is being presented. To obtain a copy of the Facilitator Guide and CD-ROM, call the FEMA Distribution Center at (800) 480-2520 or request it by writing to:

Federal Emergency Management Agency
P.O. Box 2012
Jessup, MD 20794-2012

Table of Contents

Why Prepare

There are real benefits to being prepared.

- Being prepared can reduce fear, anxiety, and losses that accompany disasters. Communities, families, and individuals should know what to do in the event of a fire and where to seek shelter during a tornado. They should be ready to evacuate their homes and take refuge in public shelters and know how to care for their basic medical needs.

- People also can reduce the impact of disasters (flood proofing, elevating a home or moving a home out of harm's way, and securing items that could shake loose in an earthquake) and sometimes avoid the danger completely.

The need to prepare is real.

- Disasters disrupt hundreds of thousands of lives every year. Each disaster has lasting effects, both to people and property.

- If a disaster occurs in your community, local government and disaster-relief organizations will try to help you, but you need to be ready as well. Local responders may not be able to reach you immediately, or they may need to focus their efforts elsewhere.

- You should know how to respond to severe weather or any disaster that could occur in your area—hurricanes, earthquakes, extreme cold, flooding, or terrorism.

- You should also be ready to be self-sufficient for at least three days. This may mean providing for your own shelter, first aid, food, water, and sanitation.

Using this guide makes preparation practical.

- This guide was developed by the Federal Emergency Management Agency (FEMA), which is the agency responsible for responding to national disasters and for helping state and local governments and individuals prepare for emergencies. It contains step-by-step advice on how to prepare for, respond to, and recover from disasters.

- Used in conjunction with information and instructions from local emergency management offices and the American Red Cross, *Are You Ready?* will give you what you need to be prepared.

Using Are You Ready? to Prepare

The main reason to use this guide is to help protect yourself and your family in the event of an emergency. Through applying what you have learned in this guide, you are taking the necessary steps to be ready when an event occurs.

Every citizen in this country is part of a national emergency management system that is all about protection–protecting people and property from all types of hazards. Think of the national emergency management system as a pyramid with you, the citizen, forming the base of the structure. At this level, you have a responsibility to protect yourself and your family by knowing what to do before, during, and after an event. Some examples of what you can do follow:

Before	• Know the risks and danger signs.
	• Purchase insurance, including flood insurance, which is not part of your homeowner's policy.
	• Develop plans for what to do.
	• Assemble a disaster supplies kit.
	• Volunteer to help others.
During	• Put your plan into action.
	• Help others.
	• Follow the advice and guidance of officials in charge of the event.
After	• Repair damaged property.
	• Take steps to prevent or reduce future loss.

You will learn more about these and other actions you should take as you progress through this guide.

It is sometimes necessary to turn to others within the local community for help. The local level is the second tier of the pyramid, and is made up of paid employees and volunteers from the private and public sectors. These individuals are engaged in preventing emergencies from happening and in being prepared to respond if something does occur. Most emergencies are handled at the local level, which puts a tremendous responsibility on the community for taking care of its citizens. Among the responsibilities faced by local officials are:

• Identifying hazards and assessing potential risk to the community.

• Enforcing building codes, zoning ordinances, and land-use management programs.

• Coordinating emergency plans to ensure a quick and effective response.

• Fighting fires and responding to hazardous materials incidents.

• Establishing warning systems.

• Stocking emergency supplies and equipment.

• Assessing damage and identifying needs.

- Evacuating the community to safer locations.

- Taking care of the injured.

- Sheltering those who cannot remain in their homes.

- Aiding recovery efforts.

If support and resources are needed beyond what the local level can provide, the community can request assistance from the state. The state may be able to provide supplemental resources such as money, equipment, and personnel to close the gap between what is needed and what is available at the local level. The state also coordinates the plans of the various jurisdictions so that activities do not interfere or conflict with each other. To ensure personnel know what to do and efforts are in agreement, the state may offer a program that provides jurisdictions the opportunity to train and exercise together.

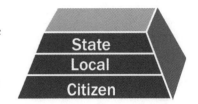

At the top of the pyramid is the federal government, which can provide resources to augment state and local efforts. These resources can be in the form of:

- Public educational materials, such as this guide, that can be used to prepare the public for protecting itself from hazards.

- Financial grants for equipment, training, exercises, personnel, and programs.

- Grants and loans to help communities respond to and recover from disasters so severe that the President of the United States has deemed them beyond state and local capabilities.

- Research findings that can help reduce losses from disaster.

- Technical assistance to help build stronger programs.

The national emergency management system is built on shared responsibilities and active participation at all levels of the pyramid. The whole system begins with you, the citizen, and your ability to follow good emergency management practices—whether at home, work, or other locations.

Are You Ready? An In-depth Guide to Citizen Preparedness is organized to help you through the process. Begin by reading Part 1 which is the core of the guide. This part provides basic information that is common to all hazards on how to create and maintain an emergency plan and disaster supplies kit.

Part 1: Basic Preparedness

- A series of worksheets to help you obtain information from the community that will form the foundation of your plan. You will need to find out about hazards that threaten the community, how the population will be warned, evacuation routes to be used in times of disaster, and the emergency plans of the community and others that will impact your plan.

- Guidance on specific content that you and your family will need to develop and include in your plan on how to escape from your residence, communicate with one another during times of disaster, shut-off household utilities, insure against financial loss, acquire basic safety skills, address special needs such as disabilities, take care of animals, and seek shelter.

- Checklists of items to consider including in your disaster supplies kit that will meet your family's needs following a disaster whether you are at home or at other locations.

Part 1 is also the gateway to the specific hazards and recovery information contained in Parts 2, 3, 4, and 5. Information from these sections should be read carefully and integrated in your emergency plan and disaster supplies kit based on the hazards that pose a threat to you and your family.

Part 2: Natural Hazards

- Floods
- Hurricanes
- Thunderstorms and lightning
- Tornadoes
- Winter storms and extreme cold
- Extreme heat
- Earthquakes
- Volcanoes
- Landslides and debris flow
- Tsunamis
- Fires
- Wildfires

Part 3: Technological Hazards

- Hazardous materials incidents
- Household chemical emergencies
- Nuclear power plant emergencies

Part 4: Terrorism

- Explosions
- Biological threats
- Chemical threats
- Nuclear blasts
- Radiological dispersion device events

Part 5: Recovering from Disaster

- Health and safety guidelines
- Returning home
- Seeking disaster assistance
- Coping with disaster
- Helping others

References

As you work through individual sections, you will see reference points. These are reminders to refer to previous sections for related information on the topic being discussed.

FEMA Publications

Throughout the guide are lists of publications available from FEMA that can help you learn more about the topics covered. To obtain these publications, call the FEMA Distribution Center at 1-800-480-2520 or request them by mail from:

Federal Emergency Management Agency
P.O. Box 2012
Jessup, MD 20794-2012

Other Publications

Other publications cited throughout this guide can be obtained by contacting the organizations below:

American Red Cross National Headquarters
2025 E Street, NW
Washington, DC 20006
Phone: (202) 303-4498
www.redcross.org/pubs/dspubs/cde.html

National Weather Service
1325 East West Highway
Silver Spring, MD 20910
www.nws.noaa.gov/education.html

Centers for Disease Control and Prevention
1600 Clifton Rd, Atlanta, GA 30333, U.S.A
Public Inquiries: (404) 639-3534 / (800) 311-3435
www.cdc.gov

U.S. Geological Survey
Information Services
P.O. Box 25286
Denver, CO 80225
1 (888) 275-8747
www.usgs.gov

Disaster Public Education Web sites

You can broaden your knowledge of disaster preparedness topics presented in this guide by reviewing information provided at various government and non-government Web sites. Provided below is a list of recommended sites. The Web address for each site reflects its home address. Searches conducted from each home site's page result in the most current and extensive list of available material for the site.

Government Sites	
Be Ready Campaign	www.ready.gov
Agency for Toxic Substances and Disease Registry	www.atsdr.cdc.gov
Centers for Disease Control and Prevention	www.cdc.gov
Citizen Corps	www.citizencorps.gov
Department of Commerce	www.doc.gov
Department of Education	www.ed.gov
Department of Energy	www.energy.gov
Department of Health and Human Services	www.hhs.gov/disasters
Department of Homeland Security	www.dhs.gov
Department of Interior	www.doi.gov
Department of Justice	www.justice.gov
Environmental Protection Agency	www.epa.gov
Federal Emergency Management Agency	www.fema.gov
Food and Drug Administration	www.fda.gov
National Oceanic and Atmospheric Administration	www.noaa.gov
National Weather Service	www.nws.noaa.gov
Nuclear Regulatory Commission	www.nrc.gov
The Critical Infrastructure Assurance Office	www.ciao.gov
The White House	www.whitehouse.gov/response
U.S. Department of Agriculture	www.usda.gov
U.S. Fire Administration	www.usfa.fema.gov
U.S. Fire Administration Kids Page	www.usfa.fema.gov/kids
U.S. Geological Survey	www.usgs.gov
U.S. Office of Personnel Management	www.opm.gov/emergency
U.S. Postal Service	www.usps.gov
USDA Forest Service Southern Research Station	www.wildfireprograms.com
Non-government Sites	
American Red Cross	www.redcross.org
Institute for Business and Home Safety	www.ibhs.org
National Fire Protection Association	www.nfpa.org
National Mass Fatalities Institute	www.nmfi.org
National Safety Compliance	www.osha-safety-training.net
The Middle East Seismological Forum	www.meieisforum.net
The Pan American Health Organization	www.disaster-info.net/SUMA

1

Basic Preparedness

In this part of the guide, you will learn preparedness strategies that are common to all disasters. You plan only once, and are able to apply your plan to all types of hazards.

When you complete Part 1, you will be able to:
- Get informed about hazards and emergencies that may affect you and your family.
- Develop an emergency plan.
- Collect and assemble disaster supplies kit.
- Learn where to seek shelter from all types of hazards.
- Identify the community warning systems and evacuation routes.
- Include in your plan required information from community and school plans.
- Learn what to do for specific hazards.
- Practice and maintain your plan.

1.1
Getting Informed

Learn about the hazards that may strike your community, the risks you face from these hazards, and your community's plans for warning and evacuation. You can obtain this information from your local emergency management office or your local chapter of the American Red Cross. Space has been provided here to record your answers.

Hazards

Ask local authorities about each possible hazard or emergency and use the worksheet that follows to record your findings and suggestions for reducing your family's risk.

Possible Hazards and Emergencies	Risk Level (None, Low, Moderate, or High)	How can I reduce my risk?
Natural Hazards		
1. Floods		
2. Hurricanes		
3. Thunderstorms and Lightning		
4. Tornadoes		
5. Winter Storms and Extreme Cold		
6. Extreme Heat		
7. Earthquakes		
8. Volcanoes		
9. Landslides and Debris Flow		
10. Tsunamis		
11. Fires		
12. Wildfires		

Technological Hazards		
1. Hazardous Materials Incidents		
2. Nuclear Power Plants		
Terrorism		
1. Explosions		
2. Biological Threats		
3. Chemical Threats		
4. Nuclear Blasts		
5. Radiological Dispersion Device (RDD)		

> You also can consult FEMA for hazard maps for your area. Go to
> www.fema.gov, select maps, and follow the directions. National hazard maps have been included with each natural hazard in Part 2 of this guide.

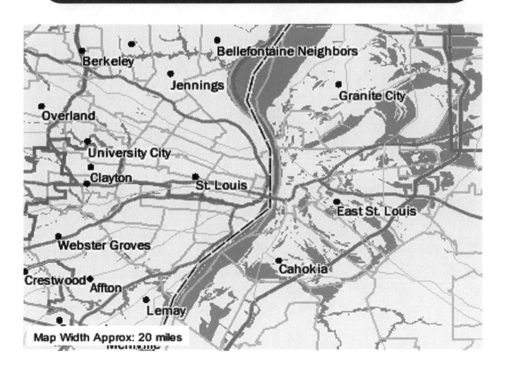

Warning Systems and Signals

The Emergency Alert System (EAS) can address the entire nation on very short notice in case of a grave threat or national emergency. Ask if your local radio and TV stations participate in the EAS.

National Oceanic & Atmospheric Administration (NOAA) Weather Radio (NWR) is a nationwide network of radio stations broadcasting continuous weather information directly from a nearby National Weather Service office to specially configured NOAA weather radio receivers. Determine if NOAA Weather Radio is available where you live. If so, consider purchasing a NOAA weather radio receiver.

Ask local authorities about methods used to warn your community.

Warning System	What should we do?
EAS	
NOAA Weather Radio	

Evacuating Yourself and Your Family

When community evacuations become necessary, local officials provide information to the public through the media. In some circumstances, other warning methods, such as sirens or telephone calls, also are used. Additionally, there may be circumstances under which you and your family feel threatened or endangered and you need to leave your home, school, or workplace to avoid these situations.

The amount of time you have to leave will depend on the hazard. If the event is a weather condition, such as a hurricane that can be monitored, you might have a day or two to get ready. However, many disasters allow no time for people to gather even the most basic necessities, which is why planning ahead is essential.

Evacuation: More Common than You Realize

Evacuations are more common than many people realize. Hundreds of times each year, transportation and industrial accidents release harmful substances, forcing thousands of people to leave their homes. Fires and floods cause evacuations even more frequently. Almost every year, people along the Gulf and Atlantic coasts evacuate in the face of approaching hurricanes.

Ask local authorities about emergency evacuation routes.

Record your specific evacuation route directions in the space provided.

Is there a map available with evacuation routes marked?　☐ Yes　☐ No

Evacuation Guidelines

Always:	If time permits:
Keep a full tank of gas in your car if an evacuation seems likely. Gas stations may be closed during emergencies and unable to pump gas during power outages. Plan to take one car per family to reduce congestion and delay.	Gather your disaster supplies kit.
Make transportation arrangements with friends or your local government if you do not own a car.	Wear sturdy shoes and clothing that provides some protection, such as long pants, long-sleeved shirts, and a cap.
Listen to a battery-powered radio and follow local evacuation instructions.	Secure your home: • Close and lock doors and windows. • Unplug electrical equipment, such as radios and televisions, and small appliances, such as toasters and microwaves. Leave freezers and refrigerators plugged in unless there is a risk of flooding.
Gather your family and go if you are instructed to evacuate immediately.	Let others know where you are going.
Leave early enough to avoid being trapped by severe weather.	
Follow recommended evacuation routes. Do not take shortcuts; they may be blocked.	
Be alert for washed-out roads and bridges. Do not drive into flooded areas.	
Stay away from downed power lines.	

Community and Other Plans

Ask local officials the following questions about your community's disaster/
emergency plans.

Does my community have a plan? ☐ Yes   ☐ No

Can I obtain a copy? ☐ Yes   ☐ No

What does the plan contain? _____

_____

How often is it updated? _____

What should I know about the plan? _____

_____

What hazards does it cover? _____

_____

In addition to finding out about your community's plan, it is important that you
know what plans are in place for your workplace and your children's school or day
care center.

1. Ask your employer about workplace policies regarding disasters and emer-
    gencies, including understanding how you will be provided emergency and
    warning information.

2. Contact your children's school or day care center to discuss their disaster pro-
    cedures.

School Emergency Plans

Know your children's school emergency plan:

- Ask how the school will communicate with families during a crisis.

- Ask if the school stores adequate food, water, and other basic supplies.

- Find out if the school is prepared to shelter-in-place if need be, and where
  they plan to go if they must get away.

In cases where schools institute procedures to shelter-in-place, you may not be
permitted to drive to the school to pick up your children. Even if you go to the
school, the doors will likely be locked to keep your children safe. Monitor local
media outlets for announcements about changes in school openings and closings,
and follow the directions of local emergency officials.

For more information on developing emergency preparedness plans for schools,
please log on to the U.S. Department of Education at www.ed.gov/emergencyplan.

Workplace Plans

If you are an employer, make sure your workplace has a building evacuation plan that is regularly practiced.

- Take a critical look at your heating, ventilation and air conditioning system to determine if it is secure or if it could feasibly be upgraded to better filter potential contaminants, and be sure you know how to turn it off if you need to.

- Think about what to do if your employees can't go home.

- Make sure you have appropriate supplies on hand.

1.2

Emergency Planning
and Checklists

Now that you've learned about what can happen and how your community is prepared to respond to emergencies, prepare your family by creating a family disaster plan. You can begin this process by gathering family members and reviewing the information you obtained in Section 1.1 (hazards, warning systems, evacuation routes and community and other plans). Discuss with them what you would do if family members are not home when a warning is issued. Additionally, your family plan should address the following:

- Escape routes.
- Family communications.
- Utility shut-off and safety.
- Insurance and vital records.
- Special needs.
- Caring for animals.
- Saftey Skills

Information on these family planning considerations are covered in the following sections.

Escape Routes

Draw a floor plan of your home. Use a blank sheet of paper for each floor. Mark two escape routes from each room. Make sure children understand the drawings. Post a copy of the drawings at eye level in each child's room.

Where to Meet

Establish a place to meet in the event of an emergency, such as a fire. Record the locations below:

	Where to meet...
Near the home	For example, the next door neighbor's telephone pole
Outside the immediate area	For example, the neighborhood grocery store parking lot

Family Communications

Your family may not be together when disaster strikes, so plan how you will contact one another. Think about how you will communicate in different situations.

Complete a contact card for each family member. Have family members keep these cards handy in a wallet, purse, backpack, etc. You may want to send one to school with each child to keep on file. Pick a friend or relative who lives out-of-state for household members to notify they are safe.

Below is a sample contact card. Copies to fill out can be found in Appendix C. Also in Appendix C is a more detailed Family Communications Plan which should be completed and posted so the contact information is readily accessible to all family members. A copy should also be included in your family disaster supplies kit.

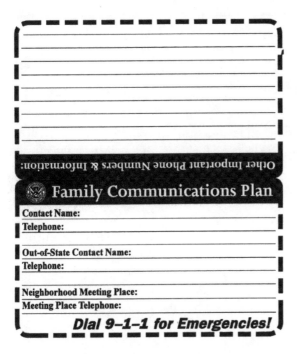

Other Important Phone Numbers & Information:

🏛 **Family Communications Plan**

Contact Name:

Telephone:

Out-of-State Contact Name:

Telephone:

Neighborhood Meeting Place:

Meeting Place Telephone:

Dial 9–1–1 for Emergencies!

Utility Shut-off and Safety

In the event of a disaster, you may be instructed to shut off the utility service at your home.

Below is some general guidance for shutting off utility service:

Modify the information provided to reflect your shut off requirements as directed by your utility company(ies).

Natural Gas

Natural gas leaks and explosions are responsible for a significant number of fires following disasters. It is vital that all household members know how to shut off natural gas.

Because there are different gas shut-off procedures for different gas meter configurations, it is important to contact your local gas company for guidance on preparation and response regarding gas appliances and gas service to your home.

When you learn the proper shut-off procedure for your meter, share the information with everyone in your household. Be sure not to actually turn off the gas when practicing the proper gas shut-off procedure.

If you smell gas or hear a blowing or hissing noise, open a window and get everyone out quickly. Turn off the gas, using the outside main valve if you can, and call the gas company from a neighbor's home.

> **CAUTION** – If you turn off the gas for any reason, a qualified professional must turn it back on. NEVER attempt to turn the gas back on yourself.

Water

Water quickly becomes a precious resource following many disasters. It is vital that all household members learn how to shut off the water at the main house valve.

- Cracked lines may pollute the water supply to your house. It is wise to shut off your water until you hear from authorities that it is safe for drinking.

- The effects of gravity may drain the water in your hot water heater and toilet tanks unless you trap it in your house by shutting off the main house valve (not the street valve in the cement box at the curb—this valve is extremely difficult to turn and requires a special tool).

Preparing to Shut Off Water

- Locate the shut-off valve for the water line that enters your house. It may look like this:

- Make sure this valve can be completely shut off. Your valve may be rusted open, or it may only partially close. Replace it if necessary.

- Label this valve with a tag for easy identification, and make sure all household members know where it is located.

Electrical sparks have the potential of igniting natural gas if it is leaking. It is wise to teach all responsible household members where and how to shut off the electricity.

Preparing to Shut Off Electricity

- Locate your electricity circuit box.

- Teach all responsible household members how to shut off the electricity to the entire house.

 FOR YOUR SAFETY: Always shut off all the individual circuits before shutting off the main circuit breaker.

Insurance and Vital Records

Obtain property, health, and life insurance if you do not have them. Review existing policies for the amount and extent of coverage to ensure that what you have in place is what is required for you and your family for all possible hazards.

Flood Insurance

If you live in a flood-prone area, consider purchasing flood insurance to reduce your risk of flood loss. Buying flood insurance to cover the value of a building and its contents will not only provide greater peace of mind, but will speed the recovery if a flood occurs. You can call 1(888)FLOOD29 to learn more about flood insurance.

Inventory Home Possessions

Make a record of your personal property, for insurance purposes. Take photos or a video of the interior and exterior of your home. Include personal belongings in your inventory.

You may also want to download the free *Household and Personal Property Inventory Book* from the University of Illinois at www.ag.uiuc.edu/~vista/abstracts/ ahouseinv.html to help you record your possessions.

Important Documents

Store important documents such as insurance policies, deeds, property records, and other important papers in a safe place, such as a safety deposit box away from your home. Make copies of important documents for your disaster supplies kit. (Information about the disaster supplies kit is covered later.)

Money

Consider saving money in an emergency savings account that could be used in any crisis. It is advisable to keep a small amount of cash or traveler's checks at home in a safe place where you can quickly access them in case of evacuation.

Special Needs

If you or someone close to you has a disability or a special need, you may have to take additional steps to protect yourself and your family in an emergency.

Disability/Special Need	Additional Steps
Hearing impaired	May need to make special arrangements to receive warnings.
Mobility impaired	May need special assistance to get to a shelter.
Single working parent	May need help to plan for disasters and emergencies.
Non-English speaking persons	May need assistance planning for and responding to emergencies. Community and cultural groups may be able to help keep people informed.
People without vehicles	May need to make arrangements for transportation.
People with special dietary needs	Should take special precautions to have an adequate emergency food supply.

Planning for Special Needs

If you have special needs:

- Find out about special assistance that may be available in your community. Register with the office of emergency services or the local fire department for assistance so needed help can be provided.

- Create a network of neighbors, relatives, friends, and coworkers to aid you in an emergency. Discuss your needs and make sure everyone knows how to operate necessary equipment.

- Discuss your needs with your employer.

- If you are mobility impaired and live or work in a high-rise building, have an escape chair.

- If you live in an apartment building, ask the management to mark accessible exits clearly and to make arrangements to help you leave the building.

- Keep specialized items ready, including extra wheelchair batteries, oxygen, catheters, medication, food for service animals, and any other items you might need.

- Be sure to make provisions for medications that require refrigeration.

- Keep a list of the type and model numbers of the medical devices you require.

Caring for Animals

Animals also are affected by disasters. Use the guidelines below to prepare a plan for caring for pets and large animals.

Guidelines for Pets

Plan for pet disaster needs by:

- Identifying shelter.

- Gathering pet supplies.

- Ensuring your pet has proper ID and up-to-date veterinarian records.

- Providing a pet carrier and leash.

Take the following steps to prepare to shelter your pet:

- Call your local emergency management office, animal shelter, or animal control office to get advice and information.

- Keep veterinary records to prove vaccinations are current.

- Find out which local hotels and motels allow pets and where pet boarding facilities are located. Be sure to research some outside your local area in case local facilities close.

- Know that, with the exception of service animals, pets are not typically permitted in emergency shelters as they may affect the health and safety of other occupants.

Guidelines for Large Animals

If you have large animals such as horses, cattle, sheep, goats, or pigs on your property, be sure to prepare before a disaster.

Use the following guidelines:

1. Ensure all animals have some form of identification.

2. Evacuate animals whenever possible. Map out primary and secondary routes in advance.

3. Make available vehicles and trailers needed for transporting and supporting each type of animal. Also make available experienced handlers and drivers.

   Note: It is best to allow animals a chance to become accustomed to vehicular travel so they are less frightened and easier to move.

4. Ensure destinations have food, water, veterinary care, and handling equipment.

5. If evacuation is not possible, animal owners must decide whether to move large animals to shelter or turn them outside.

Safety Skills

It is important that family members know how to administer first aid and CPR and how to use a fire extinguisher.

Learn First Aid and CPR

Take a first aid and CPR class. Local American Red Cross chapters can provide information about this type of training. Official certification by the American Red Cross provides, under the "good Samaritan" law, protection for those giving first aid.

Learn How to Use a Fire Extinguisher

Be sure everyone knows how to use your fire extinguisher(s) and where it is kept. You should have, at a minimum, an ABC type.

Assemble a Disaster Supplies Kit

You may need to survive on your own after a disaster. This means having your own food, water, and other supplies in sufficient quantity to last for at least three days. Local officials and relief workers will be on the scene after a disaster, but they cannot reach everyone immediately. You could get help in hours, or it might take days.

Basic services such as electricity, gas, water, sewage treatment, and telephones may be cut off for days, or even a week or longer. Or, you may have to evacuate at a moment's notice and take essentials with you. You probably will not have the opportunity to shop or search for the supplies you need.

A disaster supplies kit is a collection of basic items that members of a household may need in the event of a disaster.

Kit Locations

Since you do not know where you will be when an emergency occurs, prepare supplies for home, work, and vehicles.

Home	Work	Car
Your disaster supplies kit should contain essential food, water, and supplies for at least three days. Keep this kit in a designated place and have it ready in case you have to leave your home quickly. Make sure all family members know where the kit is kept. Additionally, you may want to consider having supplies for sheltering for up to two weeks.	This kit should be in one container, and ready to "grab and go" in case you are evacuated from your workplace. Make sure you have food and water in the kit. Also, be sure to have comfortable walking shoes at your workplace in case an evacuation requires walking long distances.	In case you are stranded, keep a kit of emergency supplies in your car. This kit should contain food, water, first aid supplies, flares, jumper cables, and seasonal supplies.

Water

Basic Preparedness

How Much Water do I Need?

You should store at least one gallon of water per person per day. A normally active person needs at least one-half gallon of water daily just for drinking.

Additionally, in determining adequate quantities, take the following into account:

- Individual needs vary, depending on age, physical condition, activity, diet, and climate.

- Children, nursing mothers, and ill people need more water.

- Very hot temperatures can double the amount of water needed.

- A medical emergency might require additional water.

How Should I Store Water?

To prepare safest and most reliable emergency supply of water, it is recommended you purchase commercially bottled water. Keep bottled water in its original container and do not open it until you need to use it.

Observe the expiration or "use by" date.

If you are preparing your own containers of water

It is recommended you purchase food-grade water storage containers from surplus or camping supplies stores to use for water storage. Before filling with water, thoroughly clean the containers with dishwashing soap and water, and rinse completely so there is no residual soap. Follow directions below on filling the container with water.

If you choose to use your own storage containers, choose two-liter plastic soft drink bottles – not plastic jugs or cardboard containers that have had milk or fruit juice in them. Milk protein and fruit sugars cannot be adequately removed from these containers and provide an environment for bacterial growth when water is stored in them. Cardboard containers also leak easily and are not designed for long-term storage of liquids. Also, do not use glass containers, because they can break and are heavy.

If storing water in plastic soda bottles, follow these steps

Thoroughly clean the bottles with dishwashing soap and water, and rinse completely so there is no residual soap.

Sanitize the bottles by adding a solution of 1 teaspoon of non-scented liquid household chlorine bleach to a quart of water. Swish the sanitizing solution in the bottle so that it touches all surfaces. After sanitizing the bottle, thoroughly rinse out the sanitizing solution with clean water.

Filling water containers

Fill the bottle to the top with regular tap water. If the tap water has been commercially treated from a water utility with chlorine, you do not need to add anything else to the water to keep it clean. If the water you are using comes from a well or water source that is not treated with chlorine, add two drops of non-scented liquid household chlorine bleach to the water.

Tightly close the container using the original cap. Be careful not to contaminate the cap by touching the inside of it with your finger. Place a date on the outside of the container so that you know when you filled it. Store in a cool, dark place.

Replace the water every six months if not using commercially bottled water.

Food

The following are things to consider when putting together your food supplies:

- Avoid foods that will make you thirsty. Choose salt-free crackers, whole grain cereals, and canned foods with high liquid content.

- Stock canned foods, dry mixes, and other staples that do not require refrigeration, cooking, water, or special preparation. You may already have many of these on hand. **Note:** Be sure to include a manual can opener.

- Include special dietary needs.

Basic Disaster Supplies Kit

The following items are recommended for inclusion in your basic disaster supplies kit:

- Three-day supply of non-perishable food.

- Three-day supply of water – one gallon of water per person, per day.

- Portable, battery-powered radio or television and extra batteries.

- Flashlight and extra batteries.

- First aid kit and manual.

- Sanitation and hygiene items (moist towelettes and toilet paper).

- Matches and waterproof container.

- Whistle.

- Extra clothing.

- Kitchen accessories and cooking utensils, including a can opener.

- Photocopies of credit and identification cards.

- Cash and coins.

- Special needs items, such as prescription medications, eye glasses, contact lens solutions, and hearing aid batteries.

- Items for infants, such as formula, diapers, bottles, and pacifiers.

- Other items to meet your unique family needs.

If you live in a cold climate, you must think about warmth. It is possible that you will not have heat. Think about your clothing and bedding supplies. Be sure to include one complete change of clothing and shoes per person, including:

- Jacket or coat.

- Long pants.

- Long sleeve shirt.

- Sturdy shoes.

- Hat, mittens, and scarf.

- Sleeping bag or warm blanket (per person).

Be sure to account for growing children and other family changes. See Appendix B for a detailed checklist of disaster supplies. You may want to add some of the items listed to your basic disaster supplies kit depending on the specific needs of your family.

Maintaining Your Disaster Supplies Kit

Just as important as putting your supplies together is maintaining them so they are safe to use when needed. Here are some tips to keep your supplies ready and in good condition:

- Keep canned foods in a dry place where the temperature is cool.

- Store boxed food in tightly closed plastic or metal containers to protect from pests and to extend its shelf life.

- Throw out any canned good that becomes swollen, dented, or corroded.

- Use foods before they go bad, and replace them with fresh supplies.

- Place new items at the back of the storage area and older ones in the front.

- Change stored food and water supplies every six months. Be sure to write the date you store it on all containers.

- Re-think your needs every year and update your kit as your family needs change.

- Keep items in airtight plastic bags and put your entire disaster supplies kit in one or two easy-to-carry containers, such as an unused trashcan, camping backpack, or duffel bag.

1.4
Shelter

Taking shelter is critical in times of disaster. Sheltering is appropriate when conditions require that you seek protection in your home, place of employment, or other location where you are when disaster strikes. Sheltering outside the hazard area would include staying with friends and relatives, seeking commercial lodging, or staying in a mass care facility operated by disaster relief groups in conjunction with local authorities.

To effectively shelter, you must first consider the hazard and then choose a place in your home or other building that is safe for that hazard. For example, for a tornado, a room should be selected that is in a basement or an interior room on the lowest level away from corners, windows, doors and outside walls. Because the safest locations to seek shelter vary by hazard, sheltering is discussed in the various hazard sections. These discussions include recommendations for sealing the shelter if the hazards warrants this type of protection.

Even though mass care shelters often provide water, food, medicine, and basic sanitary facilities, you should plan to take your disaster supplies kit with you so you will have the supplies you require. Mass care sheltering can involve living with many people in a confined space, which can be difficult and unpleasant. To avoid conflicts in this stressful situation, it is important to cooperate with shelter managers and others assisting them. Keep in mind that alcoholic beverages and weapons are forbidden in emergency shelters and smoking is restricted.

The length of time you are required to shelter may be short, such as during a tornado warning, or long, such as during a winter storm. It is important that you stay in shelter until local authorities say it is safe to leave. Additionally, you should take turns listening to radio broadcasts and maintain a 24-hour safety watch.

During extended periods of sheltering, you will need to manage water and food supplies to ensure you and your family have the required supplies and quantities. Guidance on how to accomplish this follows.

Managing Water

Essentials

1. **Allow people to drink according to their needs**. Many people need even more than the average of one-half gallon, per day. The individual amount needed depends on age, physical activity, physical condition, and time of year.

2. **Never ration water unless ordered to do so by authorities**. Drink the amount you need today and try to find more for tomorrow. Under no circumstances should a person drink less than one quart (four cups) of water each day. You can minimize the amount of water your body needs by reducing activity and staying cool.

3. **Drink water that you know is not contaminated first**. If necessary, suspicious water, such as cloudy water from regular faucets or water from streams or ponds, can be used after it has been treated. If water treatment is not possible, put off drinking suspicious water as long as possible, but do not become dehydrated.

4. **Do not drink carbonated beverages instead of drinking water.** Carbonated beverages do not meet drinking-water requirements. Caffeinated drinks and alcohol dehydrate the body, which increases the need for drinking water.

5. **Turn off the main water valves.** You will need to protect the water sources already in your home from contamination if you hear reports of broken water or sewage lines, or if local officials advise you of a problem. To close the incoming water source, locate the incoming valve and turn it to the closed position. Be sure you and other family members know how to perform this important procedure.

   • To use the water in your pipes, let air into the plumbing by turning on the faucet in your home at the highest level. A small amount of water will trickle out. Then obtain water from the lowest faucet in the home.

   • To use the water in your hot-water tank, be sure the electricity or gas is off, and open the drain at the bottom of the tank. Start the water flowing by turning off the water intake valve at the tank and turning on the hot-water faucet. Refill the tank before turning the gas or electricity back on. If the gas is turned off, a professional will be needed to turn it back on.

 Review

Section 1.2: Emergency Planning and Checklists

Water Sources

Safe Sources	Unsafe Sources
Melted ice cubes	Radiators
Water drained from the water heater (if the water heater has not been damaged)	Hot water boilers (home heating system)
Liquids from canned goods such as fruit or vegetable juices	Water beds (fungicides added to the water or chemicals in the vinyl may make water unsafe to use)
Water drained from pipes	Water from the toilet bowl or flush tank
	Swimming pools and spas (chemicals used to kill germs are too concentrated for safe drinking but can be used for personal hygiene, cleaning, and related uses)

Water Treatment

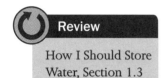

Review

How I Should Store
Water, Section 1.3

Treat all water of uncertain quality before using it for drinking, food washing or preparation, washing dishes, brushing teeth, or making ice. In addition to having a bad odor and taste, contaminated water can contain microorganisms (germs) that cause diseases such as dysentery, cholera, typhoid, and hepatitis.

There are many ways to treat water. None is perfect. Often the best solution is a combination of methods. Before treating, let any suspended particles settle to the bottom or strain them through coffee filters or layers of clean cloth.

Make sure you have the necessary materials in your disaster supplies kit for the chosen water treatment method.

There are three water treatment methods. They are as follows:

- Boiling

- Chlorination

- Distillation

These instructions are for treating water of uncertain quality in an emergency situation, when no other reliable clean water source is available, or you have used all of your stored water.

Boiling

Boiling is the safest method of treating water. In a large pot or kettle, bring water to a rolling boil for 1 full minute, keeping in mind that some water will evaporate. Let the water cool before drinking.

Boiled water will taste better if you put oxygen back into it by pouring the water back and forth between two clean containers. This also will improve the taste of stored water.

Chlorination

You can use household liquid bleach to kill microorganisms. Use only regular household liquid bleach that contains 5.25 to 6.0 percent sodium hypochlorite. Do not use scented bleaches, color safe bleaches, or bleaches with added cleaners. Because the potency of bleach diminishes with time, use bleach from a newly opened or unopened bottle.

Add 16 drops (1/8 teaspoon) of bleach per gallon of water, stir, and let stand for 30 minutes. The water should have a slight bleach odor. If it doesn't, then repeat the dosage and let stand another 15 minutes. If it still does not smell of chlorine, discard it and find another source of water.

Other chemicals, such as iodine or water treatment products sold in camping or surplus stores that do not contain 5.25 to 6.0 percent sodium hypochlorite as the only active ingredient, are not recommended and should not be used.

Distillation

While the two methods described above will kill most microbes in water, distillation will remove microbes (germs) that resist these methods, as well as heavy metals, salts, and most other chemicals.

Distillation involves boiling water and then collecting only the vapor that condenses. The condensed vapor will not include salt or most other impurities. To distill, fill a pot halfway with water. Tie a cup to the handle on the pot's lid so that the cup will hang right-side-up when the lid is upside-down (make sure the cup is not dangling into the water) and boil the water for 20 minutes. The water that drips from the lid into the cup is distilled.

Effectiveness of Water Treatment Methods

Methods	Kills Microbes	Removes other contaminants (heavy metals, salts, and most other chemicals)
Boiling	√	
Chlorination	√	
Distillation	√	√

Managing Food Supplies

Safety and Sanitation

Do:	Don't:
• Keep food in covered containers • Keep cooking and eating utensils clean • Keep garbage in closed containers and dispose outside, burying garbage if necessary • Keep your hands clean by washing them frequently with soap and water that has been boiled or disinfected • Use only pre-prepared canned baby formula for infants • Discard any food that has come into contact with contaminated floodwater • Discard any food that has been at room temperature for two hours or more • Discard any food that has an unusual odor, color, or texture	• Eat foods from cans that are swollen, dented, or corroded, even though the product may look safe to eat • Eat any food that looks or smells abnormal, even if the can looks normal • Use powdered formulas with treated water • Let garbage accumulate inside, both for fire and sanitation reasons

Note: Thawed food usually can be eaten if it is still "refrigerator cold." It can be re-frozen if it still contains ice crystals. To be safe, remember, "When in doubt, throw it out."

Cooking

- Alternative cooking sources in times of emergency include candle warmers, chafing dishes, fondue pots, or a fireplace.

- Charcoal grills and camp stoves are for outdoor use only.

- Commercially canned food may be eaten out of the can without warming.

- To heat food in a can:

    1. Remove the label.

    2. Thoroughly wash and disinfect the can. (Use a diluted solution of one part bleach to ten parts water.)

    3. Open the can before heating.

Managing without Power

Here are two options for keeping food safe if you are without power for a long period:

- Look for alternate storage space for your perishable food.

- Use dry ice. Twenty-five pounds of dry ice will keep a 10-cubic-foot freezer below freezing for 3-4 days. Use care when handling dry ice, and wear dry, heavy gloves to avoid injury.

Hazard-Specific Preparedness

There are actions that should be taken before, during, and after an event that are unique to each hazard. For example:

- Seeking a safe shelter during a tornado.

- Reducing property loss from a hurricane.

Information about the specific hazards and what to do for each is provided in Parts 2, 3, and 4. Study the material for those hazards that you identified in Section 1.1 as the ones that have happened or could happen. Share the hazard-specific information with family members and include pertinent material from these parts in your family disaster plan.

Practicing and Maintaining Your Plan

Once you have developed your plan, you need to practice and maintain it. For example, ask questions to make sure your family remembers meeting places, phone numbers, and safety rules. Conduct drills such as drop, cover, and hold on for earthquakes. Test fire alarms. Replace and update disaster supplies.

For More Information

If you require more information about any of these topics, the following are resources that may be helpful.

FEMA Publications

Disaster Preparedness Coloring Book. FEMA-243. Coloring book for ages 3-10. Also available in Spanish.

Before Disaster Strikes. FEMA A-291. Contains information about how to make sure you are financially prepared to deal with a natural disaster. Also available in Spanish.

The Adventures of Julia and Robbie: Disaster Twins. FEMA-344. A collection of disaster related stories. Includes information on preparedness and how to mitigate against disasters.

FEMA for Kids. L-229. Provides information about what FEMA (specifically fema.gov) has to offer children.

Community Shelter. FEMA 361. Contains guidelines for constructing mass shelters for public refuge in schools, hospitals, and other places.

Food and Water in an Emergency. L-210 If an earthquake, hurricane, winter storm, or other disaster strikes your community, you might not have access to food, water, and electricity for days, or even weeks. By taking some time now to store emergency food and water supplies, you can provide for your entire family. Also available online at www.fema.gov/pdf/library/f&web.pdf.

Helping Children Cope with Disaster. FEMA L-196. Helps families understand how to help children cope with disaster and its aftermath.

Assisting People with Disabilities in a Disaster. Information about helping people with disabilities in a disaster and resources for individuals with disabilities. Available online at www.fema.gov/rrr/assistf.shtm.

American Red Cross
 Publications

Facing Fear: Helping Young People Deal with Terrorism and Tragic Events. A school curriculum designed to help alleviate worries and clear up confusion about perceived and actual threats to safety. Available online at www.redcross.org/disaster/masters/facingfear, or contact your local Red Cross chapter.

2
Natural Hazards

Part 2 includes information about many types of natural hazards. Natural hazards are natural events that threaten lives, property, and other assets. Often, natural hazards can be predicted. They tend to occur repeatedly in the same geographical locations because they are related to weather patterns or physical characteristics of an area.

Natural hazards such as flood, fire, earthquake, tornado, and windstorms affect thousands of people every year. We need to know what our risks are from natrual hazards and take sensible precautions to protect ourselves, our families, and our communities.

Use Part 2 to learn about the hazards that pose a risk to you. Include the pertinent information in your family disaster plan. Specific content on each hazard consists of the characteristics of that hazard, terms associated with the hazard, measures that can be taken beforehand to avoid or lessen the impact of these events, and what individuals need to do during and after the event to protect themselves.

When you complete Part 2, you will be able to:

- Know important terms.
- Take protective measures for natural hazards.
- Identify resources for more information about natural hazards.

Floods are one of the most common hazards in the United States. Flood effects can be local, impacting a neighborhood or community, or very large, affecting entire river basins and multiple states.

However, all floods are not alike. Some floods develop slowly, sometimes over a period of days. But flash floods can develop quickly, sometimes in just a few minutes and without any visible signs of rain. Flash floods often have a dangerous wall of roaring water that carries rocks, mud, and other debris and can sweep away most things in its path. Overland flooding occurs outside a defined river or stream, such as when a levee is breached, but still can be destructive. Flooding can also occur when a dam breaks, producing effects similar to flash floods.

Be aware of flood hazards no matter where you live, but especially if you live in a low-lying area, near water or downstream from a dam. Even very small streams, gullies, creeks, culverts, dry streambeds, or low-lying ground that appear harmless in dry weather can flood. Every state is at risk from this hazard.

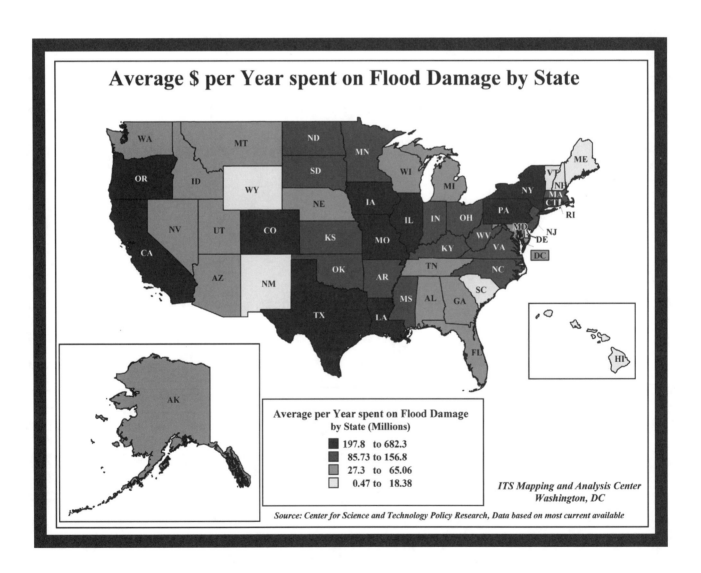

Average $ per Year spent on Flood Damage by State

Average per Year spent on Flood Damage by State (Millions)

- 197.8 to 682.3
- 85.73 to 156.8
- 27.3 to 65.06
- 0.47 to 18.38

ITS Mapping and Analysis Center Washington, DC

Source: Center for Science and Technology Policy Research, Data based on most current available

What Would You Do?

You and your family moved from a city neighborhood in San Francisco, CA, to a suburb of Phoenix, AZ. Since earthquakes were a threat in your area, you always kept some extra food, water, and other supplies on hand and maintained an earthquake insurance policy, just in case something happened. You think this kind of preparation is no longer necessary based on what your neighbors have told you. According to them, the biggest threat they face is lack of water caused by the very dry weather. You continue to see public service announcements from the federal government about flood insurance and the need to protect yourself from flood damage. Surely, there would be no need for flood insurance where you live with its bare hills, deep canyons, and dry land.

- Are you at risk for flooding, or is this more of a risk to people who live elsewhere?

  ☐ Yes   ☐ No

- Is there a need to have a disaster plan and a disaster supplies kit?

  ☐ Yes   ☐ No

- Should you consider purchasing flood insurance?

  ☐ Yes   ☐ No

Answer key
1. Yes 2. Yes 3. Yes

Know the Terms

Familiarize yourself with these terms to help identify a flood hazard:

Flood Watch
Flooding is possible. Tune in to NOAA Weather Radio, commercial radio, or television for information.

Flash Flood Watch
Flash flooding is possible. Be prepared to move to higher ground; listen to NOAA Weather Radio, commercial radio, or television for information.

Flood Warning
Flooding is occurring or will occur soon; if advised to evacuate, do so immediately.

Flash Flood Warning
A flash flood is occurring; seek higher ground on foot immediately.

Take Protective Measures

Before a Flood

To prepare for a flood, you should:

- Avoid building in a floodplain unless you elevate and reinforce your home.

- Elevate the furnace, water heater, and electric panel if susceptible to flooding.

- Install "check valves" in sewer traps to prevent flood water from backing up into the drains of your home.

- Construct barriers (levees, beams, floodwalls) to stop floodwater from entering the building.

- Seal walls in basements with waterproofing compounds to avoid seepage.

During a Flood

If a flood is likely in your area, you should:

- Listen to the radio or television for information.

- Be aware that flash flooding can occur. If there is any possibility of a flash flood, move immediately to higher ground. Do not wait for instructions to move.

- Be aware of streams, drainage channels, canyons, and other areas known to flood suddenly. Flash floods can occur in these areas with or without such typical warnings as rain clouds or heavy rain.

If you must prepare to evacuate, you should do the following:

- Secure your home. If you have time, bring in outdoor furniture. Move essential items to an upper floor.

- Turn off utilities at the main switches or valves if instructed to do so. Disconnect electrical appliances. Do not touch electrical equipment if you are wet or standing in water.

Review

See Section 1.1:
Getting Informed

If you have to leave your home, remember these evacuation tips:

- **Do not walk through moving water.** Six inches of moving water can make you fall. If you have to walk in water, walk where the water is not moving. Use a stick to check the firmness of the ground in front of you.

- **Do not drive into flooded areas.** If floodwaters rise around your car, abandon the car and move to higher ground if you can do so safely. You and the vehicle can be quickly swept away.

Driving: Flood Facts

The following are important points to remember when driving in flood conditions:
- Six inches of water will reach the bottom of most passenger cars causing loss of control and possible stalling.
- A foot of water will float many vehicles.
- Two feet of rushing water can carry away most vehicles including sport utility vehicles (SUV's) and pick-ups.

After a Flood

The following are guidelines for the period following a flood:

- Listen for news reports to learn whether the community's water supply is safe to drink.

- Avoid floodwaters; water may be contaminated by oil, gasoline, or raw sewage. Water may also be electrically charged from underground or downed power lines.

- Avoid moving water.

- Be aware of areas where floodwaters have receded. Roads may have weakened and could collapse under the weight of a car.

- Stay away from downed power lines, and report them to the power company.

- Return home only when authorities indicate it is safe.

- Stay out of any building if it is surrounded by floodwaters.

- Use extreme caution when entering buildings; there may be hidden damage, particularly in foundations.

- Service damaged septic tanks, cesspools, pits, and leaching systems as soon as possible. Damaged sewage systems are serious health hazards.

- Clean and disinfect everything that got wet. Mud left from floodwater can contain sewage and chemicals.

Additional Information

Flood Insurance

Consider the following facts:

- Flood losses are **not covered** under homeowners' insurance policies.

- FEMA manages the National Flood Insurance Program, which makes federally-backed flood insurance available in communities that agree to adopt and enforce floodplain management ordinances to reduce future flood damage.

- Flood insurance is available in most communities through insurance agents.

- There is a 30-day waiting period before flood insurance goes into effect, so don't delay.

- Flood insurance is available whether the building is in or out of the identified flood-prone area.

Knowledge Check

Decide whether the following statements are true or false. Check the appropriate column. When you have finished, check your answers using the answer key below.

T	F		Statement
☐	☐	1.	Flood emergencies occur in only 12 states.
☐	☐	2.	A "flood watch" announcement on the radio indicates that flooding is possible.
☐	☐	3.	Flash floods may occur with little warning.
☐	☐	4.	Flood risk varies from one region to another.
☐	☐	5.	National flood insurance is available only for buildings within an identified flood-prone area.
☐	☐	6.	It is safe to walk through floodwater if you can see the ground under it.
☐	☐	7.	It takes at least 3 feet of floodwater to make a motorized vehicle float.
☐	☐	8.	After flood waters recede from a roadway, the road could still be dangerous.
☐	☐	9.	To prepare for a flood emergency, you should have a NOAA Weather Radio as well as a commercial radio.

Answer key
1. False 2. True 3. True 4. True 5. False 6. False 7. False 8. True 9. True

For More Information

If you require more information about any of these topics, the following are resources that may be helpful.

FEMA Publications

- *After a Flood: The First Steps.* L-198. Information for homeowners on preparedness, safety, and recovery from a flood.

- *Homeowner's Guide to Retrofitting: Six Ways to Protect Your House from Flooding.* L-235. A brochure about obtaining information about how to protect your home from flooding.

- *Homeowner's Guide to Retrofitting: Six Ways to Protect Your House from Flooding.* FEMA-312. A detailed manual on how to protect your home from flooding.

- *About the Flood: Elevating Your Floodprone House.* FEMA-347. This publication is intended for builders, code officials and homeowners.

- *Protecting Building Utilities From Flood Damage.* FEMA-348. This publication is intended for developers, architects, engineers, builders, code officials and homeowners.

Other Publications

American Red Cross

- *Repairing Your Flooded Home.* sixty-page booklet about how to perform simple home repairs after flooding, including cleaning, sanitation, and determining which professionals to involve for various needed services. Local Red Cross chapters can order in packages of 10 as stock number A4477 for a nominal fee. Also available online at www.redcross.org/services/disaster/0,1082,0_570_,00.html

National Weather Service

- *Hurricane Flooding: A Deadly Inland Danger.* 20052. Brochure describing the impact of hurricane flooding and precautions to take. Available online at www.nws.noaa.gov/om/brochures/InlandFlooding.pdf

- *The Hidden Danger: Low Water Crossing.* 96074E. Brochure describing the hazards of driving your vehicle in flood conditions. Available online at www.nws.noaa.gov/om/brochures/TheHiddenDangerEnglish.pdf

Tornadoes

Tornadoes are nature's most violent storms. Spawned from powerful thunderstorms, tornadoes can cause fatalities and devastate a neighborhood in seconds. A tornado appears as a rotating, funnel-shaped cloud that extends from a thunderstorm to the ground with whirling winds that can reach 300 miles per hour. Damage paths can be in excess of one mile wide and 50 miles long. Every state is at some risk from this hazard.

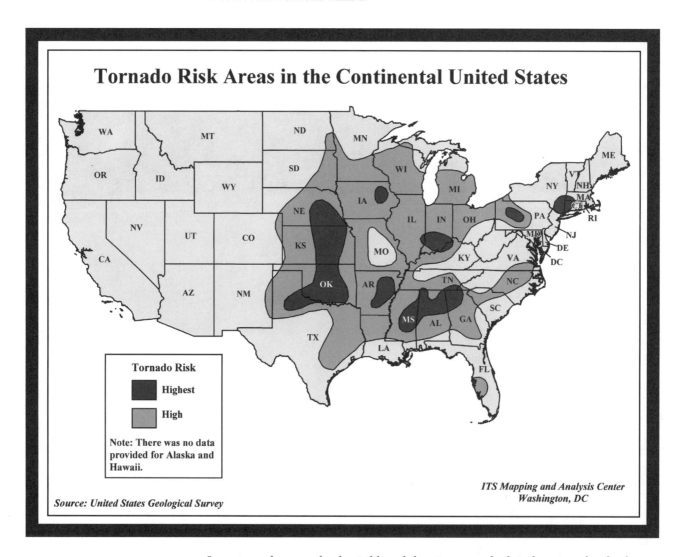

Tornado Risk Areas in the Continental United States

Tornado Risk

Highest

High

Note: There was no data provided for Alaska and Hawaii.

Source: United States Geological Survey

ITS Mapping and Analysis Center
Washington, DC

Some tornadoes are clearly visible, while rain or nearby low-hanging clouds obscure others. Occasionally, tornadoes develop so rapidly that little, if any, advance warning is possible.

Before a tornado hits, the wind may die down and the air may become very still. A cloud of debris can mark the location of a tornado even if a funnel is not visible. Tornadoes generally occur near the trailing edge of a thunderstorm. It is not uncommon to see clear, sunlit skies behind a tornado.

The following are facts about tornadoes:

- They may strike quickly, with little or no warning.

- They may appear nearly transparent until dust and debris are picked up or a cloud forms in the funnel.

- The average tornado moves Southwest to Northeast, but tornadoes have been known to move in any direction.

- The average forward speed of a tornado is 30 MPH, but may vary from stationary to 70 MPH.

- Tornadoes can accompany tropical storms and hurricanes as they move onto land.

- Waterspouts are tornadoes that form over water.

- Tornadoes are most frequently reported east of the Rocky Mountains during spring and summer months.

- Peak tornado season in the southern states is March through May; in the northern states, it is late spring through early summer.

- Tornadoes are most likely to occur between 3 p.m. and 9 p.m., but can occur at any time.

Natural Hazards

Know the Terms

Familiarize yourself with these terms to help identify a tornado hazard:

Tornado Watch
Tornadoes are possible. Remain alert for approaching storms. Watch the sky and stay tuned to NOAA Weather Radio, commercial radio, or television for information.

Tornado Warning
A tornado has been sighted or indicated by weather radar. Take shelter immediately.

Take Protective Measures

Before a Tornado

Be alert to changing weather conditions.

- Listen to NOAA Weather Radio or to commercial radio or television newscasts for the latest information.

- Look for approaching storms.

- Look for the following danger signs:

    - Dark, often greenish sky

    - Large hail

    - A large, dark, low-lying cloud (particularly if rotating)

    - Loud roar, similar to a freight train.

If you see approaching storms or any of the danger signs, be prepared to take shelter immediately.

During a Tornado

If you are under a tornado WARNING, seek shelter immediately!

If you are in:	Then:
A structure (e.g. residence, small building, school, nursing home, hospital, factory, shopping center, high-rise building)	Go to a pre-designated shelter area such as a safe room, basement, storm cellar, or the lowest building level. If there is no basement, go to the center of an interior room on the lowest level (closet, interior hallway) away from corners, windows, doors, and outside walls. Put as many walls as possible between you and the outside. Get under a sturdy table and use your arms to protect your head and neck. Do not open windows.
A vehicle, trailer, or mobile home	Get out immediately and go to the lowest floor of a sturdy, nearby building or a storm shelter. Mobile homes, even if tied down, offer little protection from tornadoes.
The outside with no shelter	• Lie flat in a nearby ditch or depression and cover your head with your hands. Be aware of the potential for flooding. • Do not get under an overpass or bridge. You are safer in a low, flat location. • Never try to outrun a tornado in urban or congested areas in a car or truck. Instead, leave the vehicle immediately for safe shelter. • Watch out for flying debris. Flying debris from tornadoes causes most fatalities and injuries.

Natural
Hazards

Preparing a Safe Room

Extreme windstorms in many parts of the country pose a serious threat to buildings and their occupants. Your residence may be built "to code," but that does not
mean it can withstand winds from extreme events such as tornadoes and major
hurricanes. The purpose of a safe room or a wind shelter is to provide a space
where you and your family can seek refuge that provides a high level of protection.
You can build a safe room in one of several places in your home:

- Your basement.

- Atop a concrete slab-on-grade foundation or garage floor.

- An interior room on the first floor.

Safe rooms built below ground level provide the greatest protection, but a safe
room built in a first-floor interior room also can provide the necessary protection.
Below-ground safe rooms must be designed to avoid accumulating water during
the heavy rains that often accompany severe windstorms.

To protect its occupants, a safe room must be built to withstand high winds and
flying debris, even if the rest of the residence is severely damaged or destroyed.
Consider the following when building a safe room:

- The safe room must be adequately anchored to resist overturning and uplift.

- The walls, ceiling, and door of the shelter must withstand wind pressure and
  resist penetration by windborne objects and falling debris.

- The connections between all parts of the safe room must be strong enough to
  resist the wind.

- Sections of either interior or exterior residence walls that are used as walls of
  the safe room, must be separated from the structure of the residence so that
  damage to the residence will not cause damage to the safe room.

Additional information about Safe Rooms avaliable from FEMA

Taking Shelter from the Storm: Building a Safe Room Inside Your House. L-233. Brochure providing details about obtaining information about how to build a wind-safe room to
withstand tornado, hurricane, and other high winds

Taking Shelter from the Storm: Building a Safe Room Inside Your House. FEMA-320. Manual with
detailed information about how to build a wind-safe room to withstand tornado,
hurricane, and other high winds

Locate the Safest Place

On the following home layout diagrams, locate the safest place to seek shelter should you not be able to evacuate.

Apartment

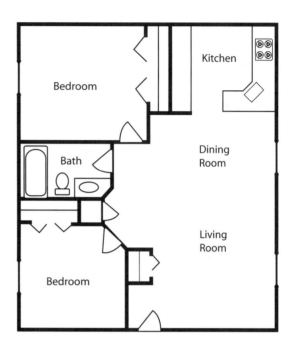

One-Story Home

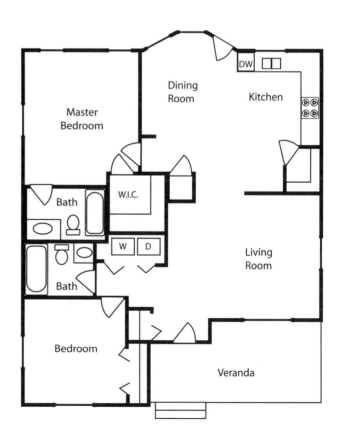

Two-Story Home

First Floor

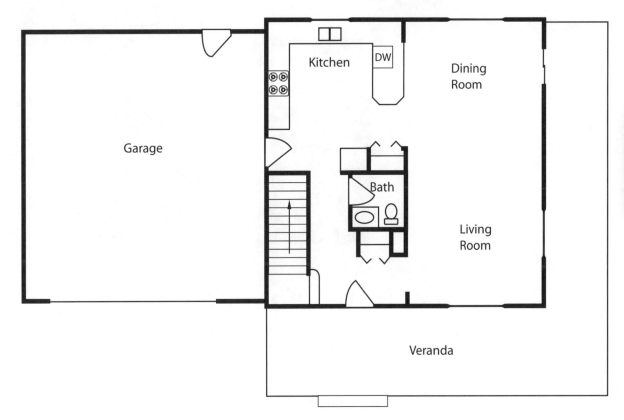

Second Floor

Natural Hazards

Answer key

Apartment: Bathroom, One-Story Home: WIC (walk in Closet), Two-Story Home: First floor bathroom

After a Tornado

Follow the instructions for recovering from a disaster in Part 5.

For More Information

If you require more information about any of these topics, the following are resources that may be helpful.

FEMA Publications

Tornado Fact Sheet. L-148. Provides safety tips for before, during, and after a tornado

Tornado Protection—Selecting Refuge Areas in Buildings. FEMA 431. Intended primarily to help building administrators, architects, and engineers select the best available refuge areas in existing schools

Hurricanes

A hurricane is a type of tropical cyclone, the generic term for a low pressure system that generally forms in the tropics. A typical cyclone is accompanied by thunderstorms, and in the Northern Hemisphere, a counterclockwise circulation of winds near the earth's surface.

All Atlantic and Gulf of Mexico coastal areas are subject to hurricanes or tropical storms. Parts of the Southwest United States and the Pacific Coast experience heavy rains and floods each year from hurricanes spawned off Mexico. The Atlantic hurricane season lasts from June to November, with the peak season from mid-August to late October.

Hurricanes can cause catastrophic damage to coastlines and several hundred miles inland. Winds can exceed 155 miles per hour. Hurricanes and tropical storms can also spawn tornadoes and microbursts, create storm surges along the coast, and cause extensive damage from heavy rainfall.

Hurricanes are classified into five categories based on their wind speed, central pressure, and damage potential (see chart). Category Three and higher hurricanes are considered major hurricanes, though Categories One and Two are still extremely dangerous and warrant your full attention.

Saffir-Simpson Hurricane Scale			
Scale Number (Category)	Sustained Winds (MPH)	Damage	Storm Surge
1	74-95	**Minimal:** Unanchored mobile homes, vegetation, and signs	4-5 feet
2	96-110	**Moderate:** All mobile homes, roofs, small craft; flooding	6-8 feet
3	111-130	**Extensive:** Small buildings; low-lying roads cut off	9-12 feet
4	131-155	**Extreme:** Roofs destroyed, trees down, roads cut off, mobile homes destroyed, beach homes flooded	13-18 feet
5	More than 155	**Catastrophic:** Most buildings destroyed, vegetation destroyed, major roads cut off, homes flooded	Greater than 18 feet

Hurricanes can produce widespread torrential rains. Floods are the deadly and destructive result. Slow moving storms and tropical storms moving into mountainous regions tend to produce especially heavy rain. Excessive rain can trigger landslides or mud slides, especially in mountainous regions. Flash flooding can occur due to intense rainfall. Flooding on rivers and streams may persist for several days or more after the storm.

Between 1970 and 1999, more people lost their lives from freshwater inland flooding associated with land falling tropical cyclones than from any other weather hazard related to tropical cyclones.

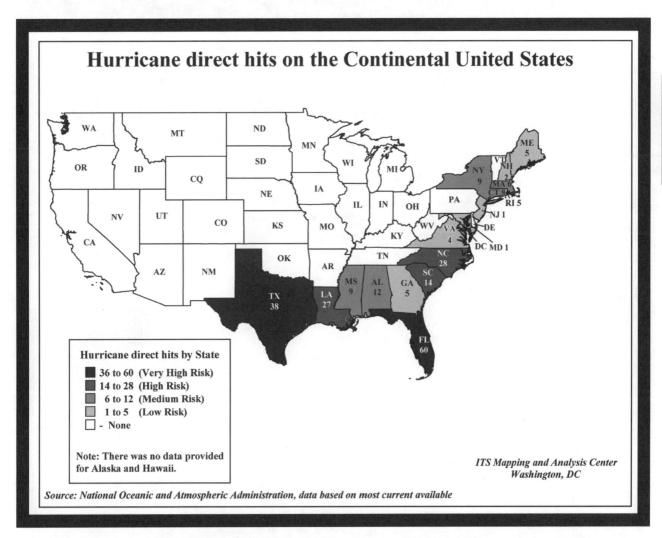

Hurricane direct hits on the Continental United States

Hurricane direct hits by State

- ■ 36 to 60 (Very High Risk)
- ■ 14 to 28 (High Risk)
- ■ 6 to 12 (Medium Risk)
- ■ 1 to 5 (Low Risk)
- □ - None

Note: There was no data provided for Alaska and Hawaii.

ITS Mapping and Analysis Center
Washington, DC

Source: National Oceanic and Atmospheric Administration, data based on most current available

Natural Hazards

Naming the Hurricane

Since 1953, Atlantic tropical storms have been named from lists originated by the National Hurricane Center and now maintained and updated by an international committee of the World Meteorological Organization. The lists featured only women's names until 1979. After that, men's and women's names were alternated. Six lists are used in rotation. Thus, the 2001 lists will be used again in 2007.

The only time there is a change in the list is if a storm is so deadly or costly that the continued use of the name would be inappropriate for reasons of sensitivity. When this occurs, the name is stricken from the list and another name is selected to replace it.

Sometimes names are changed. Lorenzo replaced Luis and Michelle replaced Marilyn. The complete lists can be found at www.nhc.noaa.gov under "Storm Names."

Know the Terms

Familiarize yourself with these terms to help identify a hurricane hazard:

Tropical Depression
An organized system of clouds and thunderstorms with a defined surface circulation and maximum sustained winds of 38 MPH (33 knots) or less. Sustained winds are defined as one-minute average wind measured at about 33 ft (10 meters) above the surface.

Tropical Storm
An organized system of strong thunderstorms with a defined surface circulation and maximum sustained winds of 39-73 MPH (34-63 knots).

Hurricane
An intense tropical weather system of strong thunderstorms with a well-defined surface circulation and maximum sustained winds of 74 MPH (64 knots) or higher.

Storm Surge
A dome of water pushed onshore by hurricane and tropical storm winds. Storm surges can reach 25 feet high and be 50-100 miles wide.

Storm Tide
A combination of storm surge and the normal tide (i.e., a 15-foot storm surge combined with a 2-foot normal high tide over the mean sea level creates a 17-foot storm tide).

Hurricane/Tropical Storm Watch
Hurricane/tropical storm conditions are possible in the specified area, usually within 36 hours. Tune in to NOAA Weather Radio, commercial radio, or television for information.

Hurricane/Tropical Storm Warning
Hurricane/tropical storm conditions are expected in the specified area, usually within 24 hours.

Short Term Watches and Warnings
These warnings provide detailed information about specific hurricane threats, such as flash floods and tornadoes.

Take Protective Measures

To prepare for a hurricane, you should take the following measures:

- Make plans to secure your property. Permanent storm shutters offer the best protection for windows. A second option is to board up windows with 5/8" marine plywood, cut to fit and ready to install. Tape does not prevent windows from breaking.

- Install straps or additional clips to securely fasten your roof to the frame structure. This will reduce roof damage.

- Be sure trees and shrubs around your home are well trimmed.

- Clear loose and clogged rain gutters and downspouts.

- Determine how and where to secure your boat.

- Consider building a safe room.

Before a Hurricane

🔁 **Review**

For more information on safe rooms See Section 2.2: Tornadoes

Natural Hazards

During a Hurricane

If a hurricane is likely in your area, you should:

- Listen to the radio or TV for information.

- Secure your home, close storm shutters, and secure outdoor objects or bring them indoors.

- Turn off utilities if instructed to do so. Otherwise, turn the refrigerator thermostat to its coldest setting and keep its doors closed.

- Turn off propane tanks.

- Avoid using the phone, except for serious emergencies.

- Moor your boat if time permits.

- Ensure a supply of water for sanitary purposes such as cleaning and flushing toilets. Fill the bathtub and other large containers with water.

You should evacuate under the following conditions:

- If you are directed by local authorities to do so. Be sure to follow their instructions.

- If you live in a mobile home or temporary structure—such shelters are particularly hazardous during hurricanes no matter how well fastened to the ground.

- If you live in a high-rise building—hurricane winds are stronger at higher elevations.

- If you live on the coast, on a floodplain, near a river, or on an inland waterway.

- If you feel you are in danger.

If you are unable to evacuate, go to your wind-safe room. If you do not have one, follow these guidelines:

- Stay indoors during the hurricane and away from windows and glass doors.

- Close all interior doors—secure and brace external doors.

- Keep curtains and blinds closed. Do not be fooled if there is a lull; it could be the eye of the storm—winds will pick up again.

- Take refuge in a small interior room, closet, or hallway on the lowest level.

- Lie on the floor under a table or another sturdy object.

⟳ Review

Guidelines for sheltering
See Section 1.4: Shelter

After a Hurricane

Follow the instructions for recovering from a disaster in Part 5.

Knowledge Check

You Make the Call

Read the following and respond to the question below. See the answer key below to check your answer.

Your neighbor said that in the event a hurricane threatens, the household would get ready by closing the windows and doors on the storm side of the house and opening the ones on the side away from the wind. They also will tape the windows to prevent damage to the glass.

Is this a good idea?

Answer Key
No! All of the doors and windows should be closed (and shuttered) throughout the duration of the hurricane. The winds in a hurricane are highly turbulent and any open window or door can be an open target for flying debris.
As for the tape, it is a waste of effort, time, and tape. It offers no strength to the glass and no protection against flying debris.

For More Information

If you require more information about any of these topics, the following are resources that may be helpful.

FEMA Publications

Against the Wind: Protecting Your Home from Hurricane and Wind Damage. FEMA-247. A guide to hurricane preparedness. Available online at www.fema.gov/txt/hazards/hurricanes/survivingthestormhurricane.txt

Community Hurricane Preparedness. IS-324. CD-ROM or Web-based training course for federal, state, and local emergency managers. Web-based version available online at http://meted.ucar.edu/hurrican/chp/index.htm

Safety Tips for Hurricanes. L 105. Publication for teachers and parents for presentation to children. To order, call 1(800)480-2520.

Other Publications

Protect Your Home against Hurricane Damage, Institute for Business and Home Safety. 110 William Street, New York, NY 20038

2.4

Thunderstorms and Lightning

All thunderstorms are dangerous. Every thunderstorm produces lightning. In the United States, an average of 300 people are injured and 80 people are killed each year by lightning. Although most lightning victims survive, people struck by lightning often report a variety of long-term, debilitating symptoms.

Other associated dangers of thunderstorms include tornadoes, strong winds, hail, and flash flooding. Flash flooding is responsible for more fatalities—more than 140 annually—than any other thunderstorm-associated hazard.

Dry thunderstorms that do not produce rain that reaches the ground are most prevalent in the western United States. Falling raindrops evaporate, but lightning can still reach the ground and can start wildfires.

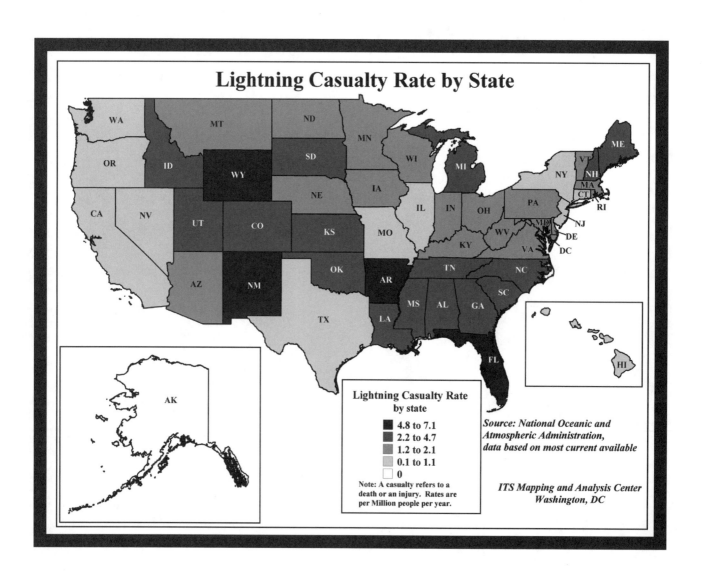

Lightning Casualty Rate by State

Lightning Casualty Rate by state

- ■ 4.8 to 7.1
- ■ 2.2 to 4.7
- ■ 1.2 to 2.1
- ■ 0.1 to 1.1
- □ 0

Note: A casualty refers to a death or an injury. Rates are per Million people per year.

Source: National Oceanic and Atmospheric Administration, data based on most current available

ITS Mapping and Analysis Center Washington, DC

The following are facts about thunderstorms:

- They may occur singly, in clusters, or in lines.

- Some of the most severe occur when a single thunderstorm affects one location for an extended time.

- Thunderstorms typically produce heavy rain for a brief period, anywhere from 30 minutes to an hour.

- Warm, humid conditions are highly favorable for thunderstorm development.

- About 10 percent of thunderstorms are classified as severe—one that produces hail at least three-quarters of an inch in diameter, has winds of 58 miles per hour or higher, or produces a tornado.

The following are facts about lightning:

- Lightning's unpredictability increases the risk to individuals and property.

- Lightning often strikes outside of heavy rain and may occur as far as 10 miles away from any rainfall.

- "Heat lightning" is actually lightning from a thunderstorm too far away for thunder to be heard. However, the storm may be moving in your direction!

- Most lightning deaths and injuries occur when people are caught outdoors in the summer months during the afternoon and evening.

- Your chances of being struck by lightning are estimated to be 1 in 600,000, but could be reduced even further by following safety precautions.

- Lightning strike victims carry no electrical charge and should be attended to immediately.

Know the Terms

Familiarize yourself with these terms to help identify a thunderstorm hazard:

Severe Thunderstorm Watch
Tells you when and where severe thunderstorms are likely to occur. Watch the sky and stay tuned to NOAA Weather Radio, commercial radio, or television for information.

Severe Thunderstorm Warning
Issued when severe weather has been reported by spotters or indicated by radar. Warnings indicate imminent danger to life and property to those in the path of the storm.

Take Protective Measures

Before Thunderstorms and Lightning

To prepare for a thunderstorm, you should do the following:

- Remove dead or rotting trees and branches that could fall and cause injury or damage during a severe thunderstorm.

- Remember the 30/30 lightning safety rule: Go indoors if, after seeing lightning, you cannot count to 30 before hearing thunder. Stay indoors for 30 minutes after hearing the last clap of thunder.

Thunderstorms

The following are guidelines for what you should do if a thunderstorm is likely in your area:

- Postpone outdoor activities.

- Get inside a home, building, or hard top automobile (not a convertible). Although you may be injured if lightning strikes your car, you are much safer inside a vehicle than outside.

- Remember, rubber-soled shoes and rubber tires provide NO protection from lightning. However, the steel frame of a hard-topped vehicle provides increased protection if you are not touching metal.

- Secure outdoor objects that could blow away or cause damage.

- Shutter windows and secure outside doors. If shutters are not available, close window blinds, shades, or curtains.

- Avoid showering or bathing. Plumbing and bathroom fixtures can conduct electricity.

- Use a corded telephone only for emergencies. Cordless and cellular telephones are safe to use.

- Unplug appliances and other electrical items such as computers and turn off air conditioners. Power surges from lightning can cause serious damage.

- Use your battery-operated NOAA Weather Radio for updates from local officials.

 Avoid the following:
- Natural lightning rods such as a tall, isolated tree in an open area
- Hilltops, open fields, the beach, or a boat on the water
- Isolated sheds or other small structures in open areas
- Anything metal—tractors, farm equipment, motorcycles, golf carts, golf clubs, and bicycles

If you are:	Then:
In a forest	Seek shelter in a low area under a thick growth of small trees.
In an open area	Go to a low place such as a ravine or valley. Be alert for flash floods.
On open water	Get to land and find shelter immediately.
Anywhere you feel your hair stand on end (which indicates that lightning is about to strike)	Squat low to the ground on the balls of your feet. Place your hands over your ears and your head between your knees. Make yourself the smallest target possible and minimize your contact with the ground. DO NOT lie flat on the ground.

Natural Hazards

After a Thunderstorm

Call 9-1-1 for medical assistance as soon as possible.

The following are things you should check when you attempt to give aid to a victim of lightning:

- **Breathing** - if breathing has stopped, begin mouth-to-mouth resuscitation.

- **Heartbeat** - if the heart has stopped, administer CPR.

- **Pulse** - if the victim has a pulse and is breathing, look for other possible injuries. Check for burns where the lightning entered and left the body. Also be alert for nervous system damage, broken bones, and loss of hearing and eyesight.

Knowledge Check

Decide whether the following statements are true or false. Check the appropriate column. When you have finished, verify your answers using the answer key below.

T	F	Statement
☐	☐	1. Every thunderstorm produces lightning.
☐	☐	2. Never touch a person struck by lightning.
☐	☐	3. Dry, cold conditions favor development of a thunderstorm.
☐	☐	4. If you can count to 25 after seeing lightning and before hearing thunder, it is safe to stay outdoors.
☐	☐	5. It is safe to use a cordless telephone during a thunderstorm.
☐	☐	6. Rubber-soled shoes and rubber tires provide protection from lightning.

For More Information

If you require more information about any of these topics, the following resource may be helpful.

Publications

National Weather Service

Facts about Lightning. 200252. Two-page factsheet for boaters. Available online at www.nws.noaa.gov/om/wcm/lightning/resources/LightningFactsSheet.pdf

Answer key:

1. True 2. False 3. False 4. False 5. True 6. False

2.5

Winter Storms and Extreme Cold

Heavy snowfall and extreme cold can immobilize an entire region. Even areas that normally experience mild winters can be hit with a major snowstorm or extreme cold. Winter storms can result in flooding, storm surge, closed highways, blocked roads, downed power lines and hypothermia.

Know the Terms

Familiarize yourself with these terms to help identify a winter storm hazard:

Freezing Rain
Rain that freezes when it hits the ground, creating a coating of ice on roads, walkways, trees, and power lines.

Sleet
Rain that turns to ice pellets before reaching the ground. Sleet also causes moisture on roads to freeze and become slippery.

Winter Storm Watch
A winter storm is possible in your area. Tune in to NOAA Weather Radio, commercial radio, or television for more information.

Winter Storm Warning
A winter storm is occurring or will soon occur in your area.

Blizzard Warning
Sustained winds or frequent gusts to 35 miles per hour or greater and considerable amounts of falling or blowing snow (reducing visibility to less than a quarter mile) are expected to prevail for a period of three hours or longer.

Frost/Freeze Warning
Below freezing temperatures are expected.

Take Protective Measures

Before Winter Storms and Extreme Cold

Review

See Section 1.3: Assemble a Disaster Supplies Kit

Include the following in your disaster supplies kit:

- Rock salt to melt ice on walkways

- Sand to improve traction

- Snow shovels and other snow removal equipment.

Prepare for possible isolation in your home by having sufficient heating fuel; regular fuel sources may be cut off. For example, store a good supply of dry, seasoned wood for your fireplace or wood-burning stove.

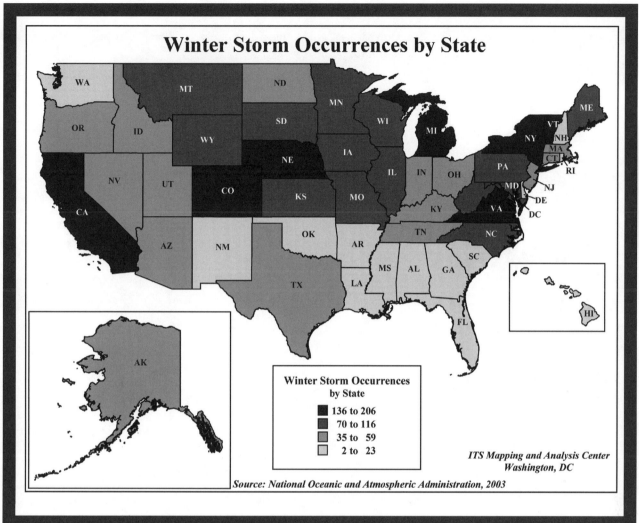

Winter Storm Occurrences by State

Winter Storm Occurrences by State
- 136 to 206
- 70 to 116
- 35 to 59
- 2 to 23

ITS Mapping and Analysis Center
Washington, DC

Source: National Oceanic and Atmospheric Administration, 2003

Winterize your home to extend the life of your fuel supply by insulating walls and attics, caulking and weather-stripping doors and windows, and installing storm windows or covering windows with plastic.

To winterize your car, attend to the following:

- Battery and ignition system should be in top condition and battery terminals clean.

- Ensure antifreeze levels are sufficient to avoid freezing.

- Ensure the heater and defroster work properly.

- Check and repair windshield wiper equipment; ensure proper washer fluid level.

- Ensure the thermostat works properly.

- Check lights and flashing hazard lights for serviceability.

- Check for leaks and crimped pipes in the exhaust system; repair or replace as necessary. Carbon monoxide is deadly and usually gives no warning.

- Check breaks for wear and fluid levels.

- Check oil for level and weight. Heavier oils congeal more at low temperatures and do not lubricate as well.

- Consider snow tires, snow tires with studs, or chains.

- Replace fuel and air filters. Keep water out of the system by using additives and maintaining a full tank of gas.

Dress for the Weather

- Wear several layers of loose fitting, lightweight, warm clothing rather than one layer of heavy clothing. The outer garments should be tightly woven and water repellent.
- Wear mittens, which are warmer than gloves.
- Wear a hat.
- Cover your mouth with a scarf to protect your lungs.

During a Winter Storm

The following are guidelines for what you should do during a winter storm or under conditions of extreme cold:

- Listen to your radio, television, or NOAA Weather Radio for weather reports and emergency information.

- Eat regularly and drink ample fluids, but avoid caffeine and alcohol.

- Avoid overexertion when shoveling snow. Overexertion can bring on a heart attack—a major cause of death in the winter. If you must shovel snow, stretch before going outside.

- Watch for signs of frostbite. These include loss of feeling and white or pale appearance in extremities such as fingers, toes, ear lobes, and the tip of the nose. If symptoms are detected, get medical help immediately.

- Watch for signs of hypothermia. These include uncontrollable shivering, memory loss, disorientation, incoherence, slurred speech, drowsiness, and apparent exhaustion. If symptoms of hypothermia are detected, get the victim to a warm location, remove wet clothing, warm the center of the body first, and give warm, non-alcoholic beverages if the victim is conscious. Get medical help as soon as possible.

- Conserve fuel, if necessary, by keeping your residence cooler than normal. Temporarily close off heat to some rooms.

- Maintain ventilation when using kerosene heaters to avoid build-up of toxic fumes. Refuel kerosene heaters outside and keep them at least three feet from flammable objects.

- Drive only if it is absolutely necessary. If you must drive, consider the following:

  - Travel in the day, don't travel alone, and keep others informed of your schedule

  - Stay on main roads; avoid back road shortcuts

If a blizzard traps you in the car, keep these guidelines in mind:

- Pull off the highway. Turn on hazard lights and hang a distress flag from the radio antenna or window.

- Remain in your vehicle where rescuers are most likely to find you. Do not set out on foot unless you can see a building close by where you know you can take shelter. Be careful; distances are distorted by blowing snow. A building may seem close, but be too far to walk to in deep snow.

- Run the engine and heater about 10 minutes each hour to keep warm. When the engine is running, open an upwind window slightly for ventilation. This will protect you from possible carbon monoxide poisoning. Periodically clear snow from the exhaust pipe.

- Exercise to maintain body heat, but avoid overexertion. In extreme cold, use road maps, seat covers, and floor mats for insulation. Huddle with passengers and use your coat for a blanket.

- Take turns sleeping. One person should be awake at all times to look for rescue crews.

- Drink fluids to avoid dehydration.

- Be careful not to waste battery power. Balance electrical energy needs—the use of lights, heat, and radio—with supply.

- Turn on the inside light at night so work crews or rescuers can see you.

- If stranded in a remote area, stomp large block letters in an open area spelling out HELP or SOS and line with rocks or tree limbs to attract the attention of rescue personnel who may be surveying the area by airplane.

- Leave the car and proceed on foot—if necessary—once the blizzard passes.

After a Winter Storm

Follow the instructions for recovering from a disaster in Part 5.

For More Information

If you require more information about any of these topics, the following are resources that may be helpful.

Publications

National Weather Service

Winter Storms...The Deceptive Killers. Brochure packed with useful information including winter storm facts, how to detect frostbite and hypothermia, what to do in a winter storm, and how to be prepared. Available online at: www.nws.noaa.gov/om/brochures/wntrstm.htm

Centers for Disease Control and Prevention

Extreme Cold: A Prevention Guide to Promote Your Personal Health and Safety. An extensive document providing information about planning ahead for cold weather, safety both indoors and outdoors in cold weather, and cold weather health conditions. Available online at: www.phppo.cdc.gov

Heat kills by pushing the human body beyond its limits. In extreme heat and high humidity, evaporation is slowed and the body must work extra hard to maintain a normal temperature.

Most heat disorders occur because the victim has been overexposed to heat or has over-exercised for his or her age and physical condition. Older adults, young children, and those who are sick or overweight are more likely to succumb to extreme heat.

Conditions that can induce heat-related illnesses include stagnant atmospheric conditions and poor air quality. Consequently, people living in urban areas may be at greater risk from the effects of a prolonged heat wave than those living in rural areas. Also, asphalt and concrete store heat longer and gradually release heat at night, which can produce higher nighttime temperatures known as the "urban heat island effect."

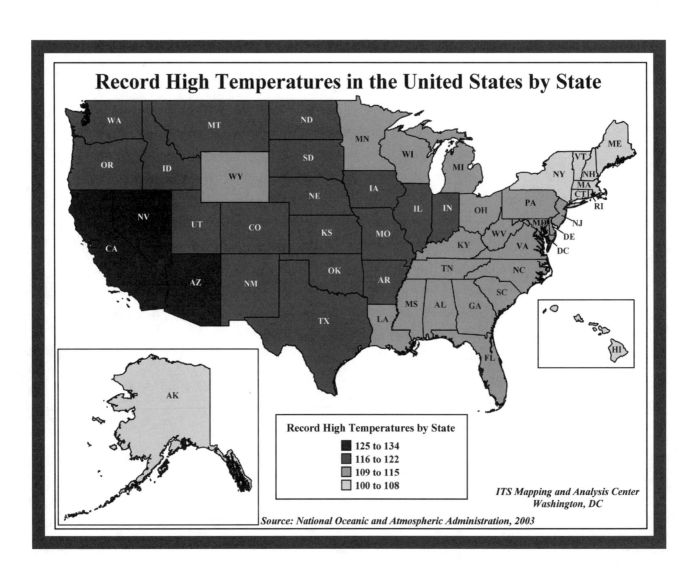

Record High Temperatures in the United States by State

Record High Temperatures by State
- 125 to 134
- 116 to 122
- 109 to 115
- 100 to 108

ITS Mapping and Analysis Center
Washington, DC

Source: National Oceanic and Atmospheric Administration, 2003

Know the Terms

Familiarize yourself with these terms to help identify an extreme heat hazard:

Heat Wave
Prolonged period of excessive heat, often combined with excessive humidity.

Heat Index
A number in degrees Fahrenheit (F) that tells how hot it feels when relative humidity is added to the air temperature. Exposure to full sunshine can increase the heat index by 15 degrees.

Heat Cramps
Muscular pains and spasms due to heavy exertion. Although heat cramps are the least severe, they are often the first signal that the body is having trouble with the heat.

Heat Exhaustion
Typically occurs when people exercise heavily or work in a hot, humid place where body fluids are lost through heavy sweating. Blood flow to the skin increases, causing blood flow to decrease to the vital organs. This results in a form of mild shock. If not treated, the victim's condition will worsen. Body temperature will keep rising and the victim may suffer heat stroke.

Heat Stroke
A life-threatening condition. The victim's temperature control system, which produces sweating to cool the body, stops working. The body temperature can rise so high that brain damage and death may result if the body is not cooled quickly.

Sun Stroke
Another term for heat stroke.

Take Protective Measures

Before Extreme Heat

To prepare for extreme heat, you should:

- Install window air conditioners snugly; insulate if necessary.

- Check air-conditioning ducts for proper insulation.

- Install temporary window reflectors (for use between windows and drapes), such as aluminum foil-covered cardboard, to reflect heat back outside.

- Weather-strip doors and sills to keep cool air in.

- Cover windows that receive morning or afternoon sun with drapes, shades, awnings, or louvers. (Outdoor awnings or louvers can reduce the heat that enters a home by up to 80 percent.)

- Keep storm windows up all year.

During a Heat Emergency

The following are guidelines for what you should do if the weather is extremely hot:

- Stay indoors as much as possible and limit exposure to the sun.

- Stay on the lowest floor out of the sunshine if air conditioning is not available.

- Consider spending the warmest part of the day in public buildings such as libraries, schools, movie theaters, shopping malls, and other community facilities. Circulating air can cool the body by increasing the perspiration rate of evaporation.

- Eat well-balanced, light, and regular meals. Avoid using salt tablets unless directed to do so by a physician.

- Drink plenty of water. Persons who have epilepsy or heart, kidney, or liver disease; are on fluid-restricted diets; or have a problem with fluid retention should consult a doctor before increasing liquid intake.

- Limit intake of alcoholic beverages.

- Dress in loose-fitting, lightweight, and light-colored clothes that cover as much skin as possible.

- Protect face and head by wearing a wide-brimmed hat.

- Check on family, friends, and neighbors who do not have air conditioning and who spend much of their time alone.

- Never leave children or pets alone in closed vehicles.

- Avoid strenuous work during the warmest part of the day. Use a buddy system when working in extreme heat, and take frequent breaks.

First Aid for Heat-Induced Illnesses

Extreme heat brings with it the possibility of heat-induced illnesses. The following table lists these illnesses, their symptoms, and the first aid treatment.

Condition	Symptoms	First Aid
Sunburn	Skin redness and pain, possible swelling, blisters, fever, headaches	• Take a shower using soap to remove oils that may block pores, preventing the body from cooling naturally. • Apply dry, sterile dressings to any blisters, and get medical attention.
Heat Cramps	Painful spasms, usually in leg and abdominal muscles; heavy sweating	• Get the victim to a cooler location. • Lightly stretch and gently massage affected muscles to relieve spasms. • Give sips of up to a half glass of cool water every 15 minutes. (Do not give liquids with caffeine or alcohol.) • Discontinue liquids, if victim is nauseated.
Heat Exhaustion	Heavy sweating but skin may be cool, pale, or flushed. Weak pulse. Normal body temperature is possible, but temperature will likely rise. Fainting or dizziness, nausea, vomiting, exhaustion, and headaches are possible.	• Get victim to lie down in a cool place. • Loosen or remove clothing. • Apply cool, wet cloths. • Fan or move victim to air-conditioned place. • Give sips of water if victim is conscious. • Be sure water is consumed slowly. • Give half glass of cool water every 15 minutes. • Discontinue water if victim is nauseated. • Seek immediate medical attention if vomiting occurs.
Heat Stroke (a severe medical emergency)	High body temperature (105+); hot, red, dry skin; rapid, weak pulse; and rapid, shallow breathing. Victim will probably not sweat unless victim was sweating from recent strenuous activity. Possible unconsciousness.	• Call 9-1-1 or emergency medical services, or get the victim to a hospital immediately. **Delay can be fatal.** • Move victim to a cooler environment. • Remove clothing. • Try a cool bath, sponging, or wet sheet to reduce body temperature. • Watch for breathing problems. • Use extreme caution. • Use fans and air conditioners.

Natural Hazards

Additional Information

An emergency water shortage can be caused by prolonged drought, poor water supply management, or contamination of a surface water supply source or aquifer.

Drought can affect vast territorial regions and large population numbers. Drought also creates environmental conditions that increase the risk of other hazards such as fire, flash flood, and possible landslides and debris flow.

Conserving water means more water available for critical needs for everyone. Appendix A contains detailed suggestions for conserving water both indoors and outdoors. Make these practices a part of your daily life and help preserve this essential resource.

After Extreme Heat

Follow the instructions for recovering from a disaster in Part 5.

Knowledge Check

You and a friend have been outdoors in the sun for some time. Shortly after coming inside, your friend complains of nausea and headache but tells you not to worry as it is probably a food allergy.

What would you advise him or her to do?

Answer: Seek immediate medical attention and discontinue intake of water.

For More Information

If you require more information about any of these topics, the following resource may be helpful.

Publications

National Weather Service

Heat Wave: A Major Summer Killer. An online brochure describing the heat index, heat disorders, and heat wave safety tips. Available online at: www.nws.noaa.gov/om/ /brochures/heat_wave.htm

Natural Hazards

Earthquakes

One of the most frightening and destructive phenomena of nature is a severe earthquake and its terrible aftereffects. An earthquake is a sudden movement of the earth, caused by the abrupt release of strain that has accumulated over a long time. For hundreds of millions of years, the forces of plate tectonics have shaped the earth, as the huge plates that form the earth's surface slowly move over, under, and past each other. Sometimes, the movement is gradual. At other times, the plates are locked together, unable to release the accumulating energy. When the accumulated energy grows strong enough, the plates break free. If the earthquake occurs in a populated area, it may cause many deaths and injuries and extensive property damage.

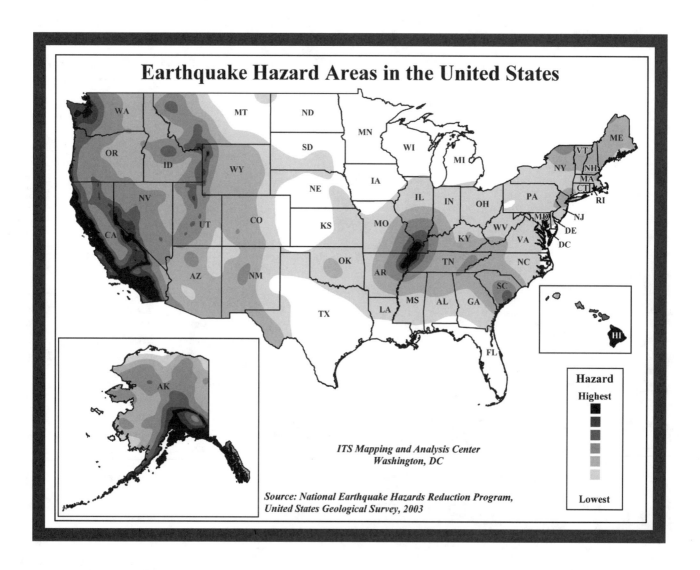

Earthquake Hazard Areas in the United States

*ITS Mapping and Analysis Center
Washington, DC*

*Source: National Earthquake Hazards Reduction Program,
United States Geological Survey, 2003*

Hazard

Highest

Lowest

Know the Terms

Familiarize yourself with these terms to help identify an earthquake hazard:

Earthquake
A sudden slipping or movement of a portion of the earth's crust, accompanied and followed by a series of vibrations.

Aftershock
An earthquake of similar or lesser intensity that follows the main earthquake.

Fault
The fracture across which displacement has occurred during an earthquake. The slippage may range from less than an inch to more than 10 yards in a severe earthquake.

Epicenter
The place on the earth's surface directly above the point on the fault where the earthquake rupture began. Once fault slippage begins, it expands along the fault during the earthquake and can extend hundreds of miles before stopping.

Seismic Waves
Vibrations that travel outward from the earthquake fault at speeds of several miles per second. Although fault slippage directly under a structure can cause considerable damage, the vibrations of seismic waves cause most of the destruction during earthquakes.

Magnitude
The amount of energy released during an earthquake, which is computed from the amplitude of the seismic waves. A magnitude of 7.0 on the Richter Scale indicates an extremely strong earthquake. Each whole number on the scale represents an increase of about 30 times more energy released than the previous whole number represents. Therefore, an earthquake measuring 6.0 is about 30 times more powerful than one measuring 5.0.

Take Protective Measures

The following are things you can do to protect yourself, your family, and your property in the event of an earthquake:

Before an Earthquake

- Repair defective electrical wiring, leaky gas lines, and inflexible utility connections. Get appropriate professional help. Do not work with gas or electrical lines yourself.

- Bolt down and secure to the wall studs your water heater, refrigerator, furnace, and gas appliances. If recommended by your gas company, have an automatic gas shut-off valve installed that is triggered by strong vibrations.

- Place large or heavy objects on lower shelves. Fasten shelves, mirrors, and large picture frames to walls. Brace high and top-heavy objects.

- Store bottled foods, glass, china, and other breakables on low shelves or in cabinets that fasten shut.

- Anchor overhead lighting fixtures.

- Be sure the residence is firmly anchored to its foundation.

- Install flexible pipe fittings to avoid gas or water leaks. Flexible fittings are more resistant to breakage.

- Locate safe spots in each room under a sturdy table or against an inside wall. Reinforce this information by moving to these places during each drill.

- Hold earthquake drills with your family members: Drop, cover, and hold on!

During an Earthquake

Minimize your movements during an earthquake to a few steps to a nearby safe place. Stay indoors until the shaking has stopped and you are sure exiting is safe.

If you are:	Then:
Indoors	• Take cover under a sturdy desk, table, or bench or against an inside wall, and hold on. If there isn't a table or desk near you, cover your face and head with your arms and crouch in an inside corner of the building. • Stay away from glass, windows, outside doors and walls, and anything that could fall, such as lighting fixtures or furniture. • Stay in bed—if you are there when the earthquake strikes—hold on and protect your head with a pillow, unless you are under a heavy light fixture that could fall. In that case, move to the nearest safe place. • Use a doorway for shelter only if it is in close proximity to you and if you know it is a strongly supported, load-bearing doorway. • Stay inside until the shaking stops and it is safe to go outside. Most injuries during earthquakes occur when people are hit by falling objects when entering into or exiting from buildings. • Be aware that the electricity may go out or the sprinkler systems or fire alarms may turn on. • DO NOT use the elevators.
Outdoors	• Stay there. • Move away from buildings, streetlights, and utility wires.

If you are:	Then:
In a moving vehicle	• Stop as quickly as safety permits and stay in the vehicle. Avoid stopping near or under buildings, trees, overpasses, and utility wires. • Proceed cautiously once the earthquake has stopped, watching for road and bridge damage.
Trapped under debris	• Do not light a match. • Do not move about or kick up dust. • Cover your mouth with a handkerchief or clothing. • Tap on a pipe or wall so rescuers can locate you. Use a whistle if one is available. Shout only as a last resort—shouting can cause you to inhale dangerous amounts of dust.

Natural Hazards

After an Earthquake

• Be prepared for aftershocks. These secondary shockwaves are usually less violent than the main quake but can be strong enough to do additional damage to weakened structures.

• Open cabinets cautiously. Beware of objects that can fall off shelves.

• Stay away from damaged areas unless your assistance has been specifically requested by police, fire, or relief organizations.

• Be aware of possible tsunamis if you live in coastal areas. These are also known as seismic sea waves (mistakenly called "tidal waves"). When local authorities issue a tsunami warning, assume that a series of dangerous waves is on the way. Stay away from the beach.

Knowledge Check

Check your knowledge about what to do during an earthquake. For each question, choose answer *A* or *B* and circle the correct response. When you have finished, check your responses using the answer key below.

What action should you take during an earthquake? The answer varies by where you are when an earthquake strikes. For each situation, pick the best course of action from the choices given.

1. At home	A. Stay inside B. Go out to the street
2. In bed	A. Stand by a window to see what is happening B. Stay in bed and protect your head with a pillow
3. In any building	A. Stand in a doorway B. Crouch in an inside corner away from the exterior wall
4. On the upper floor of an apartment building	A. Take the elevator to the ground floor as quickly as possible B. Stay in an interior room under a desk or table
5. Outdoors	A. Run into the nearest building B. Stay outside away from buildings
6. Driving a car	A. Stop the car in an open area B. Stop the car under an overpass

1. A 2. B 3. B 4. B 5. B 6. A

Answer key

For More Information

If you require more information about any of these topics, the following are resources that may be helpful.

FEMA Publications

Avoiding Earthquake Damage: A Checklist for Homeowners. Safety tips for before, during, and after an earthquake

Preparedness in High-Rise Buildings. FEMA-76. Earthquake safety tips for high-rise dwellers

Learning to Live in Earthquake Country: Preparedness in Apartments and Mobile Homes. L-143. Safety tips on earthquake preparation for residents of apartments and mobile homes

Family Earthquake Safety Home Hazard Hunt and Drill. FEMA-113. How to identify home hazards; how to conduct earthquake drills

Earthquake Preparedness: What Every Childcare Provider Should Know. FEMA 240. Publication for teachers and for presentation to children. Available online at www.fema.gov/kids/tch_eq.htm

Volcanoes

A volcano is a vent through which molten rock escapes to the earth's surface. When pressure from gases within the molten rock becomes too great, an eruption occurs. Eruptions can be quiet or explosive. There may be lava flows, flattened landscapes, poisonous gases, and flying rock and ash.

Because of their intense heat, lava flows are great fire hazards. Lava flows destroy everything in their path, but most move slowly enough that people can move out of the way.

Fresh volcanic ash, made of pulverized rock, can be abrasive, acidic, gritty, gassy, and odorous. While not immediately dangerous to most adults, the acidic gas and ash can cause lung damage to small infants, to older adults, and to those suffering from severe respiratory illnesses. Volcanic ash also can damage machinery, including engines and electrical equipment. Ash accumulations mixed with water become heavy and can collapse roofs.

Volcanic eruptions can be accompanied by other natural hazards, including earthquakes, mudflows and flash floods, rock falls and landslides, acid rain, fire, and (under special conditions) tsunamis. Active volcanoes in the U.S. are found mainly in Hawaii, Alaska, and the Pacific Northwest.

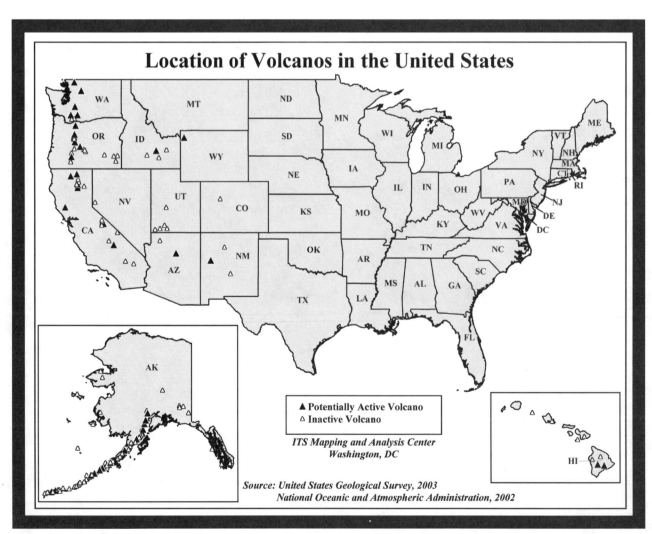

Location of Volcanos in the United States

▲ Potentially Active Volcano
△ Inactive Volcano

ITS Mapping and Analysis Center
Washington, DC

Source: United States Geological Survey, 2003
National Oceanic and Atmospheric Administration, 2002

Take Protective Measures

Before a Volcanic Eruption

- Add a pair of goggles and a disposable breathing mask for each member of the family to your disaster supplies kit.

- Stay away from active volcano sites.

During a Volcanic Eruption

The following are guidelines for what to do if a volcano erupts in your area:

- Evacuate immediately from the volcano area to avoid flying debris, hot gases, lateral blast, and lava flow.

- Be aware of mudflows. The danger from a mudflow increases near stream channels and with prolonged heavy rains. Mudflows can move faster than you can walk or run. Look upstream before crossing a bridge, and do not cross the bridge if mudflow is approaching.

- Avoid river valleys and low-lying areas.

Protection from Falling Ash

- Wear long-sleeved shirts and long pants.
- Use goggles and wear eyeglasses instead of contact lenses.
- Use a dust mask or hold a damp cloth over your face to help with breathing.
- Stay away from areas downwind from the volcano to avoid volcanic ash.
- Stay indoors until the ash has settled unless there is danger of the roof collapsing.
- Close doors, windows, and all ventilation in the house (chimney vents, furnaces, air conditioners, fans, and other vents).
- Clear heavy ash from flat or low-pitched roofs and rain gutters.
- Avoid running car or truck engines. Driving can stir up volcanic ash that can clog engines, damage moving parts, and stall vehicles.
- Avoid driving in heavy ash fall unless absolutely required. If you have to drive, keep speed down to 35 MPH or slower.

After a Volcanic Erruption Follow the instructions for recovering from a disaster in Part 5.

Knowledge Check

Read the scenario and answer the question. Check your responses with the answer key below.

Scenario

About an hour after the eruption of Mount St. Helens, ash began to fall in Yakima, a city in eastern Washington. The ash fall was so extensive and it became so dark that lights were turned on all day. It took 10 weeks to haul away the ash from Yakima's streets, sidewalks, and roofs.

Assume you were a resident of Yakima during this time. What would you need to protect yourself when going outside?

For More Information

If you require more information about any of these topics, the following are resources that may be helpful.

Publications

National Weather Service

Heat Wave: A Major Summer Killer. An online brochure describing the heat index, heat disorders, and heat wave safety tips. Available online at: www.nws.noaa.gov/om/ /brochures/heat_wave.htm

U.S. Geological Survey

Volcano Hazards Program. Website with volcano activity updates, feature stories, information about volcano hazards, and resources. Available online at: http: //volcanoes.usgs.gov

Answer key

1. Face masks 2. Goggles 3. Eyeglasses instead of contact lenses 4. Clothing to cover as much of the body as possible

Landslides and
Debris Flow (Mudslide)

Landslides occur in all U.S. states and territories. In a landslide, masses of rock, earth, or debris move down a slope. Landslides may be small or large, slow or rapid. They are activated by storms, earthquakes, volcanic eruptions, fires, and human modification of land.

Debris and mud flows are rivers of rock, earth, and other debris saturated with water. They develop when water rapidly accumulates in the ground, during heavy rainfall or rapid snowmelt, changing the earth into a flowing river of mud or "slurry." They flow can rapidly, striking with little or no warning at avalanche speeds. They also can travel several miles from their source, growing in size as they pick up trees, boulders, cars, and other materials.

Landslide problems can be caused by land mismanagement, particularly in mountain, canyon, and coastal regions. Land-use zoning, professional inspections, and proper design can minimize many landslide, mudflow, and debris flow problems.

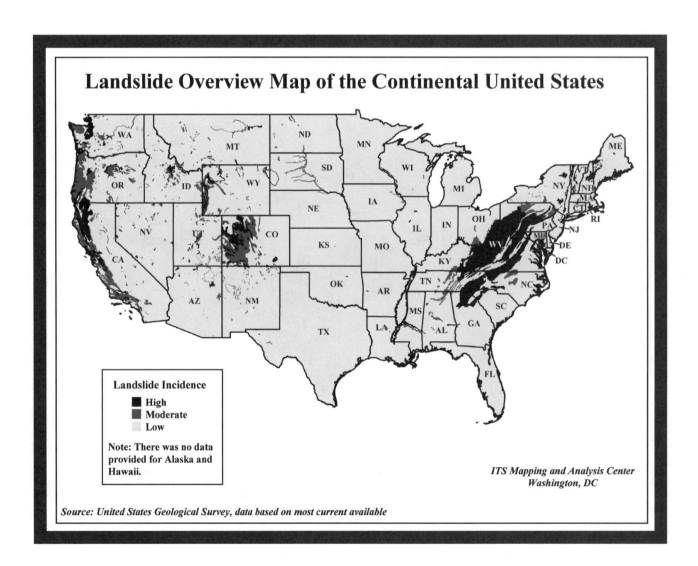

Landslide Overview Map of the Continental United States

Landslide Incidence

■ High
■ Moderate
■ Low

Note: There was no data provided for Alaska and Hawaii.

ITS Mapping and Analysis Center
Washington, DC

Source: United States Geological Survey, data based on most current available

Take Protective Measures

The following are steps you can take to protect yourself from the effects of a landslide or debris flow:

- Do not build near steep slopes, close to mountain edges, near drainage ways, or natural erosion valleys.

- Get a ground assessment of your property.

- Consult an appropriate professional expert for advice on corrective measures.

- Minimize home hazards by having flexible pipe fittings installed to avoid gas or water leaks, as flexible fittings are more resistant to breakage (only the gas company or professionals should install gas fittings).

Recognize Landslide Warning Signs

- Changes occur in your landscape such as patterns of storm-water drainage on slopes (especially the places where runoff water converges) land movement, small slides, flows, or progressively leaning trees.

- Doors or windows stick or jam for the first time.

- New cracks appear in plaster, tile, brick, or foundations.

- Outside walls, walks, or stairs begin pulling away from the building.

- Slowly developing, widening cracks appear on the ground or on paved areas such as streets or driveways.

- Underground utility lines break.

- Bulging ground appears at the base of a slope.

- Water breaks through the ground surface in new locations.

- Fences, retaining walls, utility poles, or trees tilt or move.

- A faint rumbling sound that increases in volume is noticeable as the landslide nears.

- The ground slopes downward in one direction and may begin shifting in that direction under your feet.

- Unusual sounds, such as trees cracking or boulders knocking together, might indicate moving debris.

- Collapsed pavement, mud, fallen rocks, and other indications of possible debris flow can be seen when driving (embankments along roadsides are particularly susceptible to landslides).

Natural Hazards

During a Landslide or Debris Flow

The following are guidelines for what you should do if a landslide or debris flow occurs:

- Move away from the path of a landslide or debris flow as quickly as possible.

- Curl into a tight ball and protect your head if escape is not possible.

After a Landslide or Debris Flow

The following are guidelines for the period following a landslide:

- Stay away from the slide area. There may be danger of additional slides.

- Check for injured and trapped persons near the slide, without entering the direct slide area. Direct rescuers to their locations.

- Watch for associated dangers such as broken electrical, water, gas, and sewage lines and damaged roadways and railways.

- Replant damaged ground as soon as possible since erosion caused by loss of ground cover can lead to flash flooding and additional landslides in the near future.

- Seek advice from a geotechnical expert for evaluating landslide hazards or designing corrective techniques to reduce landslide risk.

- Follow the instructions for returning home in Part 5.

Knowledge Check

Review the following information and answer the questions. Check your responses with the answer key below.

Landslides occur in all 50 states—it is estimated that they cause between 25 and 50 deaths each year in the U.S. and thousands more in vulnerable areas around the globe. The number of landslides in the United States is expected to increase.

1. What might account for the projected increase in landslides?

2. What can you do to help reverse the upward trend?

Natural Hazards

Answer Key

1. Mounting pressure for approving the development of lands subject to landslides and earth failures has increased development in these unsafe areas.

2. Work with others in the community to enact and enforce regulations that prohibit building near areas subject to landslides and mudslides. In areas where the hazard exists and development has already occurred, work to promote protective measures such as encouraging homeowners to get a professional ground assessment of their property and educating residents about the warning signs.

Tsunamis (pronounced soo-ná-mees), also known as seismic sea waves (mistakenly called "tidal waves"), are a series of enormous waves created by an underwater disturbance such as an earthquake, landslide, volcanic eruption, or meteorite. A tsunami can move hundreds of miles per hour in the open ocean and smash into land with waves as high as 100 feet or more.

From the area where the tsunami originates, waves travel outward in all directions. Once the wave approaches the shore, it builds in height. The topography of the coastline and the ocean floor will influence the size of the wave. There may be more than one wave and the succeeding one may be larger than the one before. That is why a small tsunami at one beach can be a giant wave a few miles away.

All tsunamis are potentially dangerous, even though they may not damage every coastline they strike. A tsunami can strike anywhere along most of the U.S. coastline. The most destructive tsunamis have occurred along the coasts of California, Oregon, Washington, Alaska, and Hawaii.

Earthquake-induced movement of the ocean floor most often generates tsunamis. If a major earthquake or landslide occurs close to shore, the first wave in a series could reach the beach in a few minutes, even before a warning is issued. Areas are at greater risk if they are less than 25 feet above sea level and within a mile of the shoreline. Drowning is the most common cause of death associated with a tsunami. Tsunami waves and the receding water are very destructive to structures in the run-up zone. Other hazards include flooding, contamination of drinking water, and fires from gas lines or ruptured tanks.

Know the Terms

Familiarize yourself with these terms to help identify a tsunami hazard:

Advisory
An earthquake has occurred in the Pacific basin, which might generate a tsunami.

Watch
A tsunami was or may have been generated, but is at least two hours travel time to the area in Watch status.

Warning
A tsunami was, or may have been generated, which could cause damage; therefore, people in the warned area are strongly advised to evacuate.

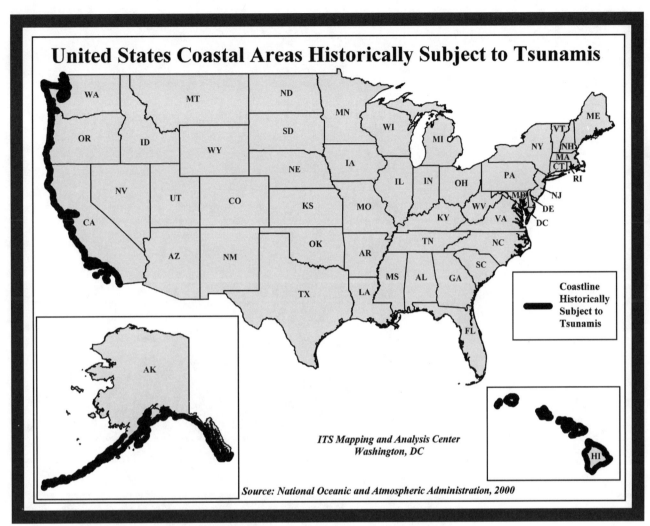

United States Coastal Areas Historically Subject to Tsunamis

Coastline Historically Subject to Tsunamis

ITS Mapping and Analysis Center
Washington, DC

Source: National Oceanic and Atmospheric Administration, 2000

Take Protective Measures

During a Tsunami

The following are guidelines for what you should do if a tsunami is likely in your area:

- Turn on your radio to learn if there is a tsunami warning if an earthquake occurs and you are in a coastal area.

- Move inland to higher ground immediately and stay there.

 If there is noticeable recession in water away from the shoreline this is nature's tsunami warning and it should be heeded. You should move away immediately.

After a Tsunami

The following are guidelines for the period following a tsunami:

- Stay away from flooded and damaged areas until officials say it is safe to return.

- Stay away from debris in the water; it may pose a safety hazard to boats and people.

Save Yourself—Not Your Possesions

Like everyone else in Maullin, Chile, Ramon Atala survived the 1960 Chile earthquake. However, he lost his life trying to save something from the tsunami that followed.

Mr. Atala was Maullin's most prosperous merchant. Outside of town, he owned a barn and a plantation of Monterey pine. In town, he owned a pier and at least one large building and also had private quarters in a waterfront warehouse.

Mr. Atala entered this warehouse between the first and second wave of the tsunami that struck Maullin. The warehouse was washed away and his body was never found.

It is unclear what he was trying to save. What is clear is that no possession is worth your life and that it is important to get to higher ground away from the coast and stay there until it is safe to return.

2.11
Fires

Each year, more than 4,000 Americans die and more than 25,000 are injured in fires, many of which could be prevented. Direct property loss due to fires is estimated at $8.6 billion annually.

To protect yourself, it is important to understand the basic characteristics of fire. Fire spreads quickly; there is no time to gather valuables or make a phone call. In just two minutes, a fire can become life-threatening. In five minutes, a residence can be engulfed in flames.

Heat and smoke from fire can be more dangerous than the flames. Inhaling the super-hot air can sear your lungs. Fire produces poisonous gases that make you disoriented and drowsy. Instead of being awakened by a fire, you may fall into a deeper sleep. Asphyxiation is the leading cause of fire deaths, exceeding burns by a three-to-one ratio.

Take Protective Measures

Before a Fire

Smoke Alarms

- Install smoke alarms. Properly working smoke alarms decrease your chances of dying in a fire by half.

- Place smoke alarms on every level of your residence. Place them outside bedrooms on the ceiling or high on the wall (4 to 12 inches from ceiling), at the top of open stairways, or at the bottom of enclosed stairs and near (but not in) the kitchen.

- Test and clean smoke alarms once a month and replace batteries at least once a year. Replace smoke alarms once every 10 years.

Escaping the Fire

- Review escape routes with your family. Practice escaping from each room.

- Make sure windows are not nailed or painted shut. Make sure security gratings on windows have a fire safety opening feature so they can be easily opened from the inside.

- Consider escape ladders if your residence has more than one level, and ensure that burglar bars and other antitheft mechanisms that block outside window entry are easily opened from the inside.

- Teach family members to stay low to the floor (where the air is safer in a fire) when escaping from a fire.

- Clean out storage areas. Do not let trash, such as old newspapers and magazines, accumulate.

Flammable Items

- Never use gasoline, benzine, naptha, or similar flammable liquids indoors.

- Store flammable liquids in approved containers in well-ventilated storage areas.

- Never smoke near flammable liquids.

- Discard all rags or materials that have been soaked in flammable liquids after you have used them. Safely discard them outdoors in a metal container.

- Insulate chimneys and place spark arresters on top. The chimney should be at least three feet higher than the roof. Remove branches hanging above and around the chimney.

Heating Sources

- Be careful when using alternative heating sources.

- Check with your local fire department on the legality of using kerosene heaters in your community. Be sure to fill kerosene heaters outside, and be sure they have cooled.

- Place heaters at least three feet away from flammable materials. Make sure the floor and nearby walls are properly insulated.

- Use only the type of fuel designated for your unit and follow manufacturer's instructions.

- Store ashes in a metal container outside and away from your residence.

- Keep open flames away from walls, furniture, drapery, and flammable items.

- Keep a screen in front of the fireplace.

- Have heating units inspected and cleaned annually by a certified specialist.

Matches and Smoking

- Keep matches and lighters up high, away from children, and, if possible, in a locked cabinet.

- Never smoke in bed or when drowsy or medicated. Provide smokers with deep, sturdy ashtrays. Douse cigarette and cigar butts with water before disposal.

Electrical Wiring

- Have the electrical wiring in your residence checked by an electrician.

- Inspect extension cords for frayed or exposed wires or loose plugs.

- Make sure outlets have cover plates and no exposed wiring.

- Make sure wiring does not run under rugs, over nails, or across high-traffic areas.

- Do not overload extension cords or outlets. If you need to plug in two or three appliances, get a UL-approved unit with built-in circuit breakers to prevent sparks and short circuits.

- Make sure insulation does not touch bare electrical wiring.

Other

- Sleep with your door closed.

- Install A-B-C-type fire extinguishers in your residence and teach family members how to use them.

- Consider installing an automatic fire sprinkler system in your residence.

- Ask your local fire department to inspect your residence for fire safety and prevention.

During a Fire

If your clothes catch on fire, you should:

- **Stop, drop, and roll**—until the fire is extinguished. Running only makes the fire burn **faster**.

To escape a fire, you should:

- **Check closed doors for heat before you open them.** If you are escaping through a closed door, use the back of your hand to feel the top of the door, the doorknob, and the crack between the door and door frame before you open it. Never use the palm of your hand or fingers to test for heat—burning those areas could impair your ability to escape a fire (i.e., ladders and crawling).

Hot Door	Cool Door
Do not open. Escape through a window. If you cannot escape, hang a white or light-colored sheet outside the window, alerting fire fighters to your presence.	Open slowly and ensure fire and/or smoke is not blocking your escape route. If your escape route is blocked, shut the door immediately and use an alternate escape route, such as a window. If clear, leave immediately through the door and close it behind you. Be prepared to crawl. Smoke and heat rise. The air is clearer and cooler near the floor.

- Crawl low under any smoke to your exit—heavy smoke and poisonous gases collect first along the ceiling.

- Close doors behind you as you escape to delay the spread of the fire.

- Stay out once you are safely out. Do not reenter. Call 9-1-1.

The following are guidelines for different circumstances in the period following a fire:

After a Fire

- If you are with burn victims, or are a burn victim yourself, call 9-1-1; cool and cover burns to reduce chance of further injury or infection.

- If you detect heat or smoke when entering a damaged building, evacuate immediately.

- If you are a tenant, contact the landlord.

- If you have a safe or strong box, do not try to open it. It can hold intense heat for several hours. If the door is opened before the box has cooled, the contents could burst into flames.

- If you must leave your home because a building inspector says the building is unsafe, ask someone you trust to watch the property during your absence.

- Follow the instructions for recovering from a disaster in Part 5.

Knowledge Check

Answer each question and check your responses using the answer key below.

1. You need to escape a fire through a closed door. What, if anything, should you do before opening the door?

2. What should you do if your clothes are on fire?

3. What actions should be taken for burn victims?

4. To reduce heating costs, you installed a wood-burning stove. What can you do to reduce the risk of fire from this heating source?

5. To escape in thick smoke, what should you do?

Answer key

1. Check the door for heat with the back of your hand
2. Stop, drop, and roll
3. Call 9-1-1 and cool and cover burns
4. Have the stove cleaned and inspected by a certified specialist
5. Crawl close to the floor

For More Information

If you require more information about any of these topics, the following are resources that may be helpful.

FEMA Publications

After the Fire: Returning to Normal. FA 046. This 16-page booklet provides information about recovering from a fire, including what to do during the first 24 hours, insurance considerations, valuing your property, replacement of valuable documents, salvage hints, fire department operations, and more. Available online at www.usfa.fema.gov/public/hfs/pubs/atf/after.shtm

Protecting Your Family From Fire. FA 130. This pamphlet was written to provide the information you need to decide what you must do to protect your family from fire. Topics include children, sleepwear, older adults, smoke detectors, escape plans, and residential sprinklers. Available online at www.usfa.fema.gov/public/hfs/pubs/hfs_pubs2.shtm

Fire Risks for the Hard of Hearing. FA 202; *Fire Risks for the Older Adult.* FA 203; *Fire Risks for the Mobility Impaired.* FA 204; *Fire Risks for the Blind or Visually Impaired.* FA 205
These reports address preparation for fire risks for populations with special challenges. All are available online at www.usfa.fema.gov/fire-service/education/education-pubs.shtm

If you live on a remote hillside or in a valley, prairie, or forest where flammable vegetation is abundant, your residence could be vulnerable to wildfires. These fires are usually triggered by lightning or accidents. Wildfires spread quickly, igniting brush, trees, and homes.

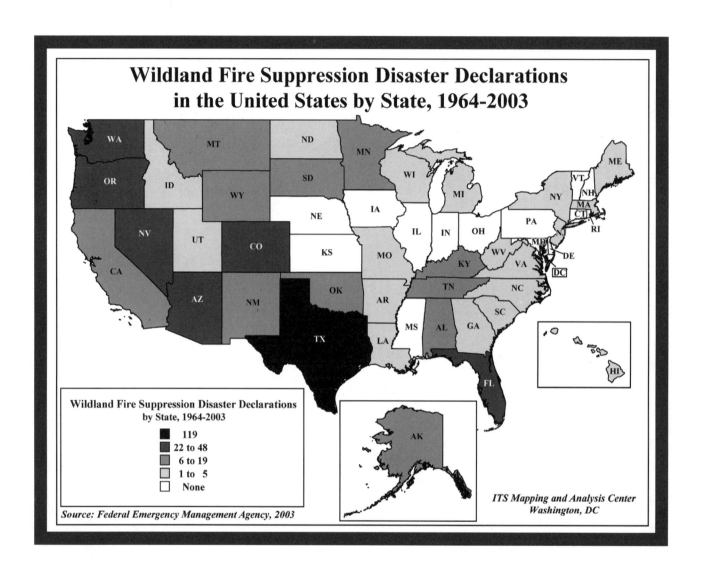

Take Protective Measures

Before a Wildfire

To prepare for wildfires, you should:

- Mark the entrance to your property with address signs that are clearly visible from the road.

- Keep lawns trimmed, leaves raked, and the roof and rain gutters free from debris such as dead limbs and leaves.

- Stack firewood at least 30 feet away from your residence.

- Store flammable materials, liquids, and solvents in metal containers outside your residence at least 30 feet away from structures and wooden fences.

- Create defensible space by thinning trees and brush within 30 feet around your residence. Beyond 30 feet, remove dead wood, debris, and low tree branches.

- Landscape your property with fire resistant plants and vegetation to prevent fire from spreading quickly. For example, hardwood trees are more fire-resistant than pine, evergreen, eucalyptus, or fir trees.

- Make sure water sources, such as hydrants, ponds, swimming pools, and wells, are accessible to the fire department.

- Use fire resistant, protective roofing and materials like stone, brick, and metal to protect your residence. Avoid using wood materials. They offer the least fire protection.

- Cover all exterior vents, attics, and eaves with metal mesh screens no larger than 6 millimeters or 1/4 inch to prevent debris from collecting and to help keep sparks out.

- Install multi-pane windows, tempered safety glass, or fireproof shutters to protect large windows from radiant heat.

- Use fire-resistant draperies for added window protection.

- Have chimneys, wood stoves, and all home heating systems inspected and cleaned annually by a certified specialist.

- Insulate chimneys and place spark arresters on top. The chimney should be at least 3 feet above the roof.

- Remove branches hanging above and around the chimney.

Follow Local Burning Laws

Before burning debris in a wooded area, make sure you notify local authorities, obtain a burning permit, and follow these guidelines:

- Use an approved incinerator with a safety lid or covering with holes no larger than 3/4 inch.

- Create at least a 10-foot clearing around the incinerator before burning debris.

- Have a fire extinguisher or garden hose on hand when burning debris.

During a Wildfire

If a wildfire threatens your home and time permits, take the following precautions:

- Shut off gas at the meter. Only a qualified professional can safely turn the gas back on.

- Seal attic and ground vents with pre-cut plywood or commercial seals.

- Turn off propane tanks.

- Place combustible patio furniture inside.

- Connect garden hose to outside taps. Place lawn sprinklers on the roof and near above-ground fuel tanks. Wet the roof.

- Wet or remove shrubs within 15 feet of your residence.

- Gather fire tools such as a rake, axe, handsaw or chainsaw, bucket, and shovel.

- Back your car into the garage or park it in an open space facing the direction of escape. Shut doors and roll up windows. Leave the key in the ignition and the car doors unlocked. Close garage windows and doors, but leave them unlocked. Disconnect automatic garage door openers.

- Open fireplace damper. Close fireplace screens.

- Close windows, vents, doors, blinds or noncombustible window coverings, and heavy drapes. Remove flammable drapes and curtains.

- Move flammable furniture into the center of the residence away from windows and sliding-glass doors.

- Close all interior doors and windows to prevent drafts.

- Place valuables that will not be damaged by water in a pool or pond.

If advised to evacuate, do so immediately. Choose a route away from the fire hazard. Watch for changes in the speed and direction of the fire and smoke.

After a Wildfire

Follow the instructions for recovering from a disaster in Part 5.

For More Information

If you require more information about any of these topics, the following resource may be helpful.

FEMA Publications

Wildfire: Are You Prepared? L-203. Wildfire safety tips, preparedness, and mitigation techniques.

3

Technological Hazards

Technological hazards include hazardous materials incidents and nuclear power plant failures. Usually, little or no warning precedes incidents involving technological hazards. In many cases, victims may not know they have been affected until many years later. For example, health problems caused by hidden toxic waste sites—like that at Love Canal, near Niagara Falls, New York—surfaced years after initial exposure.

The number of technological incidents is escalating, mainly as a result of the increased number of new substances and the opportunities for human error inherent in the use of these materials.

Use Part 3 to learn what actions to include in your family disaster plan to prepare for and respond to events involving technological hazards. Learn how to use, store, and dispose of household chemicals in a manner that will reduce the potential for injury to people and the environment.

When you complete Part 3, you will be able to:
- Recognize important terms.
- Take protective measures for technological disasters.
- Know what actions to take if an event occurs.
- Identify resources for more information about technological hazards.

Hazardous Materials Incidents

Chemicals are found everywhere. They purify drinking water, increase crop production, and simplify household chores. But chemicals also can be hazardous to humans or the environment if used or released improperly. Hazards can occur during production, storage, transportation, use, or disposal. You and your community are at risk if a chemical is used unsafely or released in harmful amounts into the environment where you live, work, or play.

Chemical manufacturers are one source of hazardous materials, but there are many others, including service stations, hospitals, and hazardous materials waste sites.

Take Protective Measures

Before a Hazardous Materials Incident

Many communities have Local Emergency Planning Committees (LEPCs) whose responsibilities include collecting information about hazardous materials in the community and making this information available to the public upon request. The LEPCs also are tasked with developing an emergency plan to prepare for and respond to chemical emergencies in the community. Ways the public will be notified and actions the public must take in the event of a release are part of the plan. Contact the LEPCs to find out more about chemical hazards and what needs to be done to minimize the risk to individuals and the community from these materials. The local emergency management office can provide contact information on the LEPCs.

You should add the following supplies to your disaster supplies kit:

- Plastic sheeting.

- Duct tape.

- Scissors.

Review

See Section 1.3: Assemble a Disaster Supplies Kit

During a Hazardous Materials Incident

Listen to local radio or television stations for detailed information and instructions. Follow the instructions carefully. You should stay away from the area to minimize the risk of contamination. Remember that some toxic chemicals are odorless.

If you are:	Then:
Asked to evacuate	Do so immediately.
Caught Outside	Stay upstream, uphill, and upwind! In general, try to go at least one-half mile (usually 8-10 city blocks) from the danger area. Do not walk into or touch any spilled liquids, airborne mists, or condensed solid chemical deposits.
In a motor vehicle	Stop and seek shelter in a permanent building. If you must remain in your car, keep car windows and vents closed and shut off the air conditioner and heater.
Requested to stay indoors	• Close and lock all exterior doors and windows. Close vents, fireplace dampers, and as many interior doors as possible. • Turn off air conditioners and ventilation systems. In large buildings, set ventilation systems to 100 percent recirculation so that no outside air is drawn into the building. If this is not possible, ventilation systems should be turned off. • Go into the pre-selected shelter room. This room should be above ground and have the fewest openings to the outside. • Seal the room by covering each window, door, and vent using plastic sheeting and duct tape. • Use material to fill cracks and holes in the room, such as those around pipes.

Technological Hazards

Shelter Safety for Sealed Rooms

Ten square feet of floor space per person will provide sufficient air to prevent carbon dioxide build-up for up to five hours, assuming a normal breathing rate while resting.

However, local officials are unlikely to recommend the public shelter in a sealed room for more than 2-3 hours because the effectiveness of such sheltering diminishes with time as the contaminated outside air gradually seeps into the shelter. At this point, evacuation from the area is the better protective action to take.

Also you should ventilate the shelter when the emergency has passed to avoid breathing contaminated air still inside the shelter.

**After a Hazardous
Materials Incident**

The following are guidelines for the period following a hazardous materials incident:

- Return home only when authorities say it is safe. Open windows and vents and turn on fans to provide ventilation.

- Act quickly if you have come in to contact with or have been exposed to hazardous chemicals. Do the following:

  - Follow decontamination instructions from local authorities. You may be advised to take a thorough shower, or you may be advised to stay away from water and follow another procedure.

  - Seek medical treatment for unusual symptoms as soon as possible.

  - Place exposed clothing and shoes in tightly sealed containers. Do not allow them to contact other materials. Call local authorities to find out about proper disposal.

  - Advise everyone who comes in to contact with you that you may have been exposed to a toxic substance.

- Find out from local authorities how to clean up your land and property.

- Report any lingering vapors or other hazards to your local emergency services office.

- Follow the instructions for recovering from a disaster in Part 5.

Household Chemical Emergencies

Nearly every household uses products containing hazardous materials or chemicals.

Cleaning Products

- Oven cleaners

- Drain cleaners

- Wood and metal cleaners and polishes

- Toilet cleaners

- Tub, tile, shower cleaners

- Bleach (laundry)

- Pool chemicals

Automotive Products

- Motor oil

- Fuel additives

- Carburetor and fuel injection cleaners

- Air conditioning refrigerants

- Starter fluids

- Automotive batteries

- Transmission and brake fluid

- Antifreeze

Lawn and Garden Products

- Herbicides

- Insecticides

- Fungicides/wood preservatives

Indoor Pesticides

- Ant sprays and baits

- Cockroach sprays and baits

- Flea repellents and shampoos

- Bug sprays

- Houseplant insecticides

- Moth repellents

- Mouse and rat poisons and baits

Workshop/Painting Supplies

- Adhesives and glues

- Furniture strippers

- Oil- or enamel-based paint

- Stains and finishes

- Paint thinners and turpentine

- Paint strippers and removers

- Photographic chemicals

- Fixatives and other solvents

Miscellaneous

- Batteries

- Mercury thermostats or thermometers

- Fluorescent light bulbs

- Driveway sealer

Other Flammable Products

- Propane tanks and other compressed gas cylinders

- Kerosene

- Home heating oil

- Diesel fuel

- Gas/oil mix

- Lighter fluid

Although the risk of a chemical accident is slight, knowing how to handle these products and how to react during an emergency can reduce the risk of injury.

Take Protective Measures

Before a Household Chemical Emergency

The following are guidelines for buying and storing hazardous household chemicals safely:

- Buy only as much of a chemical as you think you will use. Leftover material can be shared with neighbors or donated to a business, charity, or government agency. For example, excess pesticide could be offered to a greenhouse or garden center, and theater groups often need surplus paint. Some communities have organized waste exchanges where household hazardous chemicals and waste can be swapped or given away.

- Keep products containing hazardous materials in their original containers and never remove the labels unless the container is corroding. Corroding containers should be repackaged and clearly labeled.

- Never store hazardous products in food containers.

- Never mix household hazardous chemicals or waste with other products. Incompatibles, such as chlorine bleach and ammonia, may react, ignite, or explode.

Take the following precautions to prevent and respond to accidents:

- Follow the manufacturer's instructors for the proper use of the household chemical.

- Never smoke while using household chemicals.

- Never use hair spray, cleaning solutions, paint products, or pesticides near an open flame (e.g., pilot light, lighted candle, fireplace, wood burning stove, etc.) Although you may not be able to see or smell them, vapor particles in the air could catch fire or explode.

- Clean up any chemical spill immediately. Use rags to clean up the spill. Wear gloves and eye protection. Allow the fumes in the rags to evaporate outdoors, then dispose of the rags by wrapping them in a newspaper and placing them in a sealed plastic bag in your trash can.

- Dispose of hazardous materials correctly. Take household hazardous waste to a local collection program. Check with your county or state environmental or solid waste agency to learn if there is a household hazardous waste collection program in your area.

Learn to recognize the symptoms of toxic poisoning, which are as follows:

- Difficulty breathing.

- Irritation of the eyes, skin, throat, or respiratory tract.

- Changes in skin color.

- Headache or blurred vision.

- Dizziness.

- Clumsiness or lack of coordination.

- Cramps or diarrhea.

Be prepared to seek medical assistance:

- Post the number of the emergency medical services and the poison control center by all telephones. In an emergency situation, you may not have time to look up critical phone numbers. The national poison control number is (800)222-1222.

During a Household Chemical Emergency

If there is a danger of fire or explosion:

- Get out of the residence immediately. Do not waste time collecting items or calling the fire department when you are in danger. Call the fire department from outside (a cellular phone or a neighbor's phone) once you are safely away from danger.

- Stay upwind and away from the residence to avoid breathing toxic fumes.

If someone has been exposed to a household chemical:

- Find any containers of the substance that are readily available in order to provide requested information. Call emergency medical services.

- Follow the emergency operator or dispatcher's first aid instructions carefully. The first aid advice found on containers may be out of date or inappropriate. Do not give anything by mouth unless advised to do so by a medical professional.

Discard clothing that may have been contaminated. Some chemicals may not wash out completely.

Checking Your Home

There are probably many hazardous materials throughout your home. Take a tour of your home to see where these materials are located. Use the list of common hazardous household items presented earlier to guide you in your hunt. Once you have located a product, check the label and take the necessary steps to ensure that you are using, storing, and disposing of the material according to the manufacturer's directions. It is critical to store household chemicals in places where children cannot access them. Remember that products such as aerosol cans of hair spray and deodorant, nail polish and nail polish remover, toilet bowl cleaners, and furniture polishes all fall into the category of hazardous materials.

For More Information

If you require more information about any of these topics, the following are resources that may be helpful.

FEMA Publications

Household Hazardous Materials: A Guide for Citizens. IS 55. An independent study resource for parents and teachers. Web-based safety program focused on reducing the number of deaths and injuries in the home. Available online at http://training.fema.gov/emiweb/is/is55.asp

Chemical Emergencies. A pamphlet promoting awareness of chemical hazards in the home, how to prevent them, and what to do if exposed. Available online at www.fema.gov/pdf/rrr/talkdiz/chemical.pdf

Backgrounder: Hazardous Materials. 0.511. Information sheet available online at www.fema.gov/hazards/hazardousmaterials/hazmat.shtm

USFA: Factsheet: Baby-sitters Make the Right Call to EMS. 0510. Available online at www.usfa.fema.gov/public/factsheets/mtrc.shtm

Other Publications

American Red Cross

Chemical Emergencies. Extensive document describing the hazards of household chemicals and what to do in an emergency. Available online at www.redcross.org/services/disaster/0,1082,0_581_,00.html

Nuclear Power Plants

Nuclear power plants use the heat generated from nuclear fission in a contained environment to convert water to steam, which powers generators to produce electricity. Nuclear power plants operate in most states in the country and produce about 20 percent of the nation's power. Nearly 3 million Americans live within 10 miles of an operating nuclear power plant.

Although the construction and operation of these facilities are closely monitored and regulated by the Nuclear Regulatory Commission (NRC), accidents are possible. An accident could result in dangerous levels of radiation that could affect the health and safety of the public living near the nuclear power plant.

Local and state governments, federal agencies, and the electric utilities have emergency response plans in the event of a nuclear power plant incident. The plans define two "emergency planning zones." One zone covers an area within a 10-mile radius of the plant, where it is possible that people could be harmed by direct radiation exposure. The second zone covers a broader area, usually up to a 50-mile radius from the plant, where radioactive materials could contaminate water supplies, food crops, and livestock.

The potential danger from an accident at a nuclear power plant is exposure to radiation. This exposure could come from the release of radioactive material from the plant into the environment, usually characterized by a plume (cloud-like formation) of radioactive gases and particles. The major hazards to people in the vicinity of the plume are radiation exposure to the body from the cloud and particles deposited on the ground, inhalation of radioactive materials, and ingestion of radioactive materials.

Radioactive materials are composed of atoms that are unstable. An unstable atom gives off its excess energy until it becomes stable. The energy emitted is radiation. Each of us is exposed to radiation daily from natural sources, including the Sun and the Earth. Small traces of radiation are present in food and water. Radiation also is released from man-made sources such as X-ray machines, television sets, and microwave ovens. Radiation has a cumulative effect. The longer a person is exposed to radiation, the greater the effect. A high exposure to radiation can cause serious illness or death.

Minimizing Exposure to Radiation

- **Distance** - The more distance between you and the source of the radiation, the better. This could be evacuation or remaining indoors to minimize exposure.
- **Shielding** - The more heavy, dense material between you and the source of the radiation, the better.
- **Time** - Most radioactivity loses its strength fairly quickly.

If an accident at a nuclear power plant were to release radiation in your area, local authorities would activate warning sirens or another approved alert method. They also would instruct you through the Emergency Alert System (EAS) on local television and radio stations on how to protect yourself.

Know the Terms

Familiarize yourself with these terms to help identify a nuclear power plant emergency:

Notification of Unusual Event
A small problem has occurred at the plant. No radiation leak is expected. No action on your part will be necessary.

Alert
A small problem has occurred, and small amounts of radiation could leak inside the plant. This will not affect you and no action is required.

Site Area Emergency
Area sirens may be sounded. Listen to your radio or television for safety information.

General Emergency
Radiation could leak outside the plant and off the plant site. The sirens will sound. Tune to your local radio or television station for reports. Be prepared to follow instructions promptly.

Take Protective Measures

Before a Nuclear Power Plant Emergency

Obtain public emergency information materials from the power company that operates your local nuclear power plant or your local emergency services office. If you live within 10 miles of the power plant, you should receive these materials yearly from the power company or your state or local government.

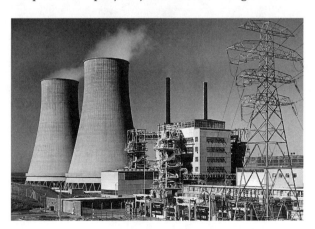

Technological Hazards

During a Nuclear Power Plant Emergency

The following are guidelines for what you should do if a nuclear power plant emergency occurs. Keep a battery-powered radio with you at all times and listen to the radio for specific instructions. Close and lock doors and windows.

If you are told to evacuate...	If you are advised to remain indoors...
• Keep car windows and vents closed; use re-circulating air.	• Turn off the air conditioner, ventilation fans, furnace, and other air intakes. • Go to a basement or other underground area, if possible. • Do not use the telephone unless absolutely necessary.

If you expect you have been exposed to nuclear radiation:

- Change clothes and shoes.

- Put exposed clothing in a plastic bag.

- Seal the bag and place it out of the way.

- Take a thorough shower.

Keep food in covered containers or in the refrigerator. Food not previously covered should be washed before being put in to containers.

After a Nuclear Power Plant Emergency

Seek medical treatment for any unusual symptoms, such as nausea, that may be related to radiation exposure.

Follow the instructions for recovering from a disaster in Part 5.

Technological Hazards Knowledge Check
Answer the following questions. Check your responses with the answer key below.

1.   What are some things you can do to reduce the threat from hazardous materials in your home?

2.   What should you do if you are caught at the scene of a hazardous materials incident?

3.   What is the telephone number for the National Poison Control Center?

4.   What are three ways to minimize radiation exposure?

5.   Are there special warning requirements for nuclear power plants? If so, what are they?

6.   What does it mean when a nuclear power plant has issued a general emergency? What actions should you take?

7.   If you are at home and instructed to shelter-in-place because of a chemical release, where will you go?

8.   If you are in a car and unable to seek shelter in a building and a chemical release occurs, you should?

9.   Who can you contact to find out about hazardous materials stored in your community?

10.   What are some common placess hazardous materials may be present in the community?

Answers:

1. a. Learn to identify hazardous materials.
   b. Follow manufacture's instructions for storage, use, and disposal.
   c. Never store hazardous products in food containers.
   d. Keep products in original containers unless the container is corroding.
   e. Never mix household hazardous chemicals or waste with other products.
   f. Take household hazardous waste to a local collection program.
   g. Never smoke while using household chemicals.
   h. Clean up spills immediately with rags.
   i. Buy only as much of a chemical as you think you will use.

2. a. Do not walk into or touch any spilled liquids, airborne mists, or condensed solid chemical deposits.
   b. Stay upstream, uphill, and upwind! In general, try to go at least one-half mile (usually 8-10 city blocks) from the danger area.

3. (800)222-1222

4. Distance, shielding, and time.

5. Yes. Nuclear power plants are required to install sirens or other approved warning systems.

6. Radiation could leak outside the plant and off the plant site. The sirens will sound. Tune to local radio or television station for reports. Be prepared to follow instructions promptly.

7. An above ground room with the fewest exterior doors and windows.

8. Keep car windows and vents closed and shut off the air conditioner or heater.

9. Local Emergency Planning Committee (LEPC). The local emergency management office can provide contact information for the LEPC.

10. Agricultural operations and farms, auto service stations and junkyards, chemical manufacturing and storage facilities, construction sites, dry cleaners, electronics manufactures, paint shops, hospitals, hazardous materials waste sites, and transportation routes.

4

Terrorism

Throughout human history, there have been many threats to the security of nations. These threats have brought about large-scale losses of life, the destruction of property, widespread illness and injury, the displacement of large numbers of people, and devastating economic loss.

Recent technological advances and ongoing international political unrest are components of the increased risk to national security.

Use Part 4 to learn what actions to include in your family disaster plan to prepare for and respond to terrorist threats.

When you complete Part 4, you will be able to:
- Recognize important terms.
- Take protective measures for terrorist threats.
- Know what actions to take if an event occurs.
- Identify resources for more information about terrorist threats.

General Information about Terrorism

Terrorism is the use of force or violence against persons or property in violation of the criminal laws of the United States for purposes of intimidation, coercion, or ransom. Terrorists often use threats to:

- Create fear among the public.

- Try to convince citizens that their government is powerless to prevent terrorism.

- Get immediate publicity for their causes.

Acts of terrorism include threats of terrorism; assassinations; kidnappings; hijackings; bomb scares and bombings; cyber attacks (computer-based); and the use of chemical, biological, nuclear and radiological weapons.

High-risk targets for acts of terrorism include military and civilian government facilities, international airports, large cities, and high-profile landmarks. Terrorists might also target large public gatherings, water and food supplies, utilities, and corporate centers. Further, terrorists are capable of spreading fear by sending explosives or chemical and biological agents through the mail.

Within the immediate area of a terrorist event, you would need to rely on police, fire, and other officials for instructions. However, you can prepare in much the same way you would prepare for other crisis events.

The following are general guidelines:

- Be aware of your surroundings.

- Move or leave if you feel uncomfortable or if something does not seem right.

- Take precautions when traveling. Be aware of conspicuous or unusual behavior. Do not accept packages from strangers. Do not leave luggage unattended. You should promptly report unusual behavior, suspicious or unattended packages, and strange devices to the police or security personnel.

- Learn where emergency exits are located in buildings you frequent. Plan how to get out in the event of an emergency.

- Be prepared to do without services you normally depend on—electricity, telephone, natural gas, gasoline pumps, cash registers, ATMs, and Internet transactions.

- Work with building owners to ensure the following items are located on each floor of the building:

  - Portable, battery-operated radio and extra batteries.

  - Several flashlights and extra batteries.

  - First aid kit and manual.

  - Hard hats and dust masks.

  - Fluorescent tape to rope off dangerous areas.

Terrorism

4.2

Explosions

Terrorists have frequently used explosive devices as one of their most common weapons. Terrorists do not have to look far to find out how to make explosive devices; the information is readily available in books and other information sources. The materials needed for an explosive device can be found in many places including variety, hardware, and auto supply stores. Explosive devices are highly portable using vehicles and humans as a means of transport. They are easily detonated from remote locations or by suicide bombers.

Conventional bombs have been used to damage and destroy financial, political, social, and religious institutions. Attacks have occurred in public places and on city streets with thousands of people around the world injured and killed.

Parcels that should make you suspicious:

- Are unexpected or from someone unfamiliar to you.
- Have no return address, or have one that can't be verified as legitimate.
- Are marked with restrictive endorsements such as "Personal," "Confidential," or "Do not X-ray."
- Have protruding wires or aluminum foil, strange odors, or stains.
- Show a city or state in the postmark that doesn't match the return address.
- Are of unusual weight given their size, or are lopsided or oddly shaped.
- Are marked with threatening language.
- Have inappropriate or unusual labeling.
- Have excessive postage or packaging material, such as masking tape and string.
- Have misspellings of common words.
- Are addressed to someone no longer with your organization or are otherwise outdated.
- Have incorrect titles or titles without a name.
- Are not addressed to a specific person.
- Have hand-written or poorly typed addressess.

Take Protective Measures

If you receive a telephoned bomb threat, you should do the following:

- Get as much information from the caller as possible.

- Keep the caller on the line and record everything that is said.

- Notify the police and the building management.

If there is an explosion, you should:

- Get under a sturdy table or desk if things are falling around you. When they stop falling, leave quickly, watching for obviously weakened floors and stairways. As you exit from the building, be especially watchful of falling debris.

- Leave the building as quickly as possible. Do not stop to retrieve personal possessions or make phone calls.

- Do not use elevators.

Once you are out:

- Do not stand in front of windows, glass doors, or other potentially hazardous areas.

- Move away from sidewalks or streets to be used by emergency officials or others still exiting the building.

During an Explosion

Review

Safety guidelines for escaping fires in Section 2.11

Terrorism

If you are trapped in debris:

- If possible, use a flashlight to signal your location to rescuers.

- Avoid unnecessary movement so you don't kick up dust.

- Cover your nose and mouth with anything you have on hand. (Dense-weave cotton material can act as a good filter. Try to breathe through the material.)

- Tap on a pipe or wall so rescuers can hear where you are.

- If possible, use a whistle to signal rescuers.

- Shout only as a last resort. Shouting can cause a person to inhale dangerous amounts of dust.

After an Explosion

Follow the instructions for recovering from a disaster in Part 5.

For More Information

If you require more information about any of these topics, the following resource may be helpful.

Publications

American Red Cross:

Terrorism, Preparing for the Unexpected. Document providing preparation guidelines for a terrorist attack or similar emergency. Available online at www.redcross.org/services/disaster/0,1082,0_589_,00.html

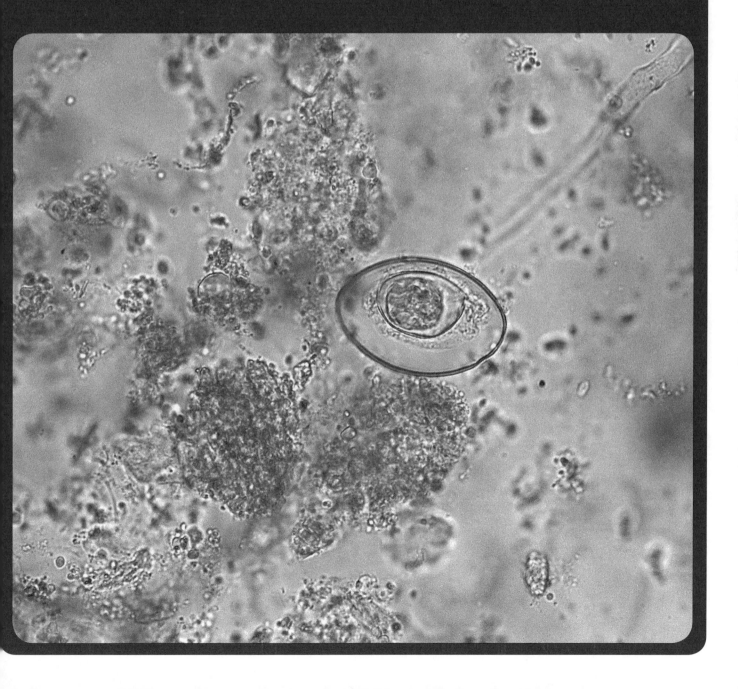

Biological agents are organisms or toxins that can kill or incapacitate people, livestock, and crops. The three basic groups of biological agents that would likely be used as weapons are bacteria, viruses, and toxins. Most biological agents are difficult to grow and maintain. Many break down quickly when exposed to sunlight and other environmental factors, while others, such as anthrax spores, are very long lived. Biological agents can be dispersed by spraying them into the air, by infecting animals that carry the disease to humans, and by contaminating food and water. Delivery methods include:

- **Aerosols**—biological agents are dispersed into the air, forming a fine mist that may drift for miles. Inhaling the agent may cause disease in people or animals.

- **Animals**—some diseases are spread by insects and animals, such as fleas, mice, flies, mosquitoes, and livestock.

- **Food and water contamination**—some pathogenic organisms and toxins may persist in food and water supplies. Most microbes can be killed, and toxins deactivated, by cooking food and boiling water. Most microbes are killed by boiling water for one minute, but some require longer. Follow official instructions.

- **Person-to-person**—spread of a few infectious agents is also possible. Humans have been the source of infection for smallpox, plague, and the Lassa viruses.

Specific information on biological agents is available at the Centers for Disease Control and Prevention's Web site, www.bt.cdc.gov.

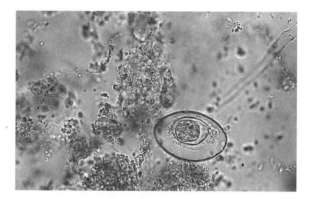

Take Protective Measures

Before a Biological Attack

The following are guidelines for what you should do to prepare for a biological threat:

- Check with your doctor to ensure all required or suggested immunizations are up to date. Children and older adults are particularly vulnerable to biological agents.

• Consider installing a High Efficiency Particulate Air (HEPA) filter in your furnace return duct. These filters remove particles in the 0.3 to 10 micron range and will filter out most biological agents that may enter your house. If you do not have a central heating or cooling system, a stand-alone portable HEPA filter can be used.

Review

Shelter
in Section 1.4

Filtration in Buildings

Building owners and managers should determine the type and level of filtration in their structures and the level of protection it provides against biological agents. The National Institute of Occupational Safety and Health (NIOSH) provides technical guidance on this topic in their publication *Guidance for Filtration and Air-Cleaning Systems to Protect Building Environments from Airborne Chemical, Biological, or Radiological Attacks.* To obtain a copy, call 1(800)35NIOSH or visit www.cdc.gov/NIOSH/publist.html and request or download NIOSH Publication 2003-136.

During a Biological Attack

Terrorism

In the event of a biological attack, public health officials may not immediately be able to provide information on what you should do. It will take time to determine what the illness is, how it should be treated, and who is in danger. Watch television, listen to radio, or check the Internet for official news and information including signs and symptoms of the disease, areas in danger, if medications or vaccinations are being distributed, and where you should seek medical attention if you become ill.

The first evidence of an attack may be when you notice symptoms of the disease caused by exposure to an agent. Be suspicious of any symptoms you notice, but do not assume that any illness is a result of the attack. Use common sense and practice good hygiene.

If you become aware of an unusual and suspicious substance nearby:

• Move away quickly.

• Wash with soap and water.

• Contact authorities.

• Listen to the media for official instructions.

• Seek medical attention if you become sick.

If you are exposed to a biological agent:

• Remove and bag your clothes and personal items. Follow official instructions for disposal of contaminated items.

• Wash yourself with soap and water and put on clean clothes.

• Seek medical assistance. You may be advised to stay away from others or even quarantined.

Using HEPA Filters

HEPA filters are useful in biological attacks. If you have a central heating and cooling system in your home with a HEPA filter, leave it on if it is running or turn the fan on if it is not running. Moving the air in the house through the filter will help remove the agents from the air. If you have a portable HEPA filter, take it with you to the internal room where you are seeking shelter and turn it on.

If you are in an apartment or office building that has a modern, central heating and cooling system, the system's filtration should provide a relatively safe level of protection from outside biological contaminants.

HEPA filters will not filter chemical agents.

After a Biological Attack

Review

Getting Informed in Section 1.1

In some situations, such as the case of the anthrax letters sent in 2001, people may be alerted to potential exposure. If this is the case, pay close attention to all official warnings and instructions on how to proceed. The delivery of medical services for a biological event may be handled differently to respond to increased demand. The basic public health procedures and medical protocols for handling exposure to biological agents are the same as for any infectious disease. It is important for you to pay attention to official instructions via radio, television, and emergency alert systems.

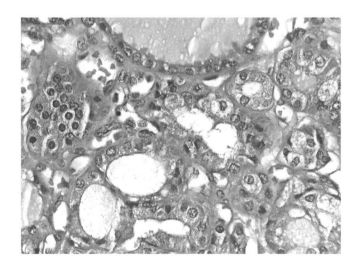

Chemical agents are poisonous vapors, aerosols, liquids, and solids that have toxic effects on people, animals, or plants. They can be released by bombs or sprayed from aircraft, boats, and vehicles. They can be used as a liquid to create a hazard to people and the environment. Some chemical agents may be odorless and tasteless. They can have an immediate effect (a few seconds to a few minutes) or a delayed effect (2 to 48 hours). While potentially lethal, chemical agents are difficult to deliver in lethal concentrations. Outdoors, the agents often dissipate rapidly. Chemical agents also are difficult to produce.

A chemical attack could come without warning. Signs of a chemical release include people having difficulty breathing; experiencing eye irritation; losing coordination; becoming nauseated; or having a burning sensation in the nose, throat, and lungs. Also, the presence of many dead insects or birds may indicate a chemical agent release.

Take Protective Measures

Before a Chemical Attack

The following are guidelines for what you should do to prepare for a chemical threat:

- Check your disaster supplies kit to make sure it includes:

  - A roll of duct tape and scissors.

  - Plastic for doors, windows, and vents for the room in which you will shelter in place. To save critical time during an emergency, pre-measure and cut the plastic sheeting for each opening.

- Choose an internal room to shelter, preferably one without windows and on the highest level.

During a Chemical Attack

The following are guidelines for what you should do in a chemical attack.

If you are instructed to remain in your home or office building, you should:

- Close doors and windows and turn off all ventilation, including furnaces, air conditioners, vents, and fans.

- Seek shelter in an internal room and take your disaster supplies kit.

- Seal the room with duct tape and plastic sheeting.

- Listen to your radio for instructions from authorities.

Review

Shelter safety for sealed rooms in Section 3.1

If you are caught in or near a contaminated area, you should:

- Move away immediately in a direction upwind of the source.

- Find shelter as quickly as possible.

After a Chemical Attack

Decontamination is needed within minutes of exposure to minimize health consequences. Do not leave the safety of a shelter to go outdoors to help others until authorities announce it is safe to do so.

A person affected by a chemical agent requires immediate medical attention from a professional. If medical help is not immediately available, decontaminate yourself and assist in decontaminating others.

Decontamination guidelines are as follows:

- Use extreme caution when helping others who have been exposed to chemical agents.

- Remove all clothing and other items in contact with the body. Contaminated clothing normally removed over the head should be cut off to avoid contact with the eyes, nose, and mouth. Put contaminated clothing and items into a plastic bag and seal it. Decontaminate hands using soap and water. Remove eyeglasses or contact lenses. Put glasses in a pan of household bleach to decontaminate them, and then rinse and dry.

- Flush eyes with water.

- Gently wash face and hair with soap and water before thoroughly rinsing with water.

- Decontaminate other body areas likely to have been contaminated. Blot (do not swab or scrape) with a cloth soaked in soapy water and rinse with clear water.

- Change into uncontaminated clothes. Clothing stored in drawers or closets is likely to be uncontaminated.

- Proceed to a medical facility for screening and professional treatment.

Terrorism

A nuclear blast is an explosion with intense light and heat, a damaging pressure wave, and widespread radioactive material that can contaminate the air, water, and ground surfaces for miles around. A nuclear device can range from a weapon carried by an intercontinental missile launched by a hostile nation or terrorist organization, to a small portable nuclear devise transported by an individual. All nuclear devices cause deadly effects when exploded, including blinding light, intense heat (thermal radiation), initial nuclear radiation, blast, fires started by the heat pulse, and secondary fires caused by the destruction.

Hazards of Nuclear Devices

The extent, nature, and arrival time of these hazards are difficult to predict. The geographical dispersion of hazard effects will be defined by the following:

- Size of the device. A more powerful bomb will produce more distant effects.

- Height above the ground the device was detonated. This will determine the extent of blast effects.

- Nature of the surface beneath the explosion. Some materials are more likely to become radioactive and airborne than others. Flat areas are more susceptible to blast effects.

- Existing meteorological conditions. Wind speed and direction will affect arrival time of fallout; precipitation may wash fallout from the atmosphere.

Radioactive Fallout

Even if individuals are not close enough to the nuclear blast to be affected by the direct impacts, they may be affected by radioactive fallout. Any nuclear blast results in some fallout. Blasts that occur near the earth's surface create much greater amounts of fallout than blasts that occur at higher altitudes. This is because the tremendous heat produced from a nuclear blast causes an up-draft of air that forms the familiar mushroom cloud. When a blast occurs near the earth's surface, millions of vaporized dirt particles also are drawn into the cloud. As the heat diminishes, radioactive materials that have vaporized condense on the particles and fall back to Earth. The phenomenon is called radioactive fallout. This fallout material decays over a long period of time, and is the main source of residual nuclear radiation.

Fallout from a nuclear explosion may be carried by wind currents for hundreds of miles if the right conditions exist. Effects from even a small portable device exploded at ground level can be potentially deadly.

Nuclear radiation cannot be seen, smelled, or otherwise detected by normal senses. Radiation can only be detected by radiation monitoring devices. This makes radiological emergencies different from other types of emergencies, such as floods or hurricanes. Monitoring can project the fallout arrival times, which will be announced through official warning channels. However, any increase in surface build-up of gritty dust and dirt should be a warning for taking protective measures.

Electromagnetic Pulse

In addition to other effects, a nuclear weapon detonated in or above the earth's atmosphere can create an electromagnetic pulse (EMP), a high-density electrical field. An EMP acts like a stroke of lightning but is stronger, faster, and shorter. An EMP can seriously damage electronic devices connected to power sources or antennas. This includes communication systems, computers, electrical appliances, and automobile or aircraft ignition systems. The damage could range from a minor interruption to actual burnout of components. Most electronic equipment within 1,000 miles of a high-altitude nuclear detonation could be affected. Battery-powered radios with short antennas generally would not be affected. Although an EMP is unlikely to harm most people, it could harm those with pacemakers or other implanted electronic devices.

Protection from a Nuclear Blast

The danger of a massive strategic nuclear attack on the United States is predicted by experts to be less likely today. However, terrorism, by nature, is unpredictable.

If there were threat of an attack, people living near potential targets could be advised to evacuate or they could decide on their own to evacuate to an area not considered a likely target. Protection from radioactive fallout would require taking shelter in an underground area or in the middle of a large building.

In general, potential targets include:

- Strategic missile sites and military bases.

- Centers of government such as Washington, DC, and state capitals.

- Important transportation and communication centers.

- Manufacturing, industrial, technology, and financial centers.

- Petroleum refineries, electrical power plants, and chemical plants.

- Major ports and airfields.

The three factors for protecting oneself from radiation and fallout are distance, shielding, and time.

- **Distance** — the more distance between you and the fallout particles, the better. An underground area such as a home or office building basement offers more protection than the first floor of a building. A floor near the middle of a high-rise may be better, depending on what is nearby at that level on which significant fallout particles would collect. Flat roofs collect fallout particles so the top floor is not a good choice, nor is a floor adjacent to a neighboring flat roof.

- **Shielding** — the heavier and denser the materials—thick walls, concrete, bricks, books and earth—between you and the fallout particles, the better.

- **Time** — fallout radiation loses its intensity fairly rapidly. In time, you will be able to leave the fallout shelter. Radioactive fallout poses the greatest threat to people during the first two weeks, by which time it has declined to about 1 percent of its initial radiation level.

Remember that any protection, however temporary, is better than none at all, and the more shielding, distance, and time you can take advantage of, the better.

Take Protective Measures

Before a Nuclear Blast

Review

Update your supplies; see Section 1.2

To prepare for a nuclear blast, you should do the following:

- Find out from officials if any public buildings in your community have been designated as fallout shelters. If none have been designated, make your own list of potential shelters near your home, workplace, and school. These places would include basements or the windowless center area of middle floors in high-rise buildings, as well as subways and tunnels.

- If you live in an apartment building or high-rise, talk to the manager about the safest place in the building for sheltering and about providing for building occupants until it is safe to go out.

- During periods of increased threat increase your disaster supplies to be adequate for up to two weeks.

Taking shelter during a nuclear blast is absolutely necessary. There are two kinds of shelters—blast and fallout. The following describes the two kinds of shelters:

- **Blast shelters** are specifically constructed to offer some protection against blast pressure, initial radiation, heat, and fire. But even a blast shelter cannot withstand a direct hit from a nuclear explosion.
- **Fallout shelters** do not need to be specially constructed for protecting against fallout. They can be any protected space, provided that the walls and roof are thick and dense enough to absorb the radiation given off by fallout particles.

Review

Shelter requirements in Section 1.4

During a Nuclear Blast

The following are guidelines for what to do in the event of a nuclear explosion.

If an attack warning is issued:

- Take cover as quickly as you can, below ground if possible, and stay there until instructed to do otherwise.

- Listen for official information and follow instructions.

If you are caught outside and unable to get inside immediately:

- Do not look at the flash or fireball—it can blind you.

- Take cover behind anything that might offer protection.

- Lie flat on the ground and cover your head. If the explosion is some distance away, it could take 30 seconds or more for the blast wave to hit.

- Take shelter as soon as you can, even if you are many miles from ground zero where the attack occurred—radioactive fallout can be carried by the winds for hundreds of miles. Remember the three protective factors: Distance, shielding, and time.

Terrorism

After a Nuclear Blast

Decay rates of the radioactive fallout are the same for any size nuclear device. However, the amount of fallout will vary based on the size of the device and its proximity to the ground. Therefore, it might be necessary for those in the areas with highest radiation levels to shelter for up to a month.

Review

Shelter requirements in Section 1.4

The heaviest fallout would be limited to the area at or downwind from the explosion, and 80 percent of the fallout would occur during the first 24 hours.

People in most of the areas that would be affected could be allowed to come out of shelter within a few days and, if necessary, evacuate to unaffected areas.

Returning to Your Home

Remember the following:

- Keep listening to the radio and television for news about what to do, where to go, and places to avoid.

- Stay away from damaged areas. Stay away from areas marked "radiation hazard" or "HAZMAT." Remember that radiation cannot be seen, smelled, or otherwise detected by human senses.

Follow the instructions for returning home in Part 5.

Radiological Dispersion Device (RDD)

Terrorist use of an RDD—often called "dirty nuke" or "dirty bomb"—is considered far more likely than use of a nuclear explosive device. An RDD combines a conventional explosive device—such as a bomb—with radioactive material. It is designed to scatter dangerous and sub-lethal amounts of radioactive material over a general area. Such RDDs appeal to terrorists because they require limited technical knowledge to build and deploy compared to a nuclear device. Also, the radioactive materials in RDDs are widely used in medicine, agriculture, industry, and research, and are easier to obtain than weapons grade uranium or plutonium.

The primary purpose of terrorist use of an RDD is to cause psychological fear and economic disruption. Some devices could cause fatalities from exposure to radioactive materials. Depending on the speed at which the area of the RDD detonation was evacuated or how successful people were at sheltering-in-place, the number of deaths and injuries from an RDD might not be substantially greater than from a conventional bomb explosion.

The size of the affected area and the level of destruction caused by an RDD would depend on the sophistication and size of the conventional bomb, the type of radioactive material used, the quality and quantity of the radioactive material, and the local meteorological conditions—primarily wind and precipitation. The area affected could be placed off-limits to the public for several months during clean-up efforts.

Take Protective Measures

Before an RDD Event

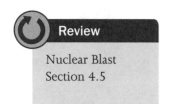

Review

Nuclear Blast
Section 4.5

There is no way of knowing how much warning time there will be before an attack by terrorists using an RDD, so being prepared in advance and knowing what to do and when is important. Take the same protective measures you would for fallout resulting from a nuclear blast.

During an RDD Event

While the explosive blast will be immediately obvious, the presence of radiation will not be known until trained personnel with specialized equipment are on the scene. Whether you are indoors or outdoors, home or at work, be extra cautious. It would be safer to assume radiological contamination has occurred—particularly in an urban setting or near other likely terrorist targets—and take the proper precautions. As with any radiation, you want to avoid or limit exposure. This is particularly true of inhaling radioactive dust that results from the explosion. As you seek shelter from any location (indoors or outdoors) and there is visual dust or other contaminants in the air, breathe though the cloth of your shirt or coat to limit your exposure. If you manage to avoid breathing radioactive dust, your proximity to the radioactive particles may still result in some radiation exposure.

If the explosion or radiological release occurs inside, get out immediately and seek safe shelter. Otherwise, if you are:

Outdoors	Indoors
• Seek shelter indoors immediately in the nearest undamaged building. • If appropriate shelter is not available, move as rapidly as is safe upwind and away from the location of the explosive blast. Then, seek appropriate shelter as soon as possible. • Listen for official instructions and follow directions.	• If you have time, turn off ventilation and heating systems, close windows, vents, fireplace dampers, exhaust fans, and clothes dryer vents. Retrieve your disaster supplies kit and a battery-powered radio and take them to your shelter room. • Seek shelter immediately, preferably underground or in an interior room of a building, placing as much distance and dense shielding as possible between you and the outdoors where the radioactive material may be. • Seal windows and external doors that do not fit snugly with duct tape to reduce infiltration of radioactive particles. Plastic sheeting will not provide shielding from radioactivity nor from blast effects of a nearby explosion. • Listen for official instructions and follow directions.

After an RDD Event

After finding safe shelter, those who may have been exposed to radioactive material should decontaminate themselves. To do this, remove and bag your clothing (and isolate the bag away from you and others), and shower thoroughly with soap and water. Seek medical attention after officials indicate it is safe to leave shelter.

Contamination from an RDD event could affect a wide area, depending on the amount of conventional explosives used, the quantity and type of radioactive material released, and meteorological conditions. Thus, radiation dissipation rates vary, but radiation from an RDD will likely take longer to dissipate due to a potentially larger localized concentration of radioactive material.

Follow these additional guidelines after an RDD event:

• Continue listening to your radio or watch the television for instructions from local officials, whether you have evacuated or sheltered-in-place.

• Do not return to or visit an RDD incident location for any reason.

• Follow the instructions for recovering from a disaster in Part 5.

Terrorism

Terrorism Knowledge Check

Answer the following questions. Check your responses with the answer key below.

1 What would you do, if you were at work and…

   a. there was an explosion in the building?

   b. you received a package in the mail that you considered suspicious?

   c. you received a telephone call that was a bomb threat?

2 If caught outside during a nuclear blast, what should you do?

3 What are the three key factors for protection from nuclear blast and fallout?

4 If you take shelter in your own home, what kind of room would be safest during a chemical or biological attack?

5 In case of a chemical attack, what extra items should you have in your disaster supplies kit?

5.   Plastic sheeting, duct tape, and scissors.
4.   An interior room on the uppermost level, preferably without windows
3.   Distance, shielding, time
     • Cover your head
     • Lay flat on the ground
     • Take cover behind anything that offers protection
2.   • Don't look at the flash
     c. Keep the caller on the line and record everything that was said
     b. Clear the area and notify the police immediately
1.   a. Shelter from falling debris under a desk and then follow evacuation procedures

Answer Key

Homeland Security Advisory System

The Homeland Security Advisory System was designed to provide a national framework and comprehensive means to disseminate information regarding the risk of terrorist acts to the following:

- Federal, state, and local authorities

- The private sector

- The American people

This system provides warnings in the form of a set of graduated "threat conditions" that increase as the risk of the threat increases. Risk includes both the probability of an attack occurring and its potential gravity. Threat conditions may be assigned for the entire nation, or they may be set for a particular geographic area or industrial sector. At each threat condition, government entities and the private sector, including businesses and schools, would implement a corresponding set of "protective measures" to further reduce vulnerability or increase response capability during a period of heightened alert.

There are five threat conditions, each identified by a description and corresponding color. Assigned threat conditions will be reviewed at regular intervals to determine whether adjustments are warranted.

Threat Conditions and Associated Protective Measures

There is always a risk of a terrorist threat. Each threat condition assigns a level of alert appropriate to the increasing risk of terrorist attacks. Beneath each threat condition are some suggested protective measures that the government, the private sector, and the public can take.

In each case, as threat conditions escalate, protective measures are added to those already taken in lower threat conditions. The measures are cumulative.

Citizen Guidance on the Homeland Security Advisory System

Low Risk

- Develop a family emergency plan. Share it with family and friends, and practice the plan. Visit www.Ready.gov for help creating a plan.
- Create an "Emergency Supply Kit" for your household.
- Be informed. Visit www.Ready.gov or obtain a copy of "Preparing Makes Sense, Get Ready Now" by calling 1-800-BE-READY.
- Know where to shelter and how to turn off utilities (power, gas, and water) to your home.
- Examine volunteer opportunities in your community, such as Citizen Corps, Volunteers in Police Service, Neighborhood Watch or others, and donate your time. Consider completing an American Red Cross first aid or CPR course , or Community Emergency Response Team (CERT) course .

Guarded Risk

- Complete recommended steps at level green.
- Review stored disaster supplies and replace items that are outdated.
- Be alert to suspicious activity and report it to proper authorities.

Elevated Risk

- Complete recommended steps at levels green and blue.
- Ensure disaster supplies are stocked and ready.
- Check telephone numbers in family emergency plan and update as necessary.
- Develop alternate routes to/from work or school and practice them.
- Continue to be alert for suspicious activity and report it to authorities.

High Risk

- Complete recommended steps at lower levels.
- Exercise caution when traveling, pay attention to travel advisories.
- Review your family emergency plan and make sure all family members know what to do.
- Be Patient. Expect some delays, baggage searches and restrictions at public buildings.
- Check on neighbors or others that might need assistance in an emergency.

Severe Risk

- Complete all recommended actions at lower levels.
- Listen to local emergency management officials.
- Stay tuned to TV or radio for current information/instructions.
- Be prepared to shelter or evacuate, as instructed.
- Expect traffic delays and restrictions.
- Provide volunteer services only as requested.
- Contact your school/business to determine status of work day.

*Developed with input from the American Red Cross.

Terrorism

Knowledge Check

1. By following the instructions in this guide, you should now have the following:

   • A family disaster plan that sets forth what you and your family need to do to prepare for and respond to all types of hazards.

   • A disaster supplies kit filled with items you would need to sustain you and your family for at least three days, maybe more.

   • Knowledge of your community warning systems and what you should do when these are activated.

   • An understanding of why evacuations are necessary and what you would need to do in the case of an evacuation.

   • Identification of where the safest shelters are for the various hazards.

   Compare the above actions with the personal action guidelines for each of the threat levels. Determine how well you are prepared for each of the five levels.

2. What is the current threat level? _____

   Hint: To determine the current threat level, check your cable news networks or visit www.dhs.gov. Keep your family informed when changes in the threat level occur, and go over the personal actions you need to take.

For More Information

If you require more information about any of these topics, the following resource may be helpful.

Publications

American Red Cross

American Red Cross: Homeland Security Advisory System Recommendations for Individuals, Families, Neighborhoods, Schools, and Businesses. Explanation of preparedness activities for each population. Available online at www.redcross.org/services/disaster/beprepared/hsas.html

Terrorism

Recovering from Disaster

Health and Safety Guidelines

Recovering from a disaster is usually a gradual process. Safety is a primary issue, as are mental and physical well-being. If assistance is available, knowing how to access it makes the process faster and less stressful. This section offers some general advice on steps to take after disaster strikes in order to begin getting your home, your community, and your life back to normal.

Your first concern after a disaster is your family's health and safety. You need to consider possible safety issues and monitor family health and well-being.

Aiding the Injured

Check for injuries. Do not attempt to move seriously injured persons unless they are in immediate danger of death or further injury. If you must move an unconscious person, first stabilize the neck and back, then call for help immediately.

- If the victim is not breathing, carefully position the victim for artificial respiration, clear the airway, and commence mouth-to-mouth resuscitation.

- Maintain body temperature with blankets. Be sure the victim does not become overheated.

- Never try to feed liquids to an unconscious person.

Health

- Be aware of exhaustion. Don't try to do too much at once. Set priorities and pace yourself. Get enough rest.

- Drink plenty of clean water.

- Eat well.

- Wear sturdy work boots and gloves.

- Wash your hands thoroughly with soap and clean water often when working in debris.

Safety Issues

- Be aware of new safety issues created by the disaster. Watch for washed out roads, contaminated buildings, contaminated water, gas leaks, broken glass, damaged electrical wiring, and slippery floors.

- Inform local authorities about health and safety issues, including chemical spills, downed power lines, washed out roads, smoldering insulation, and dead animals.

Returning Home

Returning home can be both physically and mentally challenging. Above all, use caution.

General tips:

- Keep a battery-powered radio with you so you can listen for emergency updates and news reports.

- Use a battery-powered flash light to inspect a damaged home.
  Note: The flashlight should be turned on outside before entering—the battery may produce a spark that could ignite leaking gas, if present.

- Watch out for animals, especially poisonous snakes. Use a stick to poke through debris.

- Use the phone only to report life-threatening emergencies.

- Stay off the streets. If you must go out, watch for fallen objects; downed electrical wires; and weakened walls, bridges, roads, and sidewalks.

Before You Enter Your Yome

Walk carefully around the outside and check for loose power lines, gas leaks, and structural damage. If you have any doubts about safety, have your residence inspected by a qualified building inspector or structural engineer before entering.

Do not enter if:

- You smell gas.

- Floodwaters remain around the building.

- Your home was damaged by fire and the authorities have not declared it safe.

Going Inside Your Home

When you go inside your home, there are certain things you should and should not do. Enter the home carefully and check for damage. Be aware of loose boards and slippery floors. The following items are other things to check inside your home:

- **Natural gas.** If you smell gas or hear a hissing or blowing sound, open a window and leave immediately. Turn off the main gas valve from the outside, if you can. Call the gas company from a neighbor's residence. If you shut off the gas supply at the main valve, you will need a professional to turn it back on. Do not smoke or use oil, gas lanterns, candles, or torches for lighting inside a damaged home until you are sure there is no leaking gas or other flammable materials present.

- **Sparks, broken or frayed wires.** Check the electrical system unless you are wet, standing in water, or unsure of your safety. If possible, turn off the electricity at the main fuse box or circuit breaker. If the situation is unsafe, leave the building and call for help. Do not turn on the lights until you are sure they're safe to use. You may want to have an electrician inspect your wiring.

- **Roof, foundation, and chimney cracks.** If it looks like the building may collapse, leave immediately.

- **Appliances.** If appliances are wet, turn off the electricity at the main fuse box or circuit breaker. Then, unplug appliances and let them dry out. Have appliances checked by a professional before using them again. Also, have the electrical system checked by an electrician before turning the power back on.

- **Water and sewage systems.** If pipes are damaged, turn off the main water valve. Check with local authorities before using any water; the water could be contaminated. Pump out wells and have the water tested by authorities before drinking. Do not flush toilets until you know that sewage lines are intact.

- **Food and other supplies.** Throw out all food and other supplies that you suspect may have become contaminated or come in to contact with floodwater.

- **Your basement.** If your basement has flooded, pump it out gradually (about one third of the water per day) to avoid damage. The walls may collapse and the floor may buckle if the basement is pumped out while the surrounding ground is still waterlogged.

- **Open cabinets.** Be alert for objects that may fall.

- **Clean up household chemical spills.** Disinfect items that may have been contaminated by raw sewage, bacteria, or chemicals. Also clean salvageable items.

- **Call your insurance agent.** Take pictures of damages. Keep good records of repair and cleaning costs.

Being Wary of Wildlife and Other Animals

Disaster and life threatening situations will exacerbate the unpredictable nature of wild animals. To protect yourself and your family, learn how to deal with wildlife.

Guidelines

- Do not approach or attempt to help an injured or stranded animal. Call your local animal control office or wildlife resource office.

- Do not corner wild animals or try to rescue them. Wild animals will likely feel threatened and may endanger themselves by dashing off into floodwaters, fire, and so forth.

- Do not approach wild animals that have taken refuge in your home. Wild animals such as snakes, opossums, and raccoons often seek refuge from floodwaters on upper levels of homes and have been known to remain after water recedes. If you encounter animals in this situation, open a window or provide another escape route and the animal will likely leave on its own. Do not attempt to capture or handle the animal. Should the animal stay, call your local animal control office or wildlife resource office.

- Do not attempt to move a dead animal. Animal carcasses can present serious health risks. Contact your local emergency management office or health department for help and instructions.

- If bitten by an animal, seek immediate medical attention.

Seeking Disaster Assistance

Throughout the recovery period, it is important to monitor local radio or television reports and other media sources for information about where to get emergency housing, food, first aid, clothing, and financial assistance. The following section provides general information about the kinds of assistance that may be available.

Recovering from Disaster

Direct Assistance

Direct assistance to individuals and families may come from any number of organizations, including:

- American Red Cross.

- Salvation Army.

- Other volunteer organization.

These organizations provide food, shelter, supplies and assist in clean-up efforts.

The Federal Role

In the most severe disasters, the federal government is also called in to help individuals and families with temporary housing, counseling (for post-disaster trauma), low-interest loans and grants, and other assistance. The federal government also has programs that help small businesses and farmers.

Most federal assistance becomes available when the President of the United States declares a "Major Disaster" for the affected area at the request of a state governor. FEMA will provide information through the media and community outreach about federal assistance and how to apply.

Coping with Disaster

The emotional toll that disaster brings can sometimes be even more devastating than the financial strains of damage and loss of home, business, or personal property.

Understand Disaster Events

- Everyone who sees or experiences a disaster is affected by it in some way.

- It is normal to feel anxious about your own safety and that of your family and close friends.

- Profound sadness, grief, and anger are normal reactions to an abnormal event.

- Acknowledging your feelings helps you recover.

- Focusing on your strengths and abilities helps you heal.

- Accepting help from community programs and resources is healthy.

- Everyone has different needs and different ways of coping.

- It is common to want to strike back at people who have caused great pain.

Children and older adults are of special concern in the aftermath of disasters. Even individuals who experience a disaster "second hand" through exposure to extensive media coverage can be affected.

Contact local faith-based organizations, voluntary agencies, or professional counselors for counseling. Additionally, FEMA and state and local governments of the affected area may provide crisis counseling assistance.

When adults have the following signs, they might need crisis counseling or stress management assistance:

- Difficulty communicating thoughts.

- Difficulty sleeping.

- Difficulty maintaining balance in their lives.

- Low threshold of frustration.

- Increased use of drugs/alcohol.

- Limited attention span.

- Poor work performance.

- Headaches/stomach problems.

- Tunnel vision/muffled hearing.

- Colds or flu-like symptoms.

- Disorientation or confusion.

- Difficulty concentrating.

- Reluctance to leave home.

- Depression, sadness.

- Feelings of hopelessness.

- Mood-swings and easy bouts of crying.

- Overwhelming guilt and self-doubt.

- Fear of crowds, strangers, or being alone.

Recovering from Disaster

The following are ways to ease disaster-related stress:

- Talk with someone about your feelings—anger, sorrow, and other emotions— even though it may be difficult.

- Seek help from professional counselors who deal with post-disaster stress.

- Do not hold yourself responsible for the disastrous event or be frustrated because you feel you cannot help directly in the rescue work.

- Take steps to promote your own physical and emotional healing by healthy eating, rest, exercise, relaxation, and meditation.

- Maintain a normal family and daily routine, limiting demanding responsibilities on yourself and your family.

- Spend time with family and friends.

- Participate in memorials.

- Use existing support groups of family, friends, and religious institutions.

- Ensure you are ready for future events by restocking your disaster supplies kits and updating your family disaster plan. Doing these positive actions can be comforting.

Helping Children Cope with Disaster

Disasters can leave children feeling frightened, confused, and insecure. Whether a child has personally experienced trauma, has merely seen the event on television, or has heard it discussed by adults, it is important for parents and teachers to be informed and ready to help if reactions to stress begin to occur.

Children may respond to disaster by demonstrating fears, sadness, or behavioral problems. Younger children may return to earlier behavior patterns, such as bed-wetting, sleep problems, and separation anxiety. Older children may also display anger, aggression, school problems, or withdrawal. Some children who have only indirect contact with the disaster but witness it on television may develop distress.

Who is at Risk?

For many children, reactions to disasters are brief and represent normal reactions to "abnormal events." A smaller number of children can be at risk for more enduring psychological distress as a function of three major risk factors:

- Direct exposure to the disaster, such as being evacuated, observing injuries or death of others, or experiencing injury along with fearing one's life is in danger

- Loss/grief: This relates to the death or serious injury of family or friends

- On-going stress from the secondary effects of disaster, such as temporarily living elsewhere, loss of friends and social networks, loss of personal property, parental unemployment, and costs incurred during recovery to return the family to pre-disaster life and living conditions.

What Creates Vulnerabilities in Children?

In most cases, depending on the risk factors above, distressing responses are temporary. In the absence of severe threat to life, injury, loss of loved ones, or secondary problems such as loss of home, moves, etc., symptoms usually diminish over time. For those that were directly exposed to the disaster, reminders of the disaster such as high winds, smoke, cloudy skies, sirens, or other reminders of the disaster may cause upsetting feelings to return. Having a prior history of some type of traumatic event or severe stress may contribute to these feelings.

Children's coping with disaster or emergencies is often tied to the way parents cope. They can detect adults' fears and sadness. Parents and adults can make disasters less traumatic for children by taking steps to manage their own feelings and plans for coping. Parents are almost always the best source of support for children in disasters. One way to establish a sense of control and to build confidence in children before a disaster is to engage and involve them in preparing a family disaster plan. After a disaster, children can contribute to a family recovery plan.

Review

See Section 1:
Basic preparedness

A Child's Reaction to Disaster by Age

Below are common reactions in children after a disaster or traumatic event.

Birth through 2 years. When children are pre-verbal and experience a trauma, they do not have the words to describe the event or their feelings. However, they can retain memories of particular sights, sounds, or smells. Infants may react to trauma by being irritable, crying more than usual, or wanting to be held and cuddled. The biggest influence on children of this age is how their parents cope. As children get older, their play may involve acting out elements of the traumatic event that occurred several years in the past and was seemingly forgotten.

Preschool—3 through 6 years. Preschool children often feel helpless and powerless in the face of an overwhelming event. Because of their age and small size, they lack the ability to protect themselves or others. As a result, they feel intense fear and insecurity about being separated from caregivers. Preschoolers cannot grasp the concept of permanent loss. They can see consequences as being reversible or permanent. In the weeks following a traumatic event, preschoolers' play activities may reenact the incident or the disaster over and over again.

School age—7 through 10 years. The school-age child has the ability to understand the permanence of loss. Some children become intensely preoccupied with the details of a traumatic event and want to talk about it continually. This preoccupation can interfere with the child's concentration at school and academic performance may decline. At school, children may hear inaccurate information from peers. They may display a wide range of reactions—sadness, generalized fear, or specific fears of the disaster happening again, guilt over action or inaction during the disaster, anger that the event was not prevented, or fantasies of playing rescuer.

Pre-adolescence to adolescence—11 through 18 years. As children grow older, they develop a more sophisticated understanding of the disaster event. Their responses are more similar to adults. Teenagers may become involved in dangerous, risk-taking behaviors, such as reckless driving, or alcohol or drug use. Others can become fearful of leaving home and avoid previous levels of activities. Much of adolescence is focused on moving out into the world. After a trauma, the view of the world can seem more dangerous and unsafe. A teenager may feel overwhelmed by intense emotions and yet feel unable to discuss them with others.

Recovering
from Disaster

Children's reactions are influenced by the behavior, thoughts, and feelings of adults. Adults should encourage children and adolescents to share their thoughts and feelings about the incident. Clarify misunderstandings about risk and danger by listening to children's concerns and answering questions. Maintain a sense of calm by validating children's concerns and perceptions and with discussion of concrete plans for safety.

Listen to what the child is saying. If a young child is asking questions about the event, answer them simply without the elaboration needed for an older child or adult. Some children are comforted by knowing more or less information than others; decide what level of information your particular child needs. If a child has difficulty expressing feelings, allow the child to draw a picture or tell a story of what happened.

Try to understand what is causing anxieties and fears. Be aware that following a disaster, children are most afraid that:

• The event will happen again.

• Someone close to them will be killed or injured.

• They will be left alone or separated from the family.

Reassuring Children After a Disaster

Suggestions to help reassure children include the following:

• Personal contact is reassuring. Hug and touch your children.

• Calmly provide factual information about the recent disaster and current plans for insuring their safety along with recovery plans.

• Encourage your children to talk about their feelings.

• Spend extra time with your children such as at bedtime.

• Re-establish your daily routine for work, school, play, meals, and rest.

• Involve your children by giving them specific chores to help them feel they are helping to restore family and community life.

• Praise and recognize responsible behavior.

• Understand that your children will have a range of reactions to disasters.

• Encourage your children to help update your a family disaster plan.

If you have tried to create a reassuring environment by following the steps above, but your child continues to exhibit stress, if the reactions worsen over time, or if they cause interference with daily behavior at school, at home, or with other relationships, it may be appropriate to talk to a professional. You can get professional help from the child's primary care physician, a mental health provider specializing in children's needs, or a member of the clergy.

Monitor and Limit Your Family's Exposure to the Media

News coverage related to a disaster may elicit fear and confusion and arouse anxiety in children. This is particularly true for large-scale disasters or a terrorist event where significant property damage and loss of life has occurred. Particularly for younger children, repeated images of an event may cause them to believe the event is recurring over and over.

If parents allow children to watch television or use the Internet where images or news about the disaster are shown, parents should be with them to encourage communication and provide explanations. This may also include parent's monitoring and appropriately limiting their own exposure to anxiety-provoking information.

Use Support Networks

Parents help their children when they take steps to understand and manage their own feelings and ways of coping. They can do this by building and using social support systems of family, friends, community organizations and agencies, faith-based institutions, or other resources that work for that family. Parents can build their own unique social support systems so that in an emergency situation or when a disaster strikes, they can be supported and helped to manage their reactions. As a result, parents will be more available to their children and better able to support them. Parents are almost always the best source of support for children in difficult times. But to support their children, parents need to attend to their own needs and have a plan for their own support.

Preparing for disaster helps everyone in the family accept the fact that disasters do happen, and provides an opportunity to identify and collect the resources needed to meet basic needs after disaster. Preparation helps; when people feel prepared, they cope better and so do children.

Helping Others

The compassion and generosity of the American people is never more evident than after a disaster. People want to help. Here are some general guidelines on helping others after a disaster:

- Volunteer! Check with local organizations or listen to local news reports for information about where volunteers are needed. **Note:** Until volunteers are specifically requested, stay away from disaster areas.

- Bring your own food, water, and emergency supplies to a disaster area if you are needed there. This is especially important in cases where a large area has been affected and emergency items are in short supply.

- Give a check or money order to a recognized disaster relief organization. These groups are organized to process checks, purchase what is needed, and get it to the people who need it most.

- Do not drop off food, clothing, or any other item to a government agency or disaster relief organization unless a particular item has been requested. Normally, these organizations do not have the resources to sort through the donated items.

- Donate a quantity of a given item or class of items (such as nonperishable food) rather than a mix of different items. Determine where your donation is going, how it's going to get there, who is going to unload it, and how it is going to be distributed. Without sufficient planning, much needed supplies will be left unused.

For More Information

If you require more information about any of these topics, the following are resources that may be helpful.

FEMA Publications

Helping Children Cope with Disasters. L-196. Provides information about how to prepare children for disaster and how to lessen the emotional effects of disaster.

When Disaster Strikes. L-217. Provides information about donations and volunteer organizations.

Repairing Your Flooded Home. FEMA 234. This 362-page publication provides a step-by-step guide to repairing your home and how to get help after a flood disaster. Available online at www.fema.gov/hazards/floods/lib234.shtm

After a Flood: The First Steps. L 198. Tips for staying healthy, cleaning up and repairing, and getting help after a flood. Available online at www.fema.gov/hazards/floods/aftrfld.shtm

Appendix A:
Water Conservation Tips

General

- Never pour water down the drain when there may be another use for it. Use it to water your indoor plants or garden.
- Repair dripping faucets by replacing washers. One drop per second wastes 2,700 gallons of water per year!
- Check all plumbing for leaks. Have leaks repaired by a plumber.
- Retrofit all household faucets by installing aerators with flow restrictors.
- Install an instant hot water heater on your sink.
- Insulate your water pipes to reduce heat loss and prevent them from breaking.
- Install a water-softening system only when the minerals in the water would damage your pipes. Turn the softener off while on vacation.
- Choose appliances that are more energy and water efficient.

Bathroom

- Consider purchasing a low-volume toilet that uses less than half the water of older models. **Note:** In many areas, low-volume units are required by law.
- Install a toilet displacement device to cut down on the amount of water needed to flush. Place a one-gallon plastic jug of water into the tank to displace toilet flow (do not use a brick, it may dissolve and loose pieces may cause damage to the internal parts). Be sure installation does not interfere with the operating parts.
- Replace your showerhead with an ultra-low-flow version.
- Place a bucket in the shower to catch excess water for watering plants.
- Avoid flushing the toilet unnecessarily. Dispose of tissues, insects, and other similar waste in the trash rather than the toilet.
- Avoid taking baths—take short showers—turn on water only to get wet and lather and then again to rinse off.
- Avoid letting the water run while brushing your teeth, washing your face, or shaving.

Kitchen

- Operate automatic dishwashers only when they are fully loaded. Use the "light wash" feature, if available, to use less water.
- Hand wash dishes by filling two containers—one with soapy water and the other with rinse water containing a small amount of chlorine bleach.
- Clean vegetables in a pan filled with water rather than running water from the tap.
- Start a compost pile as an alternate method of disposing of food waste or simply dispose of food in the garbage. (Kitchen sink disposals require a lot of water to operate properly).
- Store drinking water in the refrigerator. Do not let the tap run while you are waiting for water to cool.

- Avoid wasting water waiting for it to get hot. Capture it for other uses such as plant watering or heat it on the stove or in a microwave.
- Avoid rinsing dishes before placing them in the dishwasher; just remove large particles of food. (Most dishwashers can clean soiled dishes very well, so dishes do not have to be rinsed before washing)
- Avoid using running water to thaw meat or other frozen foods. Defrost food overnight in the refrigerator or use the defrost setting on your microwave oven.

Laundry

- Operate automatic clothes washers only when they are fully loaded or set the water level for the size of your load.

Outdoor Water Conservation Tips

General

- Check your well pump periodically. If the automatic pump turns on and off while water is not being used, you have a leak.
- Plant native and/or drought-tolerant grasses, ground covers, shrubs, and trees. Once established, they do not need water as frequently and usually will survive a dry period without watering. Small plants require less water to become established. Group plants together based on similar water needs.
- Install irrigation devices that are the most water efficient for each use. Micro and drip irrigation and soaker hoses are examples of efficient devices.
- Use mulch to retain moisture in the soil. Mulch also helps control weeds that compete with landscape plants for water.
- Avoid purchasing recreational water toys that require a constant stream of water.
- Avoid installing ornamental water features (such as fountains) unless they use recycled water.

Car Washing

- Use a shut-off nozzle that can be adjusted down to a fine spray on your hose.
- Use a commercial car wash that recycles water. If you wash your own car, park on the grass so that you will be watering it at the same time.

Lawn Care

- Avoid over watering your lawn. A heavy rain eliminates the need for watering for up to two weeks. Most of the year, lawns only need one inch of water per week.
- Water in several short sessions rather than one long one, in order for your lawn to better absorb moisture.
- Position sprinklers so water lands on the lawn and shrubs and not on paved areas.

- Avoid sprinklers that spray a fine mist. Mist can evaporate before it reaches the lawn. Check sprinkler systems and timing devices regularly to be sure they operate properly.
- Raise the lawn mower blade to at least three inches or to its highest level. A higher cut encourages grass roots to grow deeper, shades the root system, and holds soil moisture.
- Plant drought-resistant lawn seed.
- Avoid over-fertilizing your lawn. Applying fertilizer increases the need for water. Apply fertilizers that contain slow-release, water-insoluble forms of nitrogen.
- Use a broom or blower instead of a hose to clean leaves and other debris from your driveway or sidewalk.
- Avoid leaving sprinklers or hoses unattended. A garden hose can pour out 600 gallons or more in only a few hours.

Pool

- Install a new water-saving pool filter. A single back flushing with a traditional filter uses 180 to 250 gallons of water.
- Cover pools and spas to reduce evaporation of water.

Appendix B:
Disaster Supplies Checklists

The following list is to help you determine what to include in your disaster supplies kit that will meet your family's needs.

First Aid Supplies

Supplies	Home (√)	Vehicle (√)	Work (√)
Adhesive bandages, various sizes			
5" x 9" sterile dressing			
Conforming roller gauze bandage			
Triangular bandages			
3" x 3" sterile gauze pads			
4" x 4" sterile gauze pads			
Roll 3" cohesive bandage			
Germicidal hand wipes or waterless, alcohol-based hand sanitizer			
Antiseptic wipes			
Pairs large, medical grade, non-latex gloves			
Tongue depressor blades			
Adhesive tape, 2" width			
Antibacterial ointment			
Cold pack			
Scissors (small, personal)			
Tweezers			
Assorted sizes of safety pins			
Cotton balls			
Thermometer			
Tube of petroleum jelly or other lubricant			
Sunscreen			
CPR breathing barrier, such as a face shield			
First aid manual			

Non-Prescription and Prescription Medicine Kit Supplies

Supplies	Home (√)	Vehicle (√)	Work (√)
Aspirin and non-aspirin pain reliever			
Anti-diarrhea medication			
Antacid (for stomach upset)			
Laxative			
Vitamins			
Prescriptions			
Extra eyeglasses/contact lenses			

Sanitation and Hygiene Supplies

Item	(√)	Item	(√)
Washcloth and towel		Heavy-duty plastic garbage bags and ties for personal sanitation uses and toilet paper	
Towelettes, soap, hand sanitizer		Medium-sized plastic bucket with tight lid	
Tooth paste, toothbrushes		Disinfectant and household chlorine bleach	
Shampoo, comb, and brush		A small shovel for digging a latrine	
Deodorants, sunscreen		Toilet paper	
Razor, shaving cream			
Lip balm, insect repellent			
Contact lens solutions			
Mirror			
Feminine supplies			

Equipment and Tools

Tools	(√)	Kitchen Items	(√)
Portable, battery-powered radio or television and extra batteries		Manual can opener	
NOAA Weather Radio, if appropriate for your area		Mess kits or paper cups, plates, and plastic utensils	
Flashlight and extra batteries		All-purpose knife	
Signal flare		Household liquid bleach to treat drinking water	
Matches in a waterproof container (or waterproof matches)		Sugar, salt, pepper	
Shut-off wrench, pliers, shovel, and other tools		Aluminum foil and plastic wrap	
Duct tape and scissors		Resealable plastic bags	
Plastic sheeting		Small cooking stove and a can of cooking fuel (if food must be cooked)	
Whistle			
Small canister, ABC-type fire extinguisher		**Comfort Items**	
Tube tent		Games	
Compass		Cards	
Work gloves		Books	
Paper, pens, and pencils		Toys for kids	
Needles and thread		Foods	
Battery-operated travel alarm clock			

Food and Water

Supplies	Home (√)	Vehicle (√)	Work (√)
Water			
Ready-to-eat meats, fruits, and vegetables			
Canned or boxed juices, milk, and soup			
High-energy foods such as peanut butter, jelly, low-sodium crackers, granola bars, and trail mix.			
Vitamins			
Special foods for infants or persons on special diets			
Cookies, hard candy			
Instant coffee			
Cereals			
Powdered milk			

Clothes and Bedding Supplies

Item	(√)	(√)	(√)	(√)
Complete change of clothes				
Sturdy shoes or boots				
Rain gear				
Hat and gloves				
Extra socks				
Extra underwear				
Thermal underwear				
Sunglasses				
Blankets/sleeping bags and pillows				

Documents and Keys

Make sure you keep these items in a watertight container

Item	Stored (√)
Personal identification	
Cash and coins	
Credit cards	
Extra set of house keys and car keys	
Copies of the following:	
• Birth certificate	
• Marriage certificate	
• Driver's license	
• Social Security cards	
• Passports	
• Wills	
• Deeds	
• Inventory of household goods	
• Insurance papers	
• Immunization records	
• Bank and credit card account numbers	
• Stocks and bonds	
Emergency contact list and phone numbers	
Map of the area and phone numbers of places you could go	

Appendix C:

 **Homeland Security** # Family Communications Plan

Your family may not be together when disaster strikes, so plan how you will contact one another and review what you will do in different situations.

Out-of-State Contact Name:	Telephone Number:
Email:	Telephone Number:

Fill out the following information for each family member and keep it up to date.

Name:	Social Security Number:
Date of Birth:	Important Medical Information:
Name:	Social Security Number:
Date of Birth:	Important Medical Information:
Name:	Social Security Number:
Date of Birth:	Important Medical Information:
Name:	Social Security Number:
Date of Birth:	Important Medical Information:
Name:	Social Security Number:
Date of Birth:	Important Medical Information:
Name:	Social Security Number:
Date of Birth:	Important Medical Information:

Where to go in an emergency. Write down where your family spends the most time: work, school and other places you frequent. Schools, daycare providers, workplaces and apartment buildings should all have site-specific emergency plans.

Home
Address:
Phone Number:
Neighborhood Meeting Place:
Regional Meeting Place:

School
Address:
Phone Number:
Evacuation Location:

School
Address:
Phone Number:
Evacuation Location:

School
Address:
Phone Number:
Evacuation Location:

Work
Address:
Phone Number:
Evacuation Location:

Work
Address:
Phone Number:
Evacuation Location:

Other place you frequent:
Address:
Phone Number:
Evacuation Location:

Other place you frequent:
Address:
Phone Number:
Evacuation Location:

Important Information	Name	Telephone #	Policy #
Doctor(s):			
Other:			
Pharmacist:			
Medical Insurance:			
Homeowners/Rental Insurance:			
Veterinarian/Kennel (for pets):			

Other useful phone numbers: **9–1–1 for emergencies.**   Police Non-Emergency Phone #:

Every family member should carry a copy of this important information:

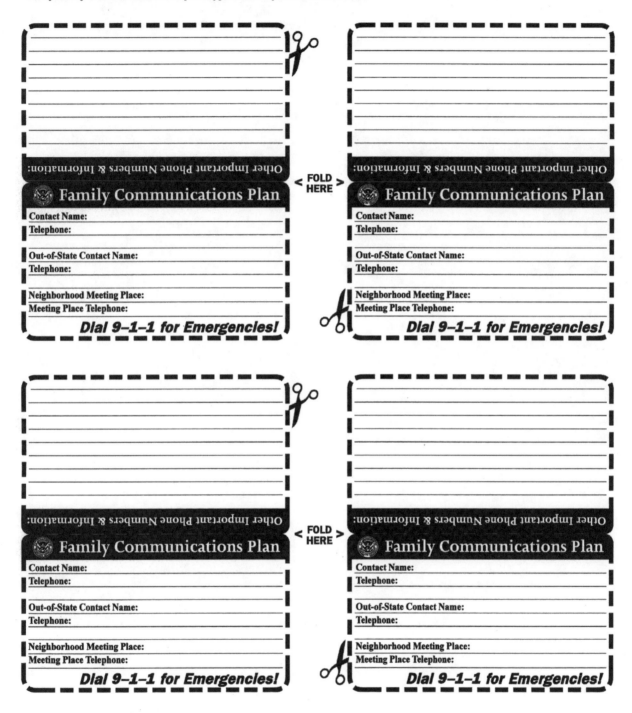

Independent Study Courses

To obtain the following Independent Study Courses from FEMA, write to:

Independent Study Program
Emergency Management Institute
16825 South Seton Avenue
Emmitsburg, MD 21727

Online: www.training.fema.gov

- IS-1   Emergency Program Manager: An Orientation to the Position
- IS-3   Radiological Emergency Management
- IS-5   Hazardous Materials: A Citizen's Orientation
- IS-7   A Citizen's Guide to Disaster Assistance
- IS-8   Building for the Earthquakes of Tomorrow: Complying with Executive Order 12699
- IS-9   Managing Floodplain Development Through the National Flood Insurance Program (NFIP)
- IS-10   Animals in Disaster—Module A, Awareness and Preparedness
- IS-11   Animals in Disaster—Module B, Community Planning
- IS-55   Hazardous Materials: A Guide for Citizens
- IS-111   Livestock in Disasters
- IS-120   An Orientation to Community Disaster Exercises
- IS-139   Exercise Design
- IS-195   Basic Incident Command System
- IS-235   Emergency Planning
- IS-240   Leadership and Influence
- IS-241   Decision Making and Problem Solving
- IS-242   Effective Communication
- IS-244   Developing and Managing Volunteers
- IS-271   Anticipating Hazardous Weather and Community Risk
- IS-275   The EOC's Role in Community Preparedness, Response and Recovery Activities
- IS-279   Engineering Principles and Practices for Retrofitting Flood-Prone Residential Structures
- IS-288   The Role of Voluntary Agencies in Emergency Management
- IS-301   Radiological Emergency Response
- IS-324   Community Hurricane Preparedness
- IS-346   An Orientation to Hazardous Materials for Medical Personnel
- IS-386   Introduction to Residential Coastal Construction
- IS-393   Introduction to Mitigation
- IS-394   Mitigation for Homeowners
- IS-513   The Professional in Emergency Management
- IS-600   Special Considerations for FEMA Public Assistance Projects
- IS-630   Introduction to the Public Assistance Process
- SS-534   Emergency Response to Terrorism (presented by the National Fire Academy–12 hours).